For Everything a Season

For Everything a Season

Mennonite Brethren in North America, 1874 - 2002

An Informal History

Paul Toews and Kevin Enns-Rempel, Editors

Copyright © 2002 by the Historical Commission, Fresno, California, USA

All rights reserved. With exception of brief excerpts for reviews, no part of this book may be reproduced, stored in a retrieval system or transmitted in whole or in part, in any form, by any means, electronic, mechanical, photocopying, recording or otherwise without prior permission of Kindred Productions.

Published simultaneously by Kindred Productions, Winnipeg, Manitoba, R2L 2E5 and Kindred Productions, Hillsboro, Kansas 67063.

Cover Design: Sandalwood Design
Book Design: The Christian Press
Printed in Canada by The Christian Press

National Library of Canada Cataloguing in Publication Data

For everything a season

ISBN 0-921788-84-3

1. Mennonite Brethren Church of North America--History. 2. Mennonites--North America--History. I. Toews, Paul. II. Enns-Rempel, Kevin.
BX8129.M373F67 2002   289.7'7   C2002-910396-7

To everything there is a season,
A time for every purpose under
    heaven;
A time to be born,
    And a time to die;
A time to plant,
    And a time to pluck
        what is planted
A time to kill,
    And a time to heal:
A time to break down
    And a time to build up
        Ecclesiastes 3:1-3

Contents

Preface	1
Mennonite Brethren Beginnings —*John B. Toews*	3
Coming to North America: The Immigrants of the 1870s —*Kevin Enns-Rempel*	15
Coming to North America: The Immigrants of the 1920s-1940s —*Abe Dueck*	29
Mennonite Brethren Theology: A Multiple Inheritance —*Lynn Jost*	43
Searching for the Right Structures —*Paul Toews*	55
From Foreign Mission to Global Partnership —*James Pankratz*	67
The Printed Path to Unity —*Wally Kroeker*	81
Embodying the Vision: Mennonite Brethren Higher Education —*Paul Toews and Abe Dueck*	95
The Dilemma of the Mennonite Brethren Writer: Having One Soul or Two? —*Katie Funk Wiebe*	109
To Improve Congregational Singing: Music in the Church —*Doreen Klassen*	121
The Life of the Congregation —*Valerie Rempel*	137
Mennonite Brethren in a Changing Society —*John H. Redekop*	151
Broadening our Horizons —*Wally Unger*	167
Afterword: A Future with Promise —*Herb Kopp*	179
Permissions	183
Authors	187

Preface

For Everything a Season marks a transition in the organized life of the Mennonite Brethren denomination. Since 1879 the dominant conference structure of the denomination has been the General Conference, the binational conference that included churches in both the United States and Canada in a variety of joint programs and in a common peoplehood. After 2002 this binational conference will be no more. Its ministries, agencies, institutions and programs are being taken over either jointly or separately by the Canadian Mennonite Brethren and United States Mennonite Brethren conferences.

The General Conference has served well the churches of Canada and the United States. It brought confessional regularity to the denomination, managed its largest programs and created shared understandings across the national boundary. It bound together peoples of differing immigrant generations, different ethnic and cultural traditions. It fostered the development of a worldwide Mennonite Brethren community that now numbers more than 250,000 persons in eighteen countries.

The demise of the General Conference as an active entity is an occasion for reflection on its history. This book provides such reflection on its origins, some of its important ministries and struggles. The varied work and agencies of the conference provided the book's organizing structure. The essays do not seek to interpret the reasons for the discontinuation of the General Conference. Another generation will make that analysis and offer an assessment as to the consequences of the decision to effectively dissolve this conference structure.

Most books are collaborative ventures. Some are more than others. *For Everything a Season* emerged from discussions between the General Conference Executive and the Historical Commission. All authors selected graciously agreed to provide the core essay for each chapter and many did so with very tight time constraints. The many sidebars and the photo selection are the work of the editors unless otherwise noted. David Giesbrecht assisted with the sidebars for chapter thirteen. Marvin Hein, Alan Peters and Larry Warkentin wrote original sidebars.

In addition to the authors of each essay other persons made significant contributions to the development of the book. Peggy Goertzen and Abe Dueck, Directors of the Centers for Mennonite Brethren Studies in Hillsboro, Kansas, and Winnipeg, Manitoba, respectively, were unfailing in their search for photographs. They also assisted various authors in finding appropriate archival and printed materials. Abe Dueck provided very special assistance in that he read each chapter and offered innumerable suggestions that strengthened the book in many ways. For years the Historical Commission's series "Perspectives on Mennonite Life and Thought" has prospered from the generous and careful attention of Marilyn Hudson of Kindred Productions. She again provided us with wise counsel, careful scrutiny of many details and saw the book through the production process.

Paul Toews and Kevin Enns-Rempel
March 2002

1

Mennonite Brethren Beginnings

John B. Toews

On January 6, 1860, eighteen villagers gathered in Elisabetthal, Molotschna Colony, to sign a document of secession that marked the beginning of the Mennonite Brethren Church. The document began by deploring the "decadent condition of the Mennonite Brotherhood" and thus for "conscience sake" the signers felt they could no longer continue within the fellowship of the existing church. It was a radical step, which grew out of a long-standing concern about the religious vitality of the Russian Mennonites.

Was the indictment correct? Can the moral decline of the mid-nineteenth century Mennonite Church in Ukraine be documented? In part yes—thanks to the diaries of David Epp (1837-1843), a deeply religious, Christ-honoring Chortitza minister. Here was a man given to prayer and the reading and studying of the Word. Throughout his diary he lamented the sins of his community. He mentioned those in his church who stole—cows, sheep, flour, eggs, fox pelts and geese. There were brothers who drank too much, fought with each other, and beat their wives. Others violated village ordinances. There were sisters and brothers, some married, some widowed, some separated and some single, who engaged in illicit sexual relations and were called to account for their actions. Epp agonized about his community. He stood in a Mennonite tradition that sought to actualize the Gospel in daily life. It was not happening.

In one of the last entries of the diaries he wrote: "Spiritually the community is in a drowsy state. Drunkenness, adultery and fornication are widespread as are lies and gossip." Almost two decades later the emerging Mennonite Brethren also complained about the prevailing state of lifestyle and morality.

Jakob Bekker, one of the signers of the Mennonite Brethren secession document of January 6, 1860, recalled how, in the early 1850s, he "guzzled liquor and sang lewd songs" at his sister's wedding. Other sources speak of widespread smoking and dancing at weddings. Jakob Wall, another signatory, related how the Lord spoke to him "when one of my comrades was snatched from the card table into eternity." When, in the secession document, the early Brethren referred to "open godlessness," people living "satanic lives" and asserted "the corruption of the whole Mennonite brotherhood" they were thinking about issues like alcoholism, nicotine addiction, card playing and dancing at weddings.

The Mennonites who came to Russia, beginning in 1789, settled in two major colonies known as Chortitza and Molotschna. They came with a set of broad-ranging privileges involving exemption from military and civilian service, the right of private land ownership, temporary exemption from taxes, complete freedom of religion and settlement in closed communities. The new immigrants were separated from the indigenous Russians and even the nearby German Lutheran and Catholic settlers. Hence the migrants retained the languages, social customs and religious practices characterizing their life in Prussia.

Recent photograph of the Rückenau Mennonite Brethren Church, built in 1883.

The frontier experience proved difficult. Land and climate differed vastly from the lowlands of the Vistula Delta. The settlers found themselves surrounded by an alien language and a different culture. Their Christian faith, so central to their lives, was sparingly nurtured by the few ministers accompanying them to the Chortitza Colony. Amid the prevailing material and spiritual insecurity they clung to what was known and familiar. For the next decades the Prussian religious patterns were rigorously observed in Russia.

One feature of that legacy involved the fusion of church and village. Once persons reached adulthood they invariably joined the church and came under its jurisdiction. Everyone—including the mayor—was a member of the elder's church and everyone—including the elder—lived in the mayor's village. The system somewhat recreated the union of church and state to which Menno Simons (1496-1561), the founder of the Mennonite movement, took such strong exception. Menno spoke of the importance of following Christ unreservedly and of the necessity of creating a Christian community that reflected this newness of life. He argued that the church consisted only of committed Christians who, of their own free will, came together and covenanted to enter into a relationship of intentional accountability and support. Adult baptism upon faith became the symbol of entry into the new community. The state had no role to play in the affairs of the new people of God. Similar demands for a radical faith were also heard in towns and cities of Germany and Switzerland. Their opponents called them Anabaptists—people who baptized a second time because they felt that their baptism as infants was meaningless.

Sixteenth-century Christianity had no understanding of a church separate from the state. Religious pluralism and religious toleration of any kind was unknown. As a result Anabaptists soon experienced persecution wherever they emerged. It is that insistence on freedom from state control that accounted for the movement of many Mennonites (or Anabaptists) from Western Europe to Prussia (now Poland) and on to Russia. Paradoxically, the nature of the settlement in Russia somewhat recreated the very structures that they had so opposed in the sixteenth-century.

In this Russian setting, where the religious and civil leadership were knit together, the church still had much to say. Major shortcomings in the community like theft, drunkenness, physical violence, contract disputes and sexual improprieties were adjudicated by a ministerial council. If the individual proved especially stubborn or if the sin was grave, the matter was

---

Excerpts from Document of Secession of the Mennonite Brethren from the Mennonite Church of Russia:

"To the total body of church elders of the Molotschna Mennonite Church!

a) We, the undersigned, have by the grace of God, recognized the decadent condition of the Mennonite Brotherhood and can, for God's and conscience' no longer continue therein; for we fear the inevitable judgment of God, since the openly godless living and their wickedness cries to God in heaven. We also fear the loss of the rights and privileges granted us by our benevolent government because the transgressions and disobedience against it increase continually. . . .

b) Therefore, we herewith completely dissociate ourselves from these decadent churches, though we pray for our brethren, that they shall be saved. We want to be innocent of the souls of the erring. . .

c) We speak here of the entire Mennonite Brotherhood, because the supreme government authorities consider it one true brotherhood.

d) In the articles, we are, according to our convictions from the holy Scripture, in agreement with our dear Menno.

e) We confess a baptism on faith, as a seal of faith; not on a memorized faith, as is the practice, but on a genuine, living faith effected by the Spirit of God. . . .

f) Regarding holy communion we confess that it serves to strengthen the faith of true believers, for they remind themselves of their mighty salvation through the death of the Lord Jesus. Yes, it is a sign that they stand in very intimate union with Jesus, their Saviour.

g) Regarding footwashing, we confess that the Lord Jesus instituted it . . . to be practiced among one another, for the blessing is in the deed, not in knowledge.

h) Teachers (preachers) may be called in two Scriptural ways: Some are chosen by God alone, without human assistance, and sent out by His Spirit, as were the prophets and apostles. . . . Others are called through the instrumentality of true believers. . . .

i) Regarding the ban, we confess that all carnal and reprobate sinners must be banned from the fellowship of believers. . . .

j) In all other articles of our confession, we are in full agreement with Menno Simons"

—*Signed by eighteen heads of households on 6 January 1860: Abraham Cornelssen, Corn. Wiens, Isaak Koop, Franz Klaassen, Abr. Wiens, Martin Klaassen, Abr. Wiens, Daniel Hoppe, August Strauss, Jakob Becker, Isaak Regehr, Andr. Voth, Jakob Wall, Joh. Claassen, Heinrich Huebert, Peter Stobbe, Abr. Peters, Diedrich Claassen.*

referred to an assembly of all adult males who belonged to the local church. Excommuni-cation from the congregation placed the individual outside of the community. In most instances such a person repented and was readmitted to the church. The arrangement worked well provided all agreed on what it meant to be a Christian and on what it meant to be the church.

Yet the system found it difficult to adjust to shifts in economic and cultural structures. What happened when wealth was based on land holding and suddenly there was not enough land, when two-thirds of your parish members possessed no land? The church could not address the growing gap between rich and poor. There was another development. Gradually the elementary school system of the day taught most of the women and men in the village to read and write. Increasingly there were those serious pilgrims who read their Bible or read books on the Bible obtained from outside the community. What if these individuals concluded

Jakob Bekker and Margaretha Wiens Bekker.
(CMBS Fresno)

that the prevailing Christian values and practices left much to be desired and demanded a church separated from the larger, less pious community? Was there a remedy if the public life of the community took a turn for the worse and its sins were not addressed?

There was possibly another issue impacting the spiritual state of the Mennonite community prior to 1860: the prevailing theology of conversion. In his diary David Epp recorded the texts of his sermons or described the spiritual state of his community. In doing so he often used the words "repentance" and "conversion." In a later diary his son, Jakob Epp, deployed the same words. Both men, but especially Jakob, portrayed an ongoing struggle for faith and salvation. "How anxious I am in my soul. Will the lord forgive me my trespasses?" Jakob confided to his diary. "Alarming doubts about the certainty of my salvation afflict my soul. . . . Poor me. I preach repentance and forgiveness of sin to the people . . . yet my own heart longs for salvation." The diaries contained many similar entries. Though risky to generalize from such slim evidence, the diaries possibly point to the then-prevailing theology of salvation. Here was the notion that you worked out your salvation with fear and trembling, that you were reluctant to speak of "salvation full and free" or of joy in the Lord. You believed in spiritual rebirth but you did not attempt to define the precise nature of the salvation experience. You struggled to affirm the sufficiency of Christ but sometimes with a sense of desperation and pessimism. Salvation was a labor of faith, one was always in

My Conversion
by Maria Dueck Martens

"Dear brothers and sisters and readers of the *Zionsbote*. Since I have been blessed and strengthened many times by reading stories of conversions, and since I felt the urge to share my conversation, . . . I will do so with God's help.

"Already at a young age the Lord worked in my life, . . . Our neighbors, the Franz Nickels . . . were converted. Their children often told stories of how life was for children who did not obey their parents. I felt I was not [obedient to my parents]. Then my mother became ill and I thought, 'your mother is going to die and you will be sent out to work as a servant.' This seemed terrible and I promised God I would behave better. But once my mother was healthy again, I went my own way.

"I heard a knocking on my heart, and when I went to bed at night I thought about my life and cried. I was always afraid during thunderstorms, and the Holy Spirit strongly warned me that I should be converted before it was too late. So I promised to follow the loving Savior if he would let me live.

"This [promise] held until my mother got sick again and died. I was eighteen years old, and as I feared, I had to go work as a servant. Satan told me that my mother had died because of my sins and that there was no salvation for me because I had gone too far. I felt abandoned by God and men. . . .

"I served at brother Johann Loepp's house. . . . They talked to me about the loving Savior, held morning and evening devotions, and prayed for me. It felt good when they prayed for me but Satan told me not to let them know, because then I would have to be baptized and I would always be sad.

"It went like this until spring, when I wanted to be 'grown up' and become a member of the Church. A dear brother told me to clean up my rotten life, or else the loving Savior would not make a covenant with me. I said I would put everything in order before I was baptized. Pentecost came and I was sprinkled, but I was not renewed. I was totally dead in sin and unhappy.

"Then I desired to marry a man who loved the Lord. My wish was fulfilled. We moved to . . . Samara and had a happy life. My husband prayed often, but the Devil told me, 'you can't pray anymore, it is too late. You should have done it when you grew up.'

"My husband hired a brother to work as a carpenter. My husband told him how he was doing and cried, and they often prayed together. Then they decided to attend devotional meetings in Pleschanowsk. Satan convinced me to sin against this brother and my husband. I hid my husband's boots and told him he should not go to the meetings. . . . My husband was quiet, went into the field and fought with God. . . . My own brother, who lived with us, said, 'God will punish you, because you did not keep your promise. You wanted a husband who loved the Lord.'

"Then my heart softened. I went to look for my husband and ask him for forgiveness. He was happy because he had found peace with God. I thought he would be embarrassed and crying, but he was happy and said, 'Pray to God and ask for forgiveness for your sins and you too will be happy.'. . . I could not understand it and did not know what to do. . . .

"The next day...the Lord brought Brother Giesbrecht from Pleschanowsk to us. . . . He told us of a woman who wanted to be converted but her husband had been against it. As a result, she became insane and had to be delivered to a mental hospital, and so both were lost. I realized this could also happen to me. . . . My husband and I prayed earnestly to God. He heard us and gave me forgiveness of my sins. . . . This happened May 24, 1892. I was happy that the Lord made me one of his children and that my name was written down in heaven. On May 30, 1892, we were buried through baptism in the death of Christ."

—Originally published in Zionsbote, *4 August 1897, p.2.*

Abraham Unger

Abraham Unger (1820-1880), an elder in the Mennonite Church in the village of Einlage in South Russia, was as responsible as anyone for the formation of the Mennonite Brethren in the Chortitza Colony, the second largest of the Mennonite Colonies. On March 4, 1862, he was baptized. Others in the village followed on March 11, which is considered the date for the establishment of the first Mennonite Brethren congregation in Chortitza. Prior to his separating from the larger Mennonite body, Unger corresponded with Johann G. Oncken, a Baptist preacher in Hamburg. That relationship and continuing contact with other German Baptists led to the introduction of Baptist beliefs and practices among the early Mennonite Brethren. That Baptist influence also created considerable tension with some of the Mennonite Brethren leaders in the larger Molotschna Colony.

process, one was "on conversion" throughout life. There was the hope of salvation but one could never be sure.

This salvation paradigm may help explain the conversion account left by Jakob Bekker. Jakob related how he was irritated by a brother-in-law who converted while working for some believers and "immediately preached repentance and conversion to us." There was also a neighbor who, in a dialogue with this new convert, asserted "that no man could be certain of his future salvation [while here on earth]. He felt that such an assertion was presumptuous." Shortly thereafter, this man died in his sleep, an event that plunged Bekker into a deep spiritual crisis. Once home he found a quiet place to pray, and as he persisted in prayer "my heart was gradually lightened and I believed my sins were forgiven." This experience occurred in 1853.

Bekker then began to attend the services of a house group. In December 1854 he attended such a service at the Abraham Mathiess residence. There Bekker experienced "intense joy for I felt absolutely certain that the Savior had also been born in me. . . . My heart leapt for joy because I knew I was a child of God."

At least two elements characterized Bekker's conversion. First the process was gradual and accompanied by intense agony. Second, it climaxed in joy and certainty of salvation. Records of later Brethren conversions documented similar patterns. In all cases the converts described a deep awareness of sin, lasting months and even years, and often specifically associated with such village activities as dancing, drinking, card playing and tobacco addiction. The process often involved persistent prayer, the seeking of counsel, reading of hymns and searching of Scripture. This agony not only contended with sin but was also a search for understanding and faith affirmation. All accounts document the end of the search. It was an intense experiential moment involving ecstasy, joy and the assurance of sins forgiven. Converts looked upon it as the most momentous event in their lives.

The context of early Brethren conversions cannot be overlooked. Converts still found themselves living in the same village, and amid traditional church structures. Conversion meant leaving family and societal patterns and defying established patterns of Mennonite spirituality. The house church now provided alternative religious nurture. At times it meant a few families engaged in Bible study or a more formal evening service in the local school with singing, Bible reading and preaching by an itinerant minister. Interaction in such a community was informal and spontaneous, and mention of it occurs repeatedly in conversion accounts.

The established Mennonite Church did not deal charitably with these new expressions of conversion and faith. During a government investigation of the early Brethren, elders Jakob Hildebrand and Gerhard Dyck submitted a somewhat defensive letter in which they sought to justify their actions against the dissidents. They reported that a house group existed as early as 1852 in Kronsweide and that in 1855 some twenty-nine families informed the local church of their desire to separate. The rebels were not only excommunicated, but nine of their leaders were

Margaretha Froese Wiens Klassen: Mother of the Mennonite Brethren Church?

We know little about the life of Margaretha Froese Wiens Klassen. Like many nineteenth-century Mennonite women, the details of her life were never recorded. Born in 1801 (apparently in Prussia), Margaretha married Abraham Wiens in 1822 and they had nine children together. Abraham died in 1844, and Margaretha married Franz Klassen in 1846. She died in Russia in 1873. Little more about her is known.

Yet Margaretha played a central role in the founding of the Mennonite Brethren Church. Four members of Margaretha's family were among the eighteen men who risked much by seceding from the Mennonite Church in Russia. At least one more son-in-law played an important role in the early church. Members of Margaretha's family, furthermore, would continue to be significant leaders in the new Mennonite Brethren Church from that time forward.

Franz Klassen, Margaretha's second husband, signed the January 1860 document, and later would be elected the first deacon of the new church. Because no elder in the established Mennonite churches of the colony would perform the ordination of new group's first elder, Franz Klassen was selected to lay hands on Heinrich Huebert, the first elder.

It was in the home of Cornelius Wiens, Margaretha's oldest son, that a private communion service took place in fall 1859, which directly led to the secession of the Brethren. Cornelius was also one of the original eighteen signers. Abraham Wiens, Margaretha's second son, also signed the document of secession. He later moved to the Kuban region of South Russia, where he helped established a new, primarily Mennonite Brethren settlement.

Margaretha's daughter Margaretha Wiens, married founder Jacob Peter Bekker. Bekker was one of the original ministers of the Mennonite Brethren Church, and wrote an important historical account of the origins of the church.

Daughter Anna Wiens married Bernhard Janzen, a leader of the Mennonite Brethren settlement in the Kuban. They migrated to the United States, where Anna died in 1895.

Despite her anonymity, Margaretha's life must have had a powerful impact on her family. They sacrificed their reputations, their fortunes, and their safety to publicly affirm their faith. Through them and Margaretha's many descendants who remain in the church today, the evidence of her faith and testimony are clearly evident.

—*Adapted from an article by Alan Peters, originally published in the* Mennonite Brethren Historical Society of the West Coast Bulletin *(November 1987).*

Johann Claassen

The life of Johann Claassen (1820-1876) combines many of the currents present at the creation of the Mennonite Brethren Church. As a young man he had associations with Johann Cornies, the most progressive person in the nineteenth-century Russian Mennonite world. In an age when many Mennonites spoke only German, he was conversant with the Russian language. In an age when most Mennonites lived in colonies he had traveled to many cities and spent considerable time in St. Petersburg, the capital of the Russian empire. At age twenty-seven he married Katharine Reimer, daughter of David Reimer, a large estate owner.

In the 1850s the Claassens were members of the Gnadenfeld, Molotschna Colony, church. This congregation was deeply influenced by European pietism, which promoted an inward spirituality, more spontaneous preaching, more exuberant singing and various kinds of renewal religious services. Pietism tended to nourish a keen sense of religious individualism.

Like other founders of the new denomination, Claassen was also deeply nurtured by Anabaptism and its concern for the church as a community of caring and witness. Claassen reached out to the new and retained the old. Pietism frequently promoted new religious, cultural and educational ideas. Anabaptism wished to preserve the deeply biblical teachings and practices of the past. Claassen combined the two: innovation and tradition, conservatism and progressivism, Anabaptism and pietism.

imprisoned and fed a diet of bread and water for up to thirteen days. The elders reported, "these persons all confessed their error and criminal activity, asked forgiveness and were readmitted as members of the church." There was an important concession: they were allowed to continue meeting in their homes, provided they caused no public disturbance.

Between 1855-1860 traditionalists and radicals in Chortitza engaged in dialogue. The secession document signatories also mentioned earlier reported house groups in the Molotschna Colony in the early 1850s that carried on a peaceable co-existence with the mother church. Eventually these revitalized Christians demanded more frequent and separate communion services, something that Elder August Lenzmann felt he could not do. When angry voices at an out-of-control church meeting demanded that the dissidents leave, they did so. House groups apparently could no longer survive within the existing community.

The emergence of radical leaders among the Brethren also contributed to the widening gulf between the two communities. Alexander Brune, a Lutheran official sent by the government to investigate the new movement, complained that some of them "carry on openly and brazenly." He mentioned a discussion with a young Gerhard Wieler who not only interrupted him, but "took a Bible from the table, placed it on top of the book I was reading to him and said: 'This is what we use for teaching, reproof and correction in righteousness.'" A bright young man, Wieler had been the Chortitza district secretary and subsequently a village school teacher in Molotschna. He left that post under pressure late in 1861. Arriving in Chortitza, he stayed with the Brethren leader Abraham Unger. Here, according to the report, he "stirred up the community" and "livened up their prayer meetings."

Wieler was a gifted, emotional man, not given to compromise. Inclined to the dramatic, he wished to define the exact patterns of the Holy Spirit's movements among the dissidents. Truth and falsehood, right and wrong, could be precisely identified. His assertive personality, combined with a doctrinaire stance, intimidated the more moderately inclined.

Wieler brought the notion of immersion baptism from the Molotschna to Chortitza and on 18 March 1862, while there was still ice on the Dnieper River, insisted on conducting a baptism. Wieler was also cited as the chief instigator of noisy late night meetings at the Abraham Unger residence. He ordered and carried out a book burning of all religious books except the Bible and insisted on aggressive door-to-door hellfire and brimstone evangelism. He upbraided a saintly elder for his inadequate preaching and, with others, called the established church a house of prostitution. Those who disagreed with him were excommunicated, including his moderate and sensible brother Johann. Radical leadership came at a high cost. It crippled the early Brethren internally and permanently alienated them from the larger Mennonite community.

The reports associated with Alexander Brune's investigation of the early Brethren were placed in an Interior Ministry file entitled *Hüpfer* (jumpers or leapers). Brune consistently used the term in all of his official correspondence and reports. He described "wild dance and the singing of worldly songs to the accompaniment of violins and accordions." In his memoirs Jakob Bekker reports how, during meetings, people leaped and jumped and shouted, "Glory! Hallelujah! Victory! Amen!" Records cited by Peter M. Friesen add to this portrait. These records describe gatherings where "they did not allow any sermons," of people dancing "until they were soaked with perspiration" and of activities characterized by "uninhibited sound and fury." When the brethren officially repented of these activities in June 1865 they made specific reference to the "wild expressions of joy," which consisted of "dancing" and "frenzy and dancing."

Despite their repentance, the Brethren could not undo the damage to their public reputation. The members of the established church long remembered the shouting, leaping and dancing. The Brethren in turn remembered the imprisonments, the beatings, and the legal attempts to deport them from Russia. Whether such memories were correct, partially correct, or false did not really matter. They served to keep the two groups apart for many decades.

As described earlier, the Brethren theology of conversion involved a profound awareness of sin, an intense struggle accompanied by a prolonged agony of soul and a moment of assurance when anxiety was replaced by inner peace. Early records portrayed individuals sharing their conversion experiences in small house groups or larger gatherings. This sharing was intended to be a source of spiritual encouragement and nurture, but it also contained possible dangers. New converts were expected to express their encounter with God using a familiar language common to the group, or the authenticity of their conversion was possibly in doubt. Members of the established church not using the same vocabulary might be suspect. Another danger may have lurked. Continually recounting the joy of salvation caused conversion to be defined primarily in terms of personal experience. Celebrating the joy of conversion again and again and consistently reaffirming "my experience" may have prompted a selfish spirituality that at times neglected the demands of discipleship.

And yet, the new church clearly did not entirely isolate the individual Christian life from the larger church community. For early Brethren believers the house church was a place of refuge. Early conversions occurred in the context of a community that welcomed individuals and made them feel comfortable. Portraits of congregational life during the first decades of the Mennonite Brethren Church at times appear almost idyllic. These gatherings were small and encouraged lay participation. Group members broadened their understanding of faith on a personal level. Openness and vulnerability typified such meetings. Early conversion accounts frequently speak of the concern shown by house church members for those seeking spiritual direction. Following conversion there was no need to search for community. Care-receivers and care-givers were connected from the very onset. Whether young or old, all were accommodated in such a setting.

Mennonites or Baptists?

"Repeatedly this question has emerged during the first fifty years of the existence of the Mennonite Brethren Church here in Russia. Every time it was answered correctly by the government and by the church: the members of the Mennonite Brethren Church are Mennonites. In spite of this, there seems to have remained a certain obscurity in some circles or possibly only among individual persons. I once was subjected to official investigation here in Halbstadt (Mennonite village in South Russia) by the honorable vice governor and by our school board which, surprisingly, was present at the occasion. The official, I might add, seemed to regard this matter as very important. He kept repeating, "Your own people, the Mennonites, *even the teachers*, call the members of the Mennonite Brethren Church, 'Baptists.' 'Whether it is due to *harmless ignorance or ignoble insult* I will not judge, but one must still ask with astonishment, 'How is that possible?'"

It is true that the Mennonite Brethren Church and the Baptists have the same mode of baptism, namely, biblical immersion. They also participate one with another in Holy Communion as guests and serve each other with sermons and by officiating in church matters. . . .

Does such an exchange of spiritual fellowship among various faiths alter the distinctive features and the name of any particular church fellowship? Certainly not! Similarly, the members of the Mennonite Brethren Church cannot be made into Baptists simply by their spiritual fellowship with them. By their birth, upbringing, confession of faith and religious distinctives as a whole, they belong to the Mennonites. They are and remain Mennonites in spite of friend or foe. To call the Mennonite Brethren Church Baptists is just as wrong as to label Mennonites collectively as Baptists, as German theologians often do."

—*by H.J. Braun, originally printed in* Friedensstimme, *5 May 1910. Translated and reprinted in* Moving Beyond Secession: Defining Russian Mennonite Brethren Mission and Identity, 1872-1922, *edited by Abe Dueck (Kindred Productions, 1997).*

Heinrich Huebert, first elder of the Mennonite Brethren Church.

The house church had other advantages. Lay-dominated services required no professional clergy. While itinerant ministers were welcomed, their presence was not necessary. The house church developed simple liturgies consisting of singing, personal testimony, Bible reading and dialogue. It was able to function with or without a building and was not dependent on a formal parish structure. Furthermore, as the Brethren were dispersed by later nineteenth-century Mennonite migrations across Russia, the house church traveled easily and efficiently. For the early Brethren the house church seemed to have all the answers. There was no reason to return to the established church.

House church spirituality allowed for healthy inner growth. It occurred in the midst of the congregation. Ordinary people sat together and related faith to the ebb and flow of everyday experience. Notions of discipleship were corporately, not individually, defined. Personal piety functioned in the context of the whole. It was difficult for artificiality or spiritual pride to survive in such a setting. A participatory discernment process prevented dominant personalities from imposing their views upon the congregation. There was an obligation toward all the people of God, not only to one's private pilgrimage. The pursuit of holiness was a congregational affair.

There was another practice enhancing the dynamic of the house church—the itinerant ministry. At the first Mennonite Brethren General Conference held in 1872, five individuals were elected to contact and nurture members scattered throughout Russia. Dedicated individuals criscrossed the land, conducting meetings and Bible studies in homes and schools. Itinerant ministers not only served as teachers and preachers but also as evangelists in the context of larger meetings or smaller gatherings in private residences. Their presence in even the most remote settlements generated a sense of belonging and identity. Conference appointment brought with it authority related to questions of doctrine, church polity and liturgical practices. Thanks to the itinerants, nineteen-century Mennonite Brethren retained an amazing uniformity in matters of worship, music and the practice of personal piety. Available sources suggest that the early Mennonite Brethren lost relatively few members and sustained a gradual church growth.

When the Brethren officially left the Mennonite Church in 1860, they also dispensed with its traditions and customs, its liturgical and worship patterns and its ecclesiastical leadership. By rejecting most of what they had known, they faced the task of creating alternative structures. German Baptists, whose evangelistic interest in Russia intensified after the mid-nineteenth century, offered this much-needed support system. They not only shared the same conversion theology with the Brethren but also offered an established church polity. The Baptists taught the early Brethren how to conduct business meetings, keep minutes and aided them in the organization of

The Birth of the Krimmer Mennonite Brethren

Jacob A. Wiebe, first elder of the KMB, was born August 6, 1836, in Margenau, South Russia. On April 11, 1857, he married Justine Friesen from Halbstadt, South Russia. (CMBS Hillboro)

The Krimmer Mennonite Brethren (KMB) also emerged during the religious ferment in South Russin in the mid-nineteenth century. Both the KMB and Mennonite Brethren understood themselves as reform movements demanding a more rigorous peity than practiced in the larger Mennonite community.

The Mennonite Brethren movement originated in the Molotschna Colony in 1860. The KMB birth was in Crimea in 1869. They both chose the name *Brüdergemeinde* (Mennonite Brethren). The KMB was soon called "*Krimmer*," German for "Crimea," to distinguish them from the Molotschna group. The name confusion and the need to distinguish on the basis of geography was indicative of the larger similarity in religious outlook.

The settlements in the Crimea were scattered and not of a colony governance structure. Hence the difficulties with the established church, that were so important to the early Mennonite Brethren, were not so for the KMB. Furthermore the entire small group migrated to Kansas in 1874, five years following its birth.

The Krimmer Mennonite Brethren Church began when Elder Jacob Wiebe and eighteen others were baptized on 21 September 1869. They were all recent emigrants from the Molotschna Colony to the Crimea. Restless with their inherited religious commitments their search led them into a temporary alliance with the *Kleine Gemeinde* (a Russian Mennonite denomination meaning "small church"). Johann Friesen and Peter Baerg of the *Kleine Gemeinde* both ministered to the small group, but refused to rebaptize them. Their need for rebaptism resulted in a movement toward independence. Although nurtured in the early years by the *Kleine Gemeinde*, their subsequent history drew them much closer to the Mennonite Brethren. In 1960 the Mennonite Brethren and Krimmer Mennonite Brethren groups merged. The merger culminated a long history of cooperation on various programs, particularly in the support of Tabor College.

a General Conference in 1872. When authorities pressed the new group to define its beliefs, the Brethren borrowed the German Baptist Confession of 1849 and, with some additions, presented it as their own in 1873. They also welcomed the Baptist hymnal *Glaubensstimme* (Voice of Faith) as more representative of their theology. Likewise the practice of immersion baptism emerged from the reading of Baptist literature. The Brethren met their Baptist friends early in their story, often meaning that they had less need of their friends in the Mennonite Church.

This cooperation continued in later decades, but not without fueling inter-Mennonite tensions. The Brethren allowed Baptists to serve as their itinerant ministers as early as 1872. They allowed Baptists to take part in communion services since they had been immersed, but refused to admit Mennonite believers baptized by pouring. Baptists could join Brethren congregations without rebaptism, a privilege not extended to other Mennonites. Similarly Baptist preachers served in Brethren congregations, a privilege rarely extended to Mennonite ministers.

What were the key issues separating the early Brethren from their fellow Mennonites? Even before the separation of 1860, members of the established church were struggling with two basic issues. The first related to Christian lifestyle. Could the whole village be Christian? Were all cradle Mennonites capable of being absorbed into the Church? Certainly the early house groups of the 1850s increasingly felt that the church could not embrace all of society. For them the Russian Mennonites were a state within a state. Alongside the church stood a civic government run by Mennonites, most of whom belonged to the church whether they attended or not or were committed or not. Such a setting made it difficult to regulate lifestyle, especially as the authority of the church was weakened by increased affluence and moral decline. There was no easy solution to the dilemma. Being Christian over centuries generated a particular Christian peoplehood that happened to be called Mennonite. Whether all in this peoplehood know what it meant to be Christian was an open question. In Russia the established church understood the problem, but resolved to work within the existing peoplehood. The varied house groups eventually concluded this was not possible, left the existing structure, and organized the Mennonite Brethren Church.

The second issue related to the meaning of theological terms. Both groups used the words "repentance" and "conversion." The one continued to think in terms of salvation with fear and trembling. It subscribed to the notion that one was in conversion throughout life, that salvation was a labor of faith. The other felt that salvation could be fully experienced, known and celebrated. Each approach was not without its hazards. The one possibly placed discipleship over experience, the other experience over discipleship.

2

Coming to North America: The Immigrants of the 1870s

Kevin Enns-Rempel

The theme of migration has run through much of the Anabaptist and Mennonite story. From their very beginnings the Anabaptists were a despised and persecuted people, and this fact forced many of them to flee the harsh treatment of civil and religious rulers. As early as 1534 the first Dutch Anabaptists had fled to the area of Danzig (today Gdańsk) in present-day Poland. Because Poland was more tolerant of religious dissent than most other regions, these Dutch Anabaptists were soon followed by Mennonites from various parts of Europe. In Poland (or Prussia, as it is sometimes called), these diverse Mennonites created their own cultural tradition alongside their distinctive religious beliefs.

The Mennonites of Poland faced a new crisis when that region came under Prussian rule in 1772. This new government was less tolerant of Mennonite refusal to participate in the military. Further acquisition of land by Mennonites was prohibited, since military obligations were tied to land ownership. These new pressures caused some Polish Mennonites to consider the idea of migration once again. At about this same time, word had gone out from Russian Empress Catherine the Great that Russia was seeking settlers for lands in "South Russia," which it recently had acquired from the Turkish Empire. Russia offered generous terms of land and religious freedom to any groups choosing to settle in this region. Many Polish Mennonites chose to accept Catherine's offer, and the first group established the Chortitza Colony along the Dnieper River in 1789. The larger Molotschna Colony was founded in 1803, and Mennonites continued to migrate into these colonies into the mid-nineteenth century. It was in the Molotschna Colony in 1860 that the Mennonite Brethren Church was born.

The new Mennonite Brethren Church had scarcely established itself when new discussions of large-scale migration began among the Russian Mennonites. Once again, the issue had to do with government policies pertaining to Mennonites and other minority groups in Russia. The Russian government had embarked on a policy of "Russification," in which these minority groups would be required to give up their special privileges and acculturate more completely into the larger Russian society. Most significantly, the government stated that Mennonites would no longer receive exemption from military service. While military service is most often cited as the chief concern leading to migration, many Mennonites were equally (or more) concerned with losing control over their schools, language, local colony governance and cultural identity. All of these issues caused some Russian Mennonites to reconsider their place in that country.

Negotiations with the Russian government eventually resulted in the establishment of an alternative service system, but even this failed to satisfy all Mennonites; a significant percentage of them began to contemplate migration. From 1873 to 1884 as many as 18,000 Mennonites in

This sod building was an early meeting place for the Kirk (Colo.) MB Church.
(CMBS Fresno)

The home of Elder Abraham Schellenberg, near Moundridge, Kansas, ca. 1890-1891. Left to right: Peter L. Schellenberg, Katharina Schellenberg, Helena Schellenberg, Maria Schellenberg.(CMBS Hillsboro)

Russia emigrated to North America, a number that represented almost one-third of the total Mennonite population in that country.

Of the 18,000 immigrants arriving in North America, nearly 8,000 settled in the Canadian province of Manitoba, and about 10,000 made their homes in Minnesota, South Dakota, Nebraska and Kansas. Canada offered more firm promises of religious freedom and military exemption than did the United States, and so in many cases the most culturally and religiously conservative Mennonites settled in Manitoba. The United States, on the other hand, offered no firm commitments regarding military service, other than a vague promise that demands for such service would be very unlikely. The fact that no widespread demand for military service had ever been made by the United States (except during its Civil War) led most of these Mennonites to believe that their pacifist beliefs would be safeguarded even without formal legal guarantees from the government.

The Mennonite Brethren, all of whom settled in the United States, made up only a small percentage of all Mennonites who migrated to North America. It is estimated that perhaps four hundred Mennonite Brethren members migrated during the years 1874-1880, representing roughly one-third of the group's membership in Russia before migration. The addition of children and other non-member individuals would have increased the size of the total Mennonite Brethren immigrant community, though it remained a tiny portion of all immigrants.

These Mennonite Brethren settlers were not only small in number, they also tended to remain isolated from the other Mennonites. This can be explained in part by the lingering mutual feelings of intolerance between Mennonite Brethren and the larger Mennonite Church in Russia. Many Mennonite Brethren still felt the sting of hostility and harassment from the larger Mennonite Church in Russia, and brought those feelings with them to North America. These other Mennonites, on the other hand, pointed to a "holier-than-thou" attitude on the part of Mennonite Brethren that caused them to hold the others at arm's length.

Anna Neuman and a friend in front of a sod house on the American prairies, undated. (CMBS Fresno)

Heinrich Voth and the first Mennonite Brethren Church in Canada

In 1883 the General Conference of Mennonite Brethren Churches sent Heinrich Voth to evangelize in Manitoba. Elder Voth accepted the work with dedication and enthusiasm. He endured hardship and persecution during the next several decades as he returned to Manitoba repeatedly.

Some in Manitoba opposed Voth and the message he preached. While traveling down a road one day he was stopped by several men and beaten quite badly; but thanks to the Lord's protection and his heavy winter clothing he was not severely injured.

In one village three leaders, including the mayor, were determined to stop Voth's preaching. They came to his meeting in a school house to capture him, then send him back to Minnesota. The only empty seats left in the building were on the platform directly behind the speaker. As they sat there waiting for the right moment to act, they heard the word of God preached clearly and fearlessly. The mayor was convicted of sin and gave his life to the Lord that evening.

Another time Voth was escorted to the United States border by some of his persecutors and forbidden to return. Undaunted, he walked back into Canada to witness and preach.

Heinrich Voth's fearlessness and determination eventually resulted in the creation of the Winkler Mennonite Brethren Church in 1886, the first Mennonite Brethren congregation in Canada.

—*Adapted from* Witness Extraordinary: A Biography of Elder Heinrich Voth, 1851-1919, *by J. A. Froese (Board of Christian Literature, 1975).*

During both the planning and implementation stages of the migration, Mennonite Brethren tended to remain on the periphery. No Mennonite Brethren representatives joined the group of twelve delegates who visited North America in 1873 to scout out potential settlement sites and negotiate with government officials. This prevented the Mennonite Brethren from making contact with American Mennonites who had established programs to assist the Russian Mennonite immigrants. Further contributing to their isolation was the fact that most Mennonite Brethren immigrants came to North America somewhat later than the first major migration waves of 1874-1875, and in poorly-organized, scattered groups. This meant that they received less assistance from the migration aid committees, most of whom had exhausted their resources with the larger, better-organized groups of earlier immigrants.

Despite their small numbers and isolation, the Mennonite Brethren did succeed in establishing eleven congregations in the United States by 1880: Ebenfeld (Marion County, Kansas), 1874; Henderson (York & Hamilton Counties, Nebraska), 1876; Turner County, South Dakota, 1876; Cottonwood County, Minnesota, 1877; Hastings (Adams County, Nebraska), 1878; Sutton (Clay County, Nebraska), 1878; Buhler (Reno County, Kansas), 1878; Culbertson (Franklin County, Nebraska), 1879; Boone County, Nebraska, 1879; Woodson County, Kansas, 1879; and Goessel (Harvey County, Kansas), 1880.

The Krimmer Mennonite Brethren Church, established in Crimea in 1869, was also gripped with the desire for migration. The Krimmer migration was unique in several ways. First, almost the entire group left Russia in a single unit of thirty-five families. This was quite different than the roughly one-third of Mennonite Brethren and Mennonite Church members who chose to migrate during these years. Second, they were among the earliest Mennonites to leave Russia, departing that country on 30 May 1874. Third, this group, more than any other, chose to organize its villages in Kansas according to the Russian Mennonite village pattern. Whereas most other Mennonites settling in the United States accepted the scattered "checkerboard" settlement pattern encouraged by government homesteading policies, the Krimmer settlers created more compact settlements in which families lived in close proximity along a common village street.

The first such village was established in Marion County, Kansas, soon after the settlers arrived there. It was named "Gnadenau" (Grace Meadow), and the KMB church there was given the same name. Two other villages, Hoffnungsthal and Alexanderfeld, were soon established in the same area, though residents of all three villages attended the Gnadenau Church. Other Krimmer churches soon followed, at Springfield, Kansas (1878), and Inman, Kansas (1879). In 1881 the KMB established its only congregation in Nebraska at Jansen.

As already noted, all Mennonite Brethren immigrants to North America during the 1870s settled in the United States. The first

A restless and ever-moving people

Mennonite Brethren communities in the late nineteenth and early twentieth centuries were characterized by considerable mobility, as families moved about in search of greener pastures. One example of this phenomenon may be found in the family of Peter T. and Katharina Duerksen. Though more extreme than most families, the Duerksens graphically illustrate the restless searching for new opportunity that was so common among Mennonite Brethren families at this time.

Peter T. Duerksen was born in 1881 in Hillsboro, Kansas, the son of Russian Mennonite Brethren immigrants who came to this country in the 1870s. In 1898, Peter's family moved to Weatherford, Oklahoma. He was married there in 1903 to Katharina Neufeld. Katharina had been born in Russia in 1883, and migrated with her parents to Hillsboro in 1891 before moving on to Oklahoma.

In 1909 Peter and Katharina Duerksen left Oklahoma, and began a remarkable odyssey across western North America that would continue for the next quarter-century. They moved first to the recently established Mennonite Brethren settlement at Escondido, California, near San Diego. A few hard winters and loss of church leadership caused the Duerksens to leave Escondido in 1915, and move north to another new Mennonite settlement at Fairmead, in Madera County. They stayed in Fairmead for about two years, and after living briefly in the nearby town of Madera, went to Reedley, California. They remained there until 1919, at which time the family left California and went to Dallas, Oregon. After only a few months, they moved to Portland and then returned south by ship to San Francisco, where they stayed briefly before settling at Lodi, California.

The 1920s were as full of movement as had been the previous decade. From about 1921 to 1924, the Duerksens lived in Reedley; then in Bakersfield until 1926. In that year they moved to a new, short-lived Mennonite settlement at Kerman, in western Fresno County. Disillusioned with that location, the Duerksens returned to Lodi later in 1926. Turning his sights further afield, Peter Duerksen moved his family to Mud Lake, Idaho, in 1927. That location did not live up to the land agent's claims, and the family moved to Salem, Oregon, in 1928. It was back to Bakersfield later that year and then on to the Fraser Valley of British Columbia in 1929. Three days of incessant rain in B.C. soured Peter Duerksen on that location, so he hooked the as-yet unloaded trailer back to their vehicle and returned to Salem. They stayed there until 1930 and then moved back to Bakersfield.

In 1931 another land agent caught Duerksen's ear and lured the family to Coldwater, Texas. Within a year, however, they had packed to move back to Oregon. But first Peter decided to visit relatives in Weatherford, Oklahoma, whom he had not seen for twenty-three years. He died of a stroke there in 1932. Katharina Duerksen and the children went ahead with the move to Dallas, but soon relocated to Salem in search of work. Within a year the family moved again to Bakersfield. In 1934 Katharina was struck by a car and killed while crossing a street, thus ending the saga of the wandering Duerksen family.

—*Based on interviews with Erma Duerksen Neufeld, Dallas, Oregon.*

Heinrich Adrian in front of his adobe house, Turner County, South Dakota. (CMBS Hillsboro)

Mennonite Brethren congregation in Canada was established not by migration from Russia, but through evangelistic efforts by these American Mennonite Brethren. Elder Heinrich Voth of Minnesota began visiting Mennonites in the West Reserve of southern Manitoba in 1884. His preaching resulted in several conversions, and in 1888 sixteen members organized the Burwalde Mennonite Brethren Church near the present-day town of Winkler.

By the end of the 1870s, the migration of Mennonite Brethren from Russia had slowed to a trickle. While others continued to migrate throughout the 1880s and 1890s, their numbers were very small. Almost all of these initial immigrants had settled in a narrow band running from north to south between the 97th and 98th meridians. Only the settlement to the northeast in Cottonwood County, Minnesota, and to the west in Culbertson, Nebraska, broke the almost perfectly straight line of Mennonite Brethren and Krimmer Mennonite Brethren settlements in North America by 1880.

Brothers Isaak, Martin and C.E. Harder making hay on their farm near Henderson, Nebraska, 1914. (CMBS Fresno)

This arrangement would remain intact for most of the 1880s. While new congregations were established, most were located in the original settlement area. Perhaps the most significant development during this decade was the establishment of several Krimmer Mennonite Brethren congregations in South Dakota. No Krimmer immigrants had settled in that state, and relatively few moved there from Kansas. These South Dakota congregations came into existence largely through Krimmer evangelistic efforts among "non-communal" Hutterites. These Hutterites had come to North America from Russia simultaneously with Mennonites, and all settled in the southeastern corner of South Dakota. Though Hutterites are known for their belief in "community of goods," a significant percentage of those who migrated from Russia at this time did not live in such communities. These non-communal Hutterites, isolated from the influence of community life, were particularly open to the influence of evangelists from nearby Mennonite groups. The Krimmer Mennonite Brethren were among the most successful in such evangelistic efforts. Elder Jacob A. Wiebe of the Gnadenau KMB Church in Kansas visited this area as early as 1884, and by 1886 several people of Hutterite background had been baptized and joined the KMB Church. Many more non-communal Hutterites joined the KMB during the ensuing years, until they became the majority of that conference's membership.

Members of the South Fairview (Okla.) MB Church in front of their meeting house, constructed in 1902. (CMBS Fresno)

Windsor Grammar School was the first meeting place of the new Reedley (Calif.) MB Church. This photo was taken in 1905.
(CMBS Fresno)

These narrowly-defined boundaries of Mennonite Brethren settlement, however, would soon change dramatically. Beginning in 1891, Mennonite Brethren individuals and families began a remarkable process of scattering across the western United States and Canada, a process that would continue almost unabated for nearly forty years. From its original base of eleven communities located in four states, Mennonite Brethren of the original 1870s immigration would establish congregations in approximately eighty-six communities across fifteen states and provinces between 1891 and 1929. This does not include the new immigrants who began arriving from Russia in the late 1920s; that story will be told in another chapter. The Krimmer Mennonite Brethren participated in this process as well, though to a much smaller extent than the Mennonite Brethren.

Why did so many Mennonite Brethren choose to uproot themselves so soon after arriving in a new homeland? They had, after all, scarcely established themselves in their original communities before many of them began moving to new and often far-flung locations. For the most part, they sought new homes for economic reasons. As more settlers, both Mennonite and otherwise, flocked to the communities where Mennonites had initially settled, available agricultural land because scarce and the prices for that land increased accordingly.

Most Mennonite Brethren farmers (and almost all of them were farmers) at the time desired to help their children establish themselves on their own farms in close proximity to the original family farm. As the land supply decreased (and the price of what was left increased), however, this goal became increasingly difficult to achieve. The fact that Mennonite Brethren families of the time commonly had six or more children (sometimes more than a dozen) meant that many of them could not fulfill the goal of farm ownership in their original communities. Subdividing farms among so many children was not a practical option, since larger farms were more viable

Members of the Henry J. Martens excursion sightseeing in Riverside, California. Martens led several groups of Mennonite land seekers to California to see land he was selling in Kern County.
(CMBS Fresno)

than small ones. Some without land of their own rented farms, though this provided less economic security than actual farm ownership. Still others left the farm and sought occupations in nearby towns. The remaining option was to seek more plentiful land elsewhere, on which extended families could re-establish themselves. This was the option pursued by many Midwestern Mennonite Brethren, and was the single largest factor fueling the migration of this period.

The first Mennonite Brethren known to have ventured out of the original 1870s settlement area was a small group from Manitoba that moved to Dallas, Oregon, in about 1891. Together with members of other Mennonite groups, they fled land shortages and harsh winters in Manitoba for the more inviting climate of Oregon's Willamette Valley. Concerned that these far-flung settlers would be lost to the church, the Mennonite Brethren conference sent Elder Heinrich Voth of Minnesota and Rev. Gerhard Wiebe of Manitoba to minister to them. In late 1891 Elder Voth helped organize the first Mennonite Brethren congregation on the West Coast. By spring of 1892 it had a membership of seventeen.

The little church would not survive long. Some members moved away within the first few years, while most others joined a nearby German Baptist congregation. By 1896 the congregation had dissolved, and not until 1904 would enough new Mennonite Brethren settlers arrive in the Dallas area to re-establish a congregation there.

At about the same time another group of Mennonite Brethren moved from Nebraska to Portland, Oregon. These were mostly "Volga Germans" who had joined the Mennonite Brethren Church in Russia shortly before the migration to North America. They for the most part settled in Hastings, Sutton, and Culbertson, Nebraska, largely separate from the "Low German" Mennonite Brethren who dominated the other original settlements. Several families from these Nebraska Volga German Mennonite Brethren groups had migrated to Portland by 1891, where they organized a congregation. By 1895 it had a membership of thirty-five, but eventually lost membership and closed in 1937.

Another small group of Mennonite Brethren at about this time set their sights on land somewhat closer to home, establishing the Kirk Mennonite Brethren Church in the eastern part of Colorado. This congregation later came to be known as the Joes Mennonite Brethren Church, and existed until 1987.

Though Oregon and Colorado were the first destinations for Mennonite Brethren land seekers, these isolated outposts were only a tentative preview of the mass movement that was soon to come. That movement began in earnest in 1892, when the first Mennonite Brethren established settlements in the newly-opened territory of Oklahoma.

The present-day state of Oklahoma became part of the United States in 1803 as part of the Louisiana Purchase. As early as 1820, this region was considered "Indian Territory," and white settlement was forbidden there. Despite these (and many other) promises to the Indians, the federal government opened Cheyenne and Arapaho land to homesteaders in April 1892. Mennonite Brethren who took up homesteads in this area eventually established communities in Okeene, Corn, Bessie and Hitchcock.

An even larger influx of settlers arrived when the Cherokee Outlet in northwestern Oklahoma was opened for settlement on 16 September 1893. Homesteads in the Cherokee Outlet were made available through a spectacular "land run," in which over 100,000 prospective settlers lined up along the northern and southern borders of the strip. At the signal, they literally raced across the line to stake out and thereby lay claim to 160-acre plots of land. Many Mennonites, including Mennonite Brethren, participated in the land run, and many were successful in claiming homesteads. A few, however, lost land when they refused to fight others who falsely asserted prior claims to land the Mennonites had staked out. By the time the dust had settled, Mennonite Brethren land runners had established communities in or near Fairview, Ringwood, Lahoma, Enid, Medford, Lookout and Coy.

Krimmer Mennonite Brethren settlers also participated in these land runs, though in far fewer numbers than Mennonite Brethren. Only two KMB congregations—at Medford and Weatherford—were established during this time, neither of which survived beyond the first few years.

Other Mennonite Brethren looked north for new lands. The most significant Canadian settlement was to the present-day province of Saskatchewan, then still a part of the North West Territories. The first Mennonite Brethren settlement there was near Laird in 1892, but many others followed over the next several years—Waldheim (1898), Dalmeny (1901), Borden (1903), Main Centre (1904), Herbert (1905), Aberdeen, Flowing Well and Hepburn (1906), Hodgeville (1907), Woodrow (1909), Rush Lake and Lichtfeld (1910), Landis (1911), Turnhill and Greenfarm (1912) and Fox Valley (1914). While some of these Canadian settlers were from Manitoba, many others crossed the border from the United States and took up settlement in a new land.

Mennonite Brethren Settlements Established Out of the 1870s Migration That Survived Twenty Years or Less:

Woodson County, Kansas: 1876-1892
Boone County, Nebraska: 1879-1899
Coffey County, Kansas: 1883-1884
Parker, South Dakota: 1896-1912
Westfield, Texas: 1897-1900
Medford, Oklahoma: 1899-1909
Pueblo, Colorado: 1902-1914
Hitchcock, Oklahoma: 1902-1919
Lahoma, Oklahoma: 1902-1919
Caddo, Oklahoma: 1905-1919
Hamilton, Kansas: 1907-ca. 1910
Nolan, Michigan: 1907-1919
Hooker, Oklahoma (KMB): 1907-1919
Henrietta, Texas: 1910-1915
Lichtfeld, Saskatchewan: 1910-1920
Landis, Saskatchewan: 1911-1912
Herington, Kansas: 1912-1925
Donald, Oregon: 1913-1915
Vinita, Oklahoma: 1913-1919
Littlefield, Texas: 1915-1923
Chinook, Montana: 1916-1923
Goodrich, North Dakota: 1916-1936
Norheim, Montana: 1917-1936
Kingwood, Oklahoma: 1918-1928
Garden City, Kansas (KMB): 1918-1936
Lake Charles, Louisiana: 1920-1923
Aberdeen, Idaho: 1920-1926
Cleveland, North Dakota: 1921-1925
Chasely, North Dakota (KMB): 1921-1932
Detroit, Michigan: 1923-1933
Tuttle, North Dakota: 1924-1936
Keenesburg, Colorado: 1927-1934
Chico, California: 1931-1932

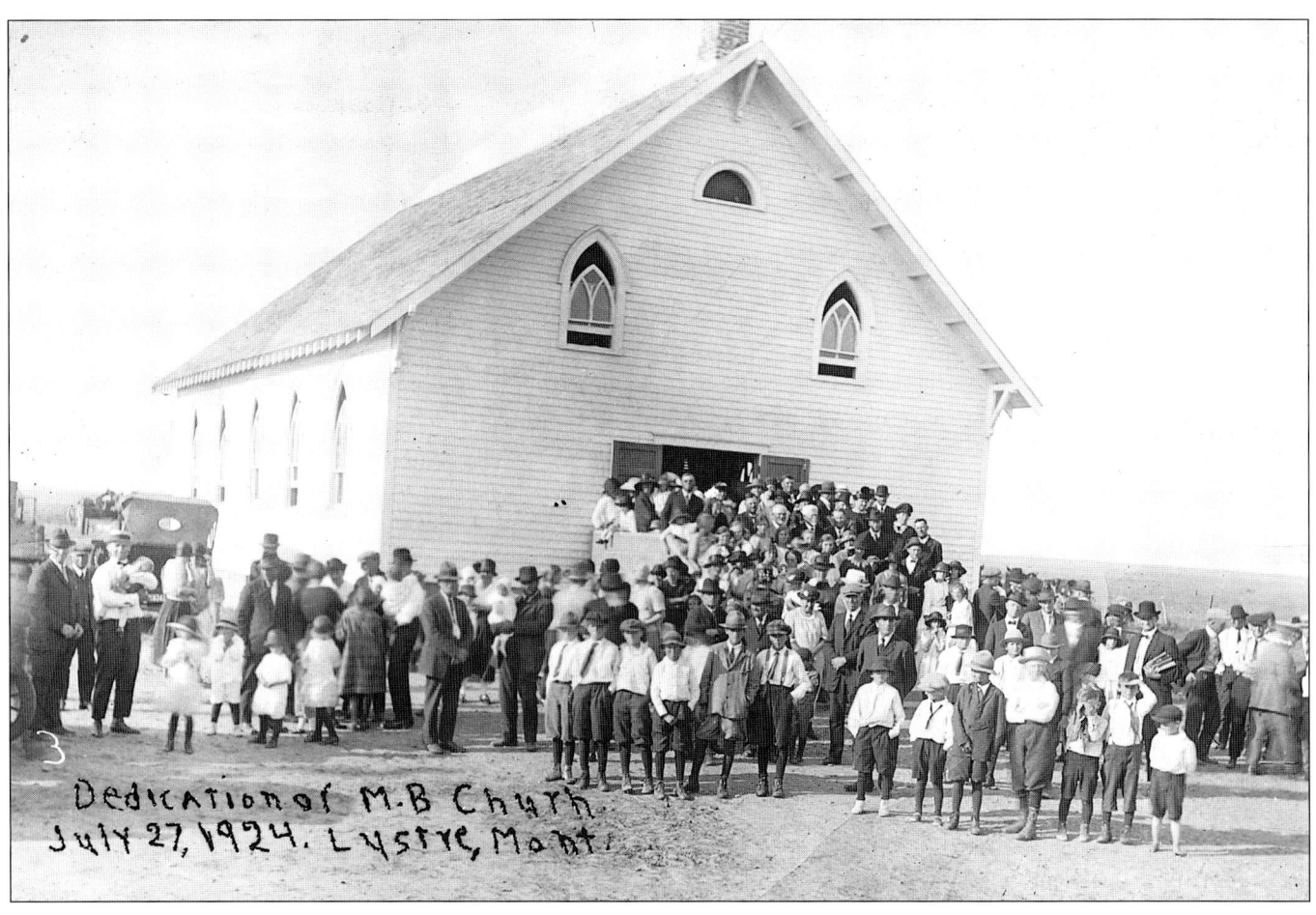

Dedication of the Lustre (Montana) MB Church, 1924.
(CMBS Fresno)

Still others went north without quite crossing into Canada. Promotional efforts by the Great Northern Railroad Company attracted many Mennonite Brethren to North Dakota, where they established settlements in Munich (1897), McClusky (1902), Mountain City (1905), Velva (1909), Goodrich (1910), Kief (1911), Dodge (1912), Cleveland (1921), Sawyer and Tuttle (1924). A similar but much smaller migration took a few Mennonite Brethren into eastern Montana beginning in 1916 and 1917.

Though few did so immediately, it was probably inevitable that large-scale Mennonite Brethren migration would eventually reach the West Coast. Other than the above-mentioned settlements in Oregon and a very short-lived community founded in Walla Walla, Washington, in 1896, West Coast settlement did not really begin until after the turn of the century. The first such significant settlement was to Reedley, California, beginning in 1904. A Mennonite Brethren congregation was established there the following year, and the new community quickly experienced rapid growth. By 1920 it had over five hundred members, and was the largest Mennonite Brethren congregation in North America. So successful was the Reedley community that it became a sort of "gold standard" by which other new Mennonite settlements were judged. Promoters of other Mennonite communities would claim that their location was "as good as Reedley" when they wished to attract the attention of potential settlers.

Other Mennonite Brethren settlements in California soon followed. Church members living in various parts of the Los Angeles Basin (some of whom had arrived already in the 1890s) pulled themselves together into a loosely-knit group and gathered for quarterly meetings beginning in 1905. Some of them ventured further south to Escondido beginning in 1907. Of particular public interest was a group of over two hundred Midwestern Mennonites (mostly Mennonite

Brethren) who purchased land in Kern County from Kansas Mennonite Brethren land agent Henry J. Martens. The town, known as Martensdale, collapsed a few months later when settlers learned that Martens had not owned the land he sold to them. Evicted by the true owners, and unable to recover the money and Midwestern land they had given to Martens, most of these now-homeless settlers started over at new locations around Bakersfield or Reedley.

California soon became the strongest magnet for Mennonite Brethren families seeking new land. Additional settlements sprang up at Fairmead (1913), Lodi (1915), Shafter (1918), Livingston (1922), Orland (1923) and Chico (1931). Krimmer Mennonite Brethren entered the state in 1910 when John Z. Kleinsasser and his extended family purchased land near Dinuba and established the Zion KMB Church—the only congregation of that conference ever founded on the West Coast.

One might have expected this West Coast settlement pattern to have extended into Canada as well, but in fact very few Mennonite Brethren of the 1870s migrations settled in British Columbia. The only congregation established there during these years was in Vanderhoof, over three hundred miles north of Vancouver. Founded in 1918, the Vanderhoof congregation disbanded only a few years later. The population of Mennonite Brethren in British Columbia, of course, would eventually grow quite large, but most of these people were part of the 1920s and 1940s migrations from the Soviet Union.

The short-lived Vanderhoof (B.C.) MB Church met in this log building.
(CMBS Fresno)

Most of these wandering Mennonite Brethren moved in a more-or-less westerly direction. That was, after all, the direction of the frontier, and a farming people such as they were naturally drawn toward the frontier. Yet a few Mennonite Brethren turned farther south and even east in their search for new settlements. Texas attracted the first such "non-conformist" settlers. Before the turn of the century there were small Mennonite Brethren communities in Westfield (north of

Building a house in the Mennonite Brethren Settlement at Lake Charles, Louisiana, in the early 1920s. (CMBS Fresno)

Houston) and the Richmond/East Bernard/Rosenberg area (southeast of Houston). Both settlements were plagued by outbreaks of malaria, and nature dealt an even harder blow on 8 September 1900 when a massive hurricane struck the Texas coast at Galveston. Two mothers and two children from the Mennonite Brethren community at Rosenberg were killed in the storm, in addition to extensive property damage. By the end of 1900 all Mennonite Brethren had apparently left these settlements.

Fifteen years would pass before more Mennonite Brethren ventured into Texas, this time to the northwestern part of the state. Congregations were eventually established at Littlefield (1915) and Coldwater (1928). The only group of Mennonite Brethren to venture back into southern Texas established a community at Premont in 1927. None of these congregations still exist today.

Even more unlikely were Mennonite Brethren settlements during this time in Michigan and Louisiana. In 1906 several families from Corn, Oklahoma, moved to Nolan, Michigan, where a Mennonite Brethren congregation was established the following year. Most families did not stay for long, and by 1919 all of them had left the area. A few years later, in 1923, several families from various other places had moved to Detroit, where a loosely-organized congregation existed for perhaps ten years. The settlement at Lake Charles, Louisiana, meanwhile, took shape in 1918. By 1920 it had a Sunday school attendance of one hundred. By 1923, however, a combination of wet weather, unfamiliar agricultural methods, and malaria, were driving most Mennonite Brethren settlers away from the area. Minister J. P. Wall left in 1924 and the congregation dissolved soon thereafter.

By the 1930s this unorganized, undisciplined movement of Mennonite Brethren across the West had for the most part come to a close. Migration into the region did not end, but it took on a different character. Subsequent migration flowed either into well-established rural communities or—more often—into urban areas. The new demands and opportunities of a wartime economy during the 1940s did much to pull Mennonite Brethren away from the search for agricultural opportunity and into the cities. They increasingly looked to occupations in industry and the professions for their livelihood, and thus the ceaseless wandering in search of greener agricultural pastures became less important. This movement of Mennonite Brethren into the cities and professions became the dominant demographic theme of the post-World War II era, and brought to a close a unique era in the history of the Mennonite Brethren Church.

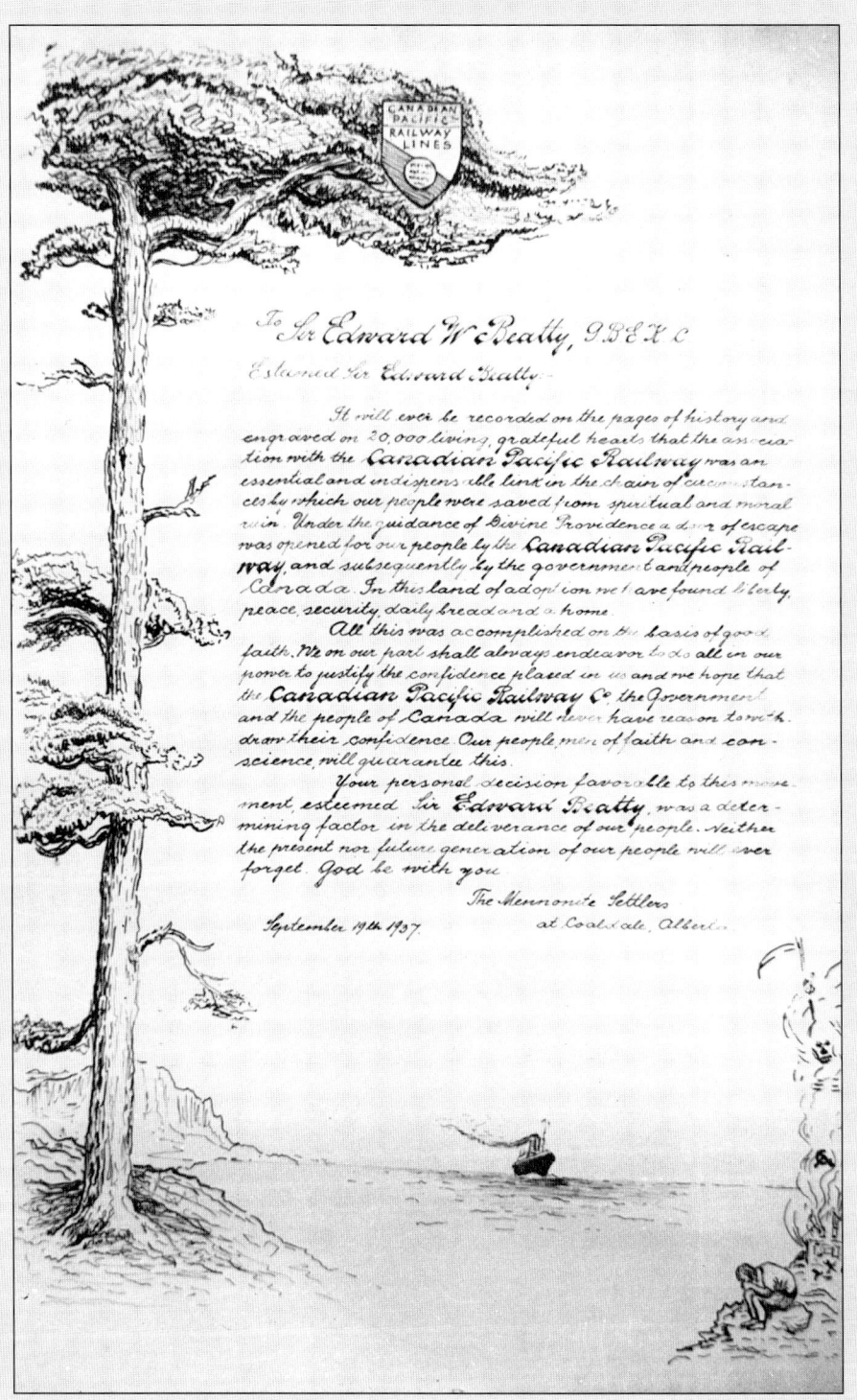

3

Coming to North America: The Immigrants of the 1920s–1940s

Abe Dueck

This proclamation was presented in 1937 to Sir Edward Beatty, President of the Canadian Pacific Railway, by Mennonite settlers of Coaldale, Alberta. It was to thank the Railway for its assistance in resettling Mennonite immigrants during the 1920s and 1930s. (CMBS Winnipeg)

While the immigrants of the 1870s were becoming established and organized in the United States and later Canada, the Mennonite Brethren Church in Russia did not remain static. The decades until World War I were years of unprecedented prosperity for Mennonites in Russia, as well as years of growth and expansion into new areas of the Russian Empire. New colonies were established in regions to the north and east in European Russia as well as in more remote areas of Asiatic Russia. Mennonite Brethren were often among the first to settle and organize new congregations in these areas.

In 1872 the Mennonite Brethren were the first to organize a conference, which became an important vehicle for communication and cooperative effort between the congregations. Mennonite Brethren became very active in mission work within the general Russian population and also began missionary work in India in 1890. Cooperation with Baptists and other evangelicals was strong. Itinerant ministers traveled many miles to minister to the scattered congregations and to develop a sense of community and common purpose. Converts were also won from the Mennonite Church (*Kirchliche*), which often caused serious tensions between the two groups. Then, in the early part of this century, a new group emerged called the Evangelical Mennonite Brethren, or *Allianz*. This group sought to bridge some of the differences between the other groups by accepting members regardless of mode of baptism. Theologically they were significantly influenced by the Plymouth Brethren and the Blankenburg Conferences in Germany, which resulted in the adoption of a dispensationalist theology by many. The *Allianz* movement had a significant impact on all Mennonites, but particularly the Mennonite Brethren.

Mennonite Brethren were in the forefront of establishing Bible schools in several locations, the most important of which was Tschongrav Bible School in Crimea. Abraham Unruh was a teacher there and was the driving force later in the organization of the Winkler Bible School (Peniel) in Canada in 1925 and the Mennonite Brethren Bible College in Winnipeg in 1944. Mennonite Brethren were also influential in the establishment of several other Bible schools that operated for brief periods in the Soviet Union in the 1920s.

In 1906, the latest year for which official statistics of Mennonite Brethren membership in Russia are available, there were approximately 5,650 members, close to 14,000 adherents, and forty-two congregations. The church was growing rapidly, with an increase of about 30 percent reported from 1905 to 1906. While this still represented a small percentage of the total Mennonite population, it was enough to cause serious concern for the other Mennonites. There were frequent

Benjamin B. Janz

Maria and Benjamin B. Janz (CMBS Fresno)

In his memoirs, a classmate of Benjamin Janz recalls a snowball fight on the grounds of the Gnadenfeld, Molotschna, high school during the early 1890s. All ran for safety as one side was vanquished, except for "little Janz" who, undaunted by the volley directed toward him, stood his ground.

Years later, when Janz was spearheading the Mennonite emigration from the Soviet Union, the exasperated chairperson of the secret police passport department in Moscow shouted at the petitioner, J. J. Thiessen: "So you come from Janz. For three years I have not crossed myself, but if I could ever free myself of Janz, I would cross myself three times!"

Here was a persistence and stubbornness that, together with the efforts of other Mennonite leaders, enabled over twenty thousand Russian Mennonites to leave Soviet Russia for Canada during the 1920s. Janz himself escaped only a few hours before his scheduled arrest by the secret police. Today Janz's surviving letters still capture the drama and tension of those days.

As a young man, Janz, against his parents' wishes, left the established Mennonite Church in Russia to join the Mennonite Brethren. Though staunchly loyal to his denomination, he was always a Mennonite ecumenist, believing that when members of a community worked together on common tasks they also built a common faith. In Russia he worked together with other Mennonites on issues related to both emigration and economic reconstruction. Once in North America he felt equally comfortable at Mennonite Central Committee gatherings or conferences relating to relief work and immigrant problems. A speaker from another Mennonite group, at a service honoring Janz's immigration work, noted that while in Russia he concluded "that Janz was a minister of our denomination. . . . Only in 1930, here in Coaldale, I learned that he was your minister, but let me tell you he is nevertheless our Benjamin Janz."

—*John B. Toews. Adapted from* Profiles of Mennonite Faith *no. 5 (Historical Commission of the Mennonite Brethren Church, 1998).*

charges that they were not really Mennonites but Baptists. On the whole, however, relationships with other Mennonites improved during the next several decades.

World War I, the Bolshevik Revolution of 1917, and the subsequent civil war and famine, resulted in severe hardship for all Mennonites. Many concluded that mass emigration was the only solution. Under very trying circumstances Mennonites in the communist Soviet Union and their brothers and sisters in America began efforts for an exodus. Benjamin B. Janz, a Mennonite Brethren leader, headed the efforts in the Soviet Union, whereas David A. Toews, a leader of the Conference of Mennonites in Central Canada, led the effort in North America. Benjamin H. Unruh, whose roots were with the Mennonite Brethren and who was in Germany at this time, was a also a major personality helping to make the migration possible.

Fleeing Terror and Beginning a New Life in Canada

By 1923 the flow of immigrants to Canada began. From 1923 to 1930 over 20,000 Mennonites settled in Canada. The doors to immigration to the United States were essentially closed by this time, although some were able to gain entry. The exact number of Mennonite Brethren among the immigrants is unknown, but they certainly made up a sizeable percentage.

This gate at the Soviet/Latvian border signified to Mennonite emigrants that they were leaving the Soviet Union on their way to new homes in Canada. (CMBS Winnipeg)

These "Russian" Mennonites (*Russländer*, as they became known in contrast to the earlier *Kanadier*) soon settled in various provinces from Ontario to British Columbia, usually in small and scattered agricultural communities, some in close proximity to Mennonites who had come earlier and others in totally new areas.

When the Mennonite Brethren of the 1920s arrived, very few Mennonite Brethren congregations existed in Canada. Those that did exist were located in southern Manitoba and in Saskatchewan. Canadian Mennonite Brethren were still a relatively insignificant force within the North American Mennonite Brethren community in 1920.

When the Russian Mennonite Brethren arrived in Canada, the relationships between the earlier arrivals and the newcomers often became quite strained. This was due to various factors. First, David Toews had made a substantial financial commitment on behalf of Canadian Mennonites to provide the guarantees to allow the Russian Mennonites to come to Canada. The Canadian Mennonites were not sure that they were in a position to provide such a substantial amount of money.

Additionally, it became obvious that a wide cultural and, to some extent, religious gap had developed between the two groups that had left Russia or the Soviet Union approximately fifty years apart. Frank Epp, in his book *Mennonites in Canada: 1920-1940*, describes the differences between the *Kanadier* and *Russländer* in general as follows:

> For the early *Kanadier* especially, the *Russländer* were too proud, too aggressive, too enthusiastic about higher education, too anxious to exercise leadership, too ready to compromise with the state, too ready to move to the cities, and too unappreciative of the pioneering done by the *Kanadier*. As far as the *Russländer* were concerned, the *Kanadier* were too withdrawn, too simple-minded, too uncultured, too weak in their High German . . . too afraid of schools and education.

The differences between the two groups of Mennonite Brethren were small compared to the differences between *Kanadier* and *Russländer* in Canada as a whole, but tensions were there nonetheless. At times the tensions were more pronounced between Mennonite Brethren in the United States and those recently arrived in Canada. The American Mennonite Brethren had already established their institutions and organizations, which the new *Russländer* Mennonite Brethren were now expected to adopt and fit into. The structure of the General Conference was already in place and Canada represented only one of four districts. Tabor College (in Hillsboro, Kansas) had become the educational institution for all Mennonite Brethren, and a foreign mission board with head office also in Hillsboro was the sending agency for all missionaries from North America. The Russian Mennonite Brethren had to leave their institutions behind and accept new institutions and organizations that they had not helped to shape.

The period from the 1920s until the 1950s was a time of adjustment and of sorting out the new realities in Canada. Sometimes this meant attempting to transplant or reincarnate what they had left behind. The new immigrants soon established Bible schools in every region where they settled and also organized provincial conferences. Only one essentially Mennonite Brethren Bible school existed before the 1920s, at Herbert, Saskatchewan, where prominent Americans like John

Finding One's Way in a New World

"Deacon Peter Block had been the first Mennonite to come to Wapiti: he cleared the way for the others. When he had come, the wilderness, now thinned every winter for firewood and better grazing, stood as forest, and the only settlers were several Englishmen grubbing a few acres from the fastness. The Wiens family came three years later, in 1930, and together with Block and the others who followed, formed the Wapiti Mennonite Church. . . . Forty years before, Wiens had been. . . serenely at ease in the Mennonite community life of Central Russia. The upheavals of Russian life after 1917 that drove him to America with his family had wrenched him from his roots. He had lived his lifetime in Russia: his sons built the farm in Canada. For him, the Canadian bush disrupted the whole order of things, for though one could succeed with some Russian Mennonite farming methods, most past standards seemed barely authoritative. Farming villages were impossible, married children had to settle far and farther from their parents, the family was splintered, the English language intruded itself. Yet if practical difficulties alone had been involved, Wiens might have regained himself. There was more, however. In Russia behaviour for him, the last of eight boys, had always been clear: right was right and wrong was wrong. Any situation could be quickly placed into one or the other category. Here, the people scattered into the Canadian bush live, according to accepted Mennonite standards, such nonchalantly sinful lives that when Wiens was among them . . . he felt as if the foundation of all morality was sliced from beneath him."

—From Peace Shall Destroy Many, by Rudy Wiebe (Eerdmans, 1962), pp. 20-21.

F. Harms and William Bestvater were most influential in the early years. The *Russländer* now led in establishing a thriving school at Winkler, Manitoba, which emphasized the training of ministers and Sunday school teachers, in contrast to the predominant missions emphasis at Herbert. Although the Winkler Mennonite Brethren Church had its roots with *Kanadier*, the *Russländer* soon became the leading force and the first instructors at the Bible school were all former teachers at the Tschongrav Bible School. In the next decades education became one of the leading concerns of the new immigrants. They were the major impetus behind the establishment of about twenty Bible schools between 1925 and 1946, five high schools, and the Mennonite Brethren Bible College in 1944.

In publication also the new immigrants soon made their presence felt. The *Mennonitische Rundschau* in time became the preferred paper for these immigrants. They were not yet ready for *The Christian Leader*, the English language publication of the General Conference, and they felt that the *Zionsbote* did not adequately speak to their needs. Later they experimented with their own English-language periodicals, such as the *Mennonite Observer*. Finally, in 1962, Canadian Mennonite Brethren began their own official English publication, the *Mennonite Brethren Herald*.

The question of publications illustrated one of the most important issues between Mennonite Brethren immigrants of the 1870s and the 1920s. The earlier immigrants, both Americans and the relatively few Canadians, had already progressed a long way in the language transition from German to English when the new immigrants arrived. For many of the new arrivals the German language came to be regarded as an important vehicle to enable them to retain their religious (and cultural) identity. Hence they felt that the American institutions could not really meet their needs.

The new immigrants also felt that they were at a disadvantage because they had to fit into existing organizations and ways of doing things. This was particularly true of foreign missions. The Mennonite Brethren Board of Foreign Mission was based in Kansas, where most General Conference agencies were headquartered. The new immigrants often felt that they were not adequately represented on the board because the structures and election procedures had not caught up with the new reality of a truly bi-national conference. Their own candidates for missions were

Members of Canadian Mennonite Brethren congregations joined together to support Canadian missionaries in the Afrika-Missionsverein. *These women were members of the* Näh-Verein *(sewing circle) at Kitchener, Ontario, which raised money for Africa missions.*
(CMBS Fresno)

Sister Anna

Anna Thiessen was known to most as "*Schwester* Anna" or "Sister Anna"—a very appropriate name, since she became a sister to around two thousand young Mennonite women in Winnipeg from the 1920s to 1950s.

The work for which she became well-known arose as many Mennonite immigrant families, with little money and heavy travel debts, began to leave their daughters in Winnipeg to work as domestic servants while they moved on to establish farms in the country. Anna, who had begun working in the Mennonite Brethren City Mission in Winnipeg in 1915, found that these Mennonite girls, some working for as little as three dollars a month, were lonely in the city and had nowhere to go on their weekly half-day off. She invited them to meet at her apartment. In time, these gatherings became so crowded with girls that the line went down the stairs. To accommodate them, she rented a third and fourth room, but even that was too little space.

Anna brought the situation to the attention of the conference, which purchased a sixteen-room house on Mountain Avenue where she could work full-time with these girls. Every Thursday evening some seventy-five to one hundred girls gathered there for singing, Bible study, and visiting. The name "Mary Martha Home" was chosen to express the ideals of worship and service, characteristics that Anna certainly exemplified.

Thiessen's role was varied. She found jobs for girls, provided accommodations as they waited for jobs, escorted them to their first places of work, and often served as a mediator between girls and their employers. She encouraged the girls to develop ties with each other and with the North End Mennonite Brethren Church. Parents, understandably reluctant to let their daughters go away to work in the city, were reassured that there was someone there to look after their physical and spiritual needs.

Anna had a stern, sober appearance, which people sometimes found formidable at first. But the warmth of her heart inevitably superseded that first impression. Though straightforward and strict, she also was loving and kind, and was always concerned about the girls' welfare. She had strong prohibitions against young men coming near the home to court any of the girls, but was often the first to congratulate a girl who became engaged.

(CMBS Winnipeg)

Anna's strictness paid off. The Mary Martha Home had a reputation for providing honest, hard-working girls, and the phone often rang with requests for them. These girls basically ran the households for many of Winnipeg's most wealthy and influential families.

Sister Anna worked as the matron of the Mary Martha Home until 1951 and continued her presence there until 1959. "Her girls" continued to visit her in the nursing home where she later lived, sometimes bringing their lunches as in the old days. She died in 1977 at the age of eighty-five.

—*Adapted from* Looking Back in Faith: A Commemorative Collection of Photos and Writing to Mark the Centennial of Mennonite Brethren in Manitoba, 1888-1988, *edited by Helmut Huebert, Harold Jantz, John Longhurst (Manitoba Mennonite Brethren Centennial Committee, 1988).*

either bypassed, it seemed, or unfairly expected to receive their credentials at Tabor College. Education in the Canadian Bible schools was not deemed adequate by the Americans. As a result some of the Canadians established their own mission society named the *Afrika–Missionsverein* (Africa Mission Society), which sent out several missionaries before the organization was eventually incorporated under the Mennonite Brethren Board of Foreign Missions in 1943.

Another unique aspect of the immigration pattern of the 1920s was that there were concentrations of *Allianz* or Evangelical Mennonite Brethren in several locations. This was particularly true in Ontario where the Kitchener church, initially called the Molotschna Mennonite Brethren Church, became the mother church of the provincial conference. The *Allianz* orientation, with open communion and recognition of non-immersion baptism, predominated. This created considerable difficulty when the Ontario Conference sought to join the General and Canadian conferences. Ontario finally joined the General Conference as a new district in 1939, giving up its more open policies. In 1946 Ontario joined the Canadian Conference and therefore no longer was a separate district within the General Conference.

In Alberta, the Namaka congregation was the mother congregation of groups of *Allianz*-minded Mennonite Brethren in places like Linden, Gem, and Crowfoot. For a time they formed a separate Evangelical Mennonite Brethren Conference in Alberta, although they simultaneously worked cooperatively with the Alberta Mennonite Brethren Conference in some areas. They also joined the Evangelical Mennonite Brethren *(Bruderthaler)* of North America for a short period, but eventually discontinued that membership and became full members of the Mennonite Brethren Conference.

World War II and Its Aftermath

World War II brought new circumstances that shaped the Mennonite Brethren church in different ways in the United States and Canada. First, the Mennonite bodies in the two countries were faced with different laws and policies respecting their nonresistant position. Negotiations with the respective governments had to proceed independently and in concert with other Mennonite groups. Although there was certainly a great deal of dialogue across the international boundary on the fundamental issues, some issues had to be handled separately because the two governments had different laws and policies dealing with conscientious objectors. Furthermore, the Russian Mennonites had experienced service in the Russian forestry camps as well as in the medical corps during World War I. This often meant that they had different views about what kind of services they could render to their country than the earlier Mennonite groups both in Canada and the United States.

Between the migrations of the 1920s and after the Second World War Russian Mennonite society underwent an even more radical transformation than that between the migrations of the 1870s and 1920s. Those who remained in the Soviet Union experienced intense trial, persecution and economic hardship. Restrictions on public worship and all public practice of religion became so severe that religious life became almost completely decimated. Churches were closed and children indoctrinated in atheism in the state-run schools. There was careful surveillance of home life and any efforts to teach religious values in the home was severely punished. Many church leaders and intellectuals were sent into exile, where every effort was made to break their spirits. Those who went into exile were often never heard from again. Mothers bore the burden of raising their families and often showed remarkable courage and stamina in resisting the authorities, maintaining their faith, and passing it on to their children.

Mennnite refugees fleeing from Ukraine toward Poland during World War II. (CMBS Winnipeg)

The rise of Nazi Germany under Hitler and the outbreak of World War II brought still more turmoil and uncertainty to the Mennonites in the Soviet Union. Mennonites were regarded with suspicion by the Soviet government because of their German connections. This distrust of the German population had also been there during World War I because Mennonites were German-speaking and had many close ties with Germany. Because of the difficulty this created for them during World War I as well as later, Mennonites made strong efforts to reassert their Dutch lineage, hoping that this would make life easier for them. But it was impossible for them to escape the taint of being regarded as Germans.

In June 1941 German armies invaded Russia. They quickly swept over many areas where the Mennonites had lived, such as Chortitza and Molotschna. The Soviets tried to evacuate these areas to the east before the Germans arrived and succeeded to a considerable extent, especially with the settlements east of the Dnieper River such as Molotschna. But in places like Chortitza most of the Mennonites remained and so lived under German occupation for some time. A period of relative tranquility ensued. Many churches reopened. This brief respite ended, however, with the defeat of the Germans at Stalingrad and subsequent retreat from Ukraine. Now the danger was even greater. Mennonites, along with other ethnic Germans, began a difficult trek west along with the retreating German armies in 1943. About 35,000 Mennonites fled their homeland, hoping to escape the certain fate of those who might be captured by Soviet forces bent on revenge. The hardships of the trek were almost unimaginable. They traveled in a cold and unforgiving climate, often with overloaded wagons that broke down, and many had to make their way on foot. Some of the more fortunate went by train. Their fate was still uncertain when the war ended in 1945. Many had been overtaken by the Soviet army and were shipped back, not to their former home in Ukraine, but further east and north where suffering and death awaited them. Some ended up in the Soviet zones from where they were forcibly repatriated. Women were raped and others killed. In all, about 23,000 Mennonites were repatriated to the Soviet Union. Some refugees ended up in areas occupied by Western allies and were rounded up to be returned to the Soviet forces. A group that ended up in Berlin escaped by what they regarded as the miraculous intervention of God. Many spent years in refugee camps, hoping that they would be allowed to join relatives and friends in Canada and elsewhere.

Eventually, over 7,700 Mennonite refugees were allowed to come to Canada. This migration began in 1947 and ended in 1951, with the largest number coming in 1948. There are no statistics available concerning the number of these who joined Mennonite Brethren churches. The United States remained closed to these refugees. While most preferred to come to Canada, for some the only alternative was South America.

The impact of the new arrivals on the Mennonite Brethren Church in Canada is difficult to assess. Their numbers were smaller and they came into a situation where organizations and institutions were already well defined. This differed from the earlier wave of 1920s immigrants,

Map showing the approximate migration route of Mennonites leaving the Soviet Union in 1943-1945.

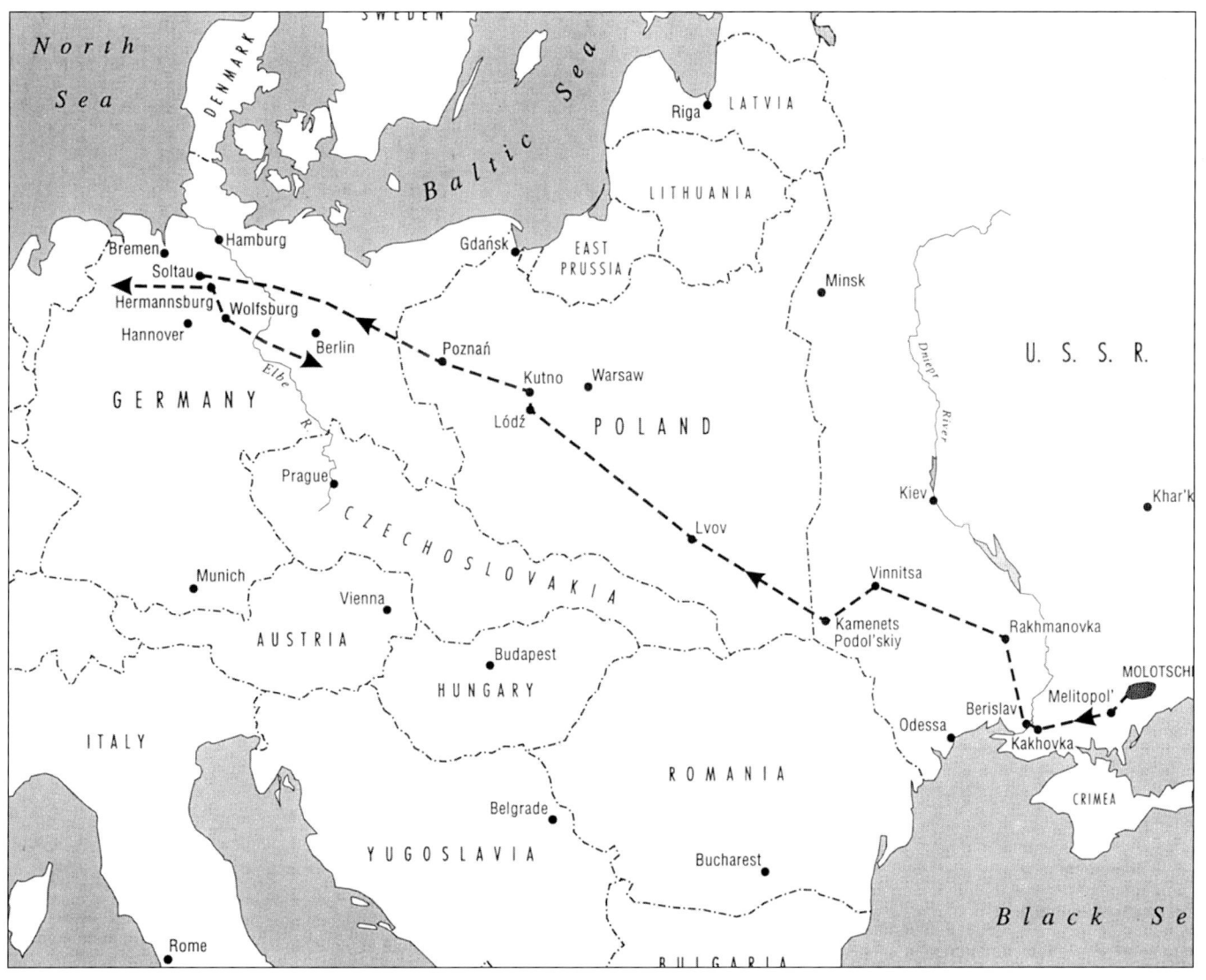

C. F. Klassen: helping his people

It was a Sunday morning in early autumn in Bavaria, West Germany. The year was 1945. A car was driving through a quiet village near the Czech border, stopping frequently as its driver and passenger got out and looked around, searching for something or someone. Suddenly, strains of a hymn could be heard on the morning air. "Wess ich den Weg auch nicht, Du weisst ihn wohl."("Even when I don't know the way, You certainly do.") Excitedly, the passenger exclaimed, "Those are my people—let's go to them."

The little group of Russian Mennonite refugees were crowded into a farm cottage with wide-open windows. They were comforting their hearts with familiar songs from their lost homeland villages in Russia, when a tall, handsome man strode into the room. Imagine their surprise and joy when they learned that C. F. Klassen was "one of them," who had left Russia and gone to Canada in 1928. Now he had come to post-war Germany, "seeking his brethren," he said. He offered them the help of the Mennonite family in North America through Mennonite Central Committee (MCC) to find a new home after the horrors of the Second World War.

As the refugees gathered around him bombarding him with questions, they were surprised to discover he could tell them all about relatives in Canada—which town or village they had settled in, what they were working at—sometimes the names of their children. How could this be?

They learned that Klassen, after helping thousands of Mennonites flee Russia in the 1920s, had been busy during the war years in Canada collecting the money borrowed from the Canadian Pacific Railway and the government to resettle in Canada. It was a difficult task but he did it cheerfully. Now it took on a new significance. He could comfort these dislocated people with news of loved ones. And he could put them in touch with those who would help them in turn to reach a new homeland. Humbly, he thanked God for His ways.

C. F. Klassen knew what it meant to be a stranger and pilgrim on earth. In Russia he had seen Mennonite village life destroyed through social unrest, famine and civil war. He had acted as an intermediary between his people and the government in Moscow and later between them and western Mennonites who had sent them relief in the famine years. He sought to give his life to relieve suffering wherever he found it, whether it was food for the hungry, escape from tyranny, or to assist in resettlement to a new land. He showed God's love and mercy to people whose lives had been ravaged by war and revolution, famine and disease.

—*Adapted from* Profiles of Mennonite Faith *no. 8, by Herb & Maureen Klassen (Historical Commission of the Mennonite Brethren Church, 1999).*

A Mennonite farmer working the fields in the Coldale, Alberta, area.
(CMBS Winnipeg)

who came to Canada when there were still very few institutions and where they quickly formed the majority. While most of the new immigrants initially settled in rural areas and helped in the agricultural industry, many soon found their way into urban areas such as Winnipeg, Vancouver and Kitchener. Some congregations received disproportionate numbers. Large numbers also entered the Bible schools and the Mennonite Brethren Bible College in Winnipeg.

Earlier settlers were usually quite generous hosts. In Coaldale, Alberta, the congregation invited the new immigrants to attend the Bible school free of charge, while in other cases relatives or friends sponsored them.

One impact of the new arrivals was to slow the language transition from German to English, which was just getting underway in Canada and was already essentially complete in the United States. In this way the immigrants probably accentuated the divergence between the United States and Canada, because now, for the second time, a wave of immigrants had come to North America and settled almost entirely in Canada. The new immigrants learned the English language rather quickly, however, and did not become an organized force to slow the language transition. Furthermore, many of the young people in this group also attended US institutions like Tabor College and the Mennonite Brethren Biblical Seminary in Fresno.

One of the unique features of these immigrants was that often families consisted of only mothers with their children. Many of the men had been taken away by the Communists and had died in captivity or were never heard from again. The responsibility of raising the children and being the economic providers fell to the women, who often experienced much hardship. Furthermore, women did not have a significant voice in the congregations, and therefore these families were quite powerless in matters that affected them deeply. In general, over the next several decades, very few of the post-World War II immigrants moved into positions of influence and power in the Canadian Conference. Many of them, however, became well-educated and entered the professional world as teachers, nurses or professors. Others became very successful as business entrepreneurs.

In addition to the two waves of immigration from the Soviet Union, there were many immigrants who came to Canada from South America, particularly Paraguay and Brazil, during the last half-century. Because they did not immigrate in larger groups and there are no reliable statistics, they have not been adequately recognized and their influence is not easily assessed. Larger urban areas such as Winnipeg and the lower Fraser Valley were usually the recipients of these immigrants and many became active in the construction industry or joined the urban labor force, especially in factories owned by Mennonites. Their influence was felt most strongly in selected churches, where their presence also slowed the language transition and otherwise resulted in more traditional worship services.

The Canadian Mennonite Brethren Mosaic

Canadian Mennonite Brethren, until recent decades, have been defined in large measure by three separate waves of immigration and more scattered immigration at other times. During their times of separation prior to arrival in Canada, very different political, cultural, and religious experiences shaped each group. Some of these differences continue to influence forms of worship as

The Mennonite Brethren Church at Sardis, B.C., one of many congregations established by immigrants to Canada during and after the 1920s.

(CMBS Winnipeg)

well as family and social life. The result might be characterized as a mosaic to which even more diversity has been added with the arrival of many other ethnic and cultural groups who have joined the Mennonite Brethren family in Canada. The diversity sometimes has resulted in misunderstanding and tension. But at its best, diversity has been a source of strength and richness, contributing to a positive witness within Canadian society. Mennonite Brethren in Canada are in a unique position to welcome those who are suffering and persecuted in many countries of the world because of their own experiences of hardship that brought them to a country of opportunity and freedom.

Members of the Canadian Mennonite Board of Colonization. This board played a major role in assisting Mennonite immigrants arriving in Canada. (CMBS Fresno)

4

Mennonite Brethren Theology: A Multiple Inheritance

Lynn Jost

The Mennonite Brethren Church is an evangelical-Anabaptist renewal movement, a missionary church with emphasis on personal conversion within a community of disciples. It claims a Bible-centered approach historically focused on theology, ethics and ecclesiology. A simple hermeneutic—"What does the Bible say?"—has often been invoked as a denominational strength. While this no doubt is true, it has also opened the church to various—and sometimes conflicting—theological emphases. Multiple theological currents have been present since the creation of the Mennonite Brethren Church in 1860. This multiple inheritance has enriched the church, but it has also been the source of some weakness. The tendency toward fragmentation and pluralism have frequently surfaced in the history of the church.

The three primary religious currents that have shaped Mennonite Brethren are Anabaptism, pietism, and evangelicalism. Each of these are complex movements in themselves, but their main characteristics help us to understand how Mennonite Brethren have come to be who they are today.

Anabaptism

The Mennonites of South Russia were largely the biological and spiritual descendants of the Dutch Mennonites of the sixteenth century led by Menno Simons. Menno, rooted in the Brethren of the Common Life and Catholic piety (in contrast to the Swiss Anabaptist roots in the Zwinglian reformation), emphasized personal conversion and the nature of the church. In succeeding centuries, as Mennonites migrated to Prussia and then to southern Russia, they experienced many changes. The original vitality of faith and practice subsided. Mennonites had been attracted to Russia by the availability of large tracts of land where they could develop closed settlements and control their own schools and other institutions as well as receive exemption from military service. But their isolation led to religious formalism and a loss of their missionary vision.

The Mennonite Brethren document of secession strongly asserts that the early brethren sought to restore the Mennonite Church of Russia to its New Testament ideal. That document decried the decadent condition of the Mennonite church. It explicitly declared that the new movement was "in full agreement with Menno Simons." Using frequent biblical references and citing Menno again and again, the document outlined specific concerns: the ordinances of the church (baptism, the Lord's Supper, and foot washing) were to be practiced within a pure church of converted disciples living a holy lifestyle; church leaders were to live circumspectly in light of their calling; and church discipline (the ban) was to be practiced by the church. Personal conversion and a life of discipleship were to characterize church members. These concerns were

Participants at the Mennonite Brethren ministers' course held at Mennonite Brethren Bible College in Winnipeg, 1957. These courses were important forums for shaping Mennonite Brethren theological understandings.
(CMBS Fresno)

rooted in their understanding of the New Testament and the nature of sixteenth-century Anabaptism.

In addition to the focus on conversion, the Mennonite Brethren followed Menno in emphasizing church discipline to enforce personal piety and a literal biblical hermeneutic. The Anabaptist emphasis on ethical commitment to discipleship within a covenant community of peacemakers was central to early Mennonite Brethren practical theology.

Lutheran Pietism

Peter M. Friesen, the prominent historian of the Russian Mennonites, identified two reformers who contributed to the founding of the Mennonite Brethren church. Menno, he claimed, was the builder of the spiritual house, and Eduard Wuest, a Lutheran pietist, refurbished an impoverished structure. Wuest came to the Russian Mennonite colonies in the 1850s, preaching the need for personal conversion, an experience of repentance from sins, and a joyous assurance of salvation. His pietist preaching led to many conversions. The renewal provided a spark that challenged the more formal and traditional religious practices of the mother church. With pietism came a renewed emphasis on personal conversion, devotional piety, Bible reading, prayer, free religious expression and emotional release.

The pietistic revival did not come about in a vacuum. In the decades prior to Wuest's arrival in Russia, Mennonites in several centers experienced intellectual and spiritual renewal. In Ohrloff, teacher Tobias Voth organized prayer meetings, mission meetings and a Christian Literature Society. At Gnadenfeld, *Bibelstunden* (Bible study discussion hours) and prayer meetings in small group home fellowships contributed to the renewal of members, many of whom later became Mennonite Brethren leaders. The Russian Mennonite colonies were ripe for a renewal movement.

Baptists and Evangelicals

A third religious current that influenced the early Mennonite Brethren Church was mediated through German Baptists. The early Mennonite Brethren movement was not well defined and often chaotic in nature. Theological understandings and ecclesiastical practices were still very fluid. Mennonite Brethren became very vulnerable to the excesses of some of their leaders. The dead formalism that some experienced in their mother church gave way to uncontrolled extremism. The young Mennonite Brethren church experienced a movement known as the *Froeliche Richtung* (joyous movement) between 1862 and 1865, with excessive emotional expression and indiscriminate exercise of the ban against respected church leaders.

In order to bring some order and stability to the movement, Abraham Unger, an elder in the Einlage village church, invited Johann Gerhard Oncken, the founder of the German Baptists, to southern Russia. He and another Baptist leader, August Liebig, introduced Baptist congregational polity to the Mennonite Brethren. Unger even published a Confession of Faith, which was essentially the German Baptist Confession with some distinctive Mennonite beliefs added. This German Baptist influence positively contributed to peaceful resolution of some early governance

---

"Biblical or Systematic Theology?"

The 1957 General Conference authorized the publication of three books: one on Mennonite Brethren history, one on Mennonite Brethren polity and one on Mennonite Brethren theology. J. B. Toews was asked to write the one on theology. In 1995 he reflected on the task and why the book was never written. His position confirms comments by various Mennonite Brethren leaders over many years that ours has been a "biblical" theology rather than a "systematic" theology.

"I was asked to prepare a book on 'Mennonite Brethren Theology (Biblical Doctrine).' I worked on it, as my schedule allowed, for the next several years and prepared a tentative outline. I read all the writing of Mennonite Brethren in the *Friedensstimme* in Russia, the *Zionsbote* in North America and other papers by Mennonite Brethren to gain insights into the various trends in our history. My conclusion, after all this research, was that Mennonite Brethren had an implicit biblical theology: they believed in the Bible and found the answers for faith and life as needs demanded."

—*From* JB: A Twentieth-Century Mennonite Pilgrim, *by J. B. Toews (Center for Mennonite Brethren Studies-Fresno, 1995)*

issues. It also resulted in continuing cooperation between the two groups. The first Mennonite Brethren foreign missionaries went to India under joint sponsorship with the Baptists, and many Russian church leaders received theological training from the Baptist seminary in Hamburg.

The Baptist influence however, also threatened the Anabaptist/Mennonite identity of the young church. Other Mennonites often labeled Mennonite Brethren as Baptists. Government officials threatened to withdraw their special privileges as Mennonites and to place them under the same restrictions as other groups who were defined as sects. Indeed, the Baptist influence encouraged some Mennonite Brethren to question Mennonite understandings of biblical nonresistance and the Baptist emphasis on individual conversion tended to reduce the emphasis on discipleship.

In later years the Russian Mennonites, especially Mennonite Brethren, were also influenced by the Plymouth Brethren movement, which had its institutional center in Blankenburg, Germany. Mennonite leaders frequently attended the prophetic conferences at Blankenburg, which had a heavy emphasis on eschatology and dispensational theology. Plymouth Brethren speakers were also invited to gatherings in various churches and estates in southern Russia.

Balancing the Theological Triangle

The three major currents that have shaped Mennonite Brethren have each helped to enrich the movement. Anabaptism formed the ecclesiastical foundation for Mennonite Brethren. Mennonite Brethren considered Anabaptism to be a biblical movement, especially because of Menno's emphasis on new birth, holy living and the church as a community of disciples. Pietism offered the promise of engaging the heart. Traditional forms of worship were replaced by joyous personal experiences of redeeming grace. Pietism reinforced Menno's emphasis on personal conversion, whereas its weak ecclesiology was counterbalanced by the strong emphasis on the nature of the church by Anabaptists. Baptists offered both a practical theology (congregational polity and foreign mission organization) and a systematic theology (a ready-made confession of faith and the theological curriculum of the Hamburg seminary).

The literal biblical hermeneutic of the early Mennonite Brethren worked well enough in solving most ethical issues. The Bible had clear enough answers for most questions. As years went by, however, the Anabaptist hermeneutic became less familiar to Mennonite Brethren Bible teachers and preachers, and was replaced by an evangelical systematic theology.

Early Trends and Influences in North America

When Mennonite Brethren began moving to North America in the 1870s they did not diverge significantly from

---

A Theological Autobiography

"One often-debated question was the security of the believer. 'Eternal security' was considered a heresy. We knew nothing about Calvinism or Arminianism, but we knew that the warnings of Scripture had to be taken seriously. This often led to a lack of assurance and robbed us of much joy and peace.

"Sanctification was very central in the church's teaching, and at times it was understood as perfectionism. Since none of us measured up, we often felt like giving up. It was clearly stated that we were saved by grace, but the strong emphasis on holy living and good deeds caused us to wonder whether we would be able to stand in the final judgment or whether, like the five foolish maidens, we would find the door shut.

"Conversion was generally understood as a crisis experience, and those who had come into the kingdom in a more gentle way, not kicking and screaming, would have to do a lot of explaining . . . when it came to baptism. . . .

"One theological issue that earned me personally much criticism was my failure to uphold the dispensational approach to the Bible. Some thought I had become a modernist because I no longer held to a pretribulation rapture. In fact I was Anabaptist in this regard. I took the Sermon on the Mount seriously, which Scofield had relegated to the coming millennium. I didn't have to speculate on who or what the treasure in the field or the pearl of great price was, because I interpreted all the parables of Jesus as Kingdom parables. The most bitter attacks came when it was discovered that I put little stock in political developments in modern Israel, which is largely godless; and when I pointed out that the line in the New Testament is no longer drawn between Jew and Gentile, but between people of faith and unfaith."

—Adapted from David Ewert's "Theological Autobiography" in Bridging Troubled Waters: The Mennonite Brethren at Mid-Twentieth Century *(Kindred Productions, 1995).*

their roots. The first official convention of the General Conference of Mennonite Brethren in North America met in 1879 for inspirational Bible teaching and to plan cooperative mission work. Home missions involved sending evangelists and elders to strengthen existing churches and to plant new congregations. Foreign mission work began as a cooperative venture with the American

Baptists in India. Elder Abraham Schellenberg served as conference moderator and provided a leading voice in favor of cooperation between churches in the work of missions, education, and publications. Evangelists, including Peter H. Wedel, N. N. Hiebert, and John F. Harms, were appointed to visit the scattered congregations.

The Anabaptist concern for ethical faithfulness is evident in the issues that were discussed. The church was committed to a separation from the world, as evidenced by high standards of Christian life and discipleship. Issues debated included insurance policies, political involvement, marriage to non-church members, and leadership questions.

Several factors promoted theological unity among Mennonite Brethren. Their common culture and language often isolated them from their neighbors. Their simple biblicism helped them to resolve issues of faith and life. No systematic grid for reading the Bible was needed because of their shared culture. Furthermore, although Mennonite Brethren followed a democratic congregational rule, a few leading elders largely controlled denominational life. The later division of the conference into district conferences (1909) limited the centralizing control of the elders and opened the way to growing diversity.

The need for biblical training for Mennonite Brethren leaders and missionaries soon became evident in North America. Pastors and missionaries turned to two primary sources—Baptist

Bible teacher conferences in Canada were intstrumental in focusing the theology set forth in Mennonite Brethren Bible schools. This group of teachers met in Saskatoon in 1941. (CMBS Winnipeg)

seminaries and the Bible school movement. Many of the early missionaries and college Bible instructors were trained at Rochester Seminary in New York and at Southern Baptist Seminary in Louisville, Kentucky. These schools helped nurture a missionary vision and biblical emphasis and contributed practical instruction in evangelism, Christian education and theology. On the other hand, the hierarchical concept of church ministry and polity became accepted as the pattern at home and abroad. An emphasis on Anabaptist theology was neglected. The New Testament concept of multiple church leaders and calling out leaders from within the congregation was replaced by a polity governed by professional clergy.

Bible institutes, particularly the Bible Institute of Los Angeles, Moody Bible Institute in Chicago, and Northwestern Bible Institute and Seminary in Minneapolis, had a profound influence on the spiritual development of a generation of leaders. Their emphasis on Bible content, missionary motivation, a simple hermeneutic, the experiential reality of Christ as Savior, and the work of the Holy Spirit as a second act of grace became sustaining influences in spiritual life. Evangelism, however, tended to emphasize the benefits of salvation while neglecting the notions of service, accountability and discipleship.

Exposure to the Bible institute movement also opened Mennonite Brethren to the fundamentalist influence. Mennonite Brethren trained in the Bible institutes emerged with a concern for propositional truth in the battle against modernism, which focused on biblical inerrancy, the virgin birth, the physical resurrection of Jesus, and the imminent return of Christ. A dispensational eschatology was taught in most of these institutions.

Fundamentalism made its impact on Mennonite Brethren in a variety of ways, particularly by means of radio and the print media. Periodicals such as John Rice's *The Sword of the Lord* and Gerald Winrod's *Defender* became household literature among Mennonite Brethren. Fundamentalist textbooks, notably R. A. Torrey's *What the Bible Teaches* and James M. Gray's *Synthetic Bible Studies*, served as doctrinal guides for Mennonite Brethren pastors, teachers and educational curricula. Fundamentalist and pietist writings provided devotional material for Mennonite Brethren homes.

One of the leaders whose influence was widespread in the Mennonite Brethren Church in the 1920s and 1930s was William Bestvater. Bestvater emphasized missionary outreach, biblical study, and personal conversion. His influence spread widely through his teaching at Herbert (Sask.) Bible School and Tabor College, his writing in textbooks and periodicals, and his itinerant evangelism. Bestvater was a powerful speaker and his advocacy of dispensational theology influenced the Mennonite Brethren church for half a century or more.

Developments in Russia Until the 1920s

While Mennonite Brethren were becoming established in North America, the Russian Mennonite Brethren Church was also developing. Gradually the relationships between Mennonite Brethren and the Mennonite Church (referred to as *Kirchliche*) improved and there was cooperation in an organization known as the General Conference of Mennonite Churches in Russia. Mennonite Brethren were among the leaders in education, land settlement, health care, publications, and church life.

Anna and William Bestvater. He was well-known for his lectures on dispensational theology.
(CMBS Fresno)

Abraham H. Unruh

Abraham H. Unruh (1878-1961) was an outstanding Mennonite Brethren minister, teacher, and Bible expositor in Russia and Canada. In 1920 he was asked to join the newly-founded Bible school in Tschongrav, Crimea. Unruh taught there until 1924 when the Soviet authorities closed it. He immigrated to Canada in 1925 and began a Bible school in Winkler, Manitoba with his former colleagues.

In 1944 the Canadian Mennonite Brethren Conference established the Mennonite Brethren Bible College in Winnipeg and Unruh became the first president (1944-1945). He taught there until his retirement in 1956 and remained very active in Conference boards and as an eloquent preacher in the Canadian constituency.

According to his biographer, David Ewert, "anyone who met Unruh for the first time was struck by his physique. He was quite literally head and shoulders above other men. His physical dimensions, coupled with a dignified bearing, gave him a patriarchal appearance. . . .

"[Unruh] was physically not too well coordinated. Those responsibilities in the home which demanded some degree of physical dexterity were conveniently left to his wife. She . . . could handle a snowshovel as well as any man. The neighbors . . . recount with delight the drama which the Unruhs staged when they put up storm windows in fall. . . . Mrs. Unruh was up on the ladder removing screens, cleaning windows, and putting on the storm windows, while the doctor of divinity stood on the ground watching. Abraham was content to hold the ladder while dear Tina took care of the rest. But they got along famously. . . .

"[He] was careful in the observance of the Lord's day, but not in a pharisaical way. Once when a brother did some necessary work on Sunday and excused himself by a reference to the words of Jesus about the donkey that fell into the well on the Sabbath, Unruh commented: 'Good enough!' 'But,' he added, 'if the donkey falls in every Sunday, perhaps you should sell the donkey.'"

—*Adapted in part from* Stalwart for the Truth: The Life and Legacy of A. H. Unruh, *by David Ewert (Board of Christian Literature, 1975)*

(CMBS Winnipeg)

Jacob W. Reimer was an influential teacher and Bible expositor among Mennonite Brethren in Russia, the United States and Canada. (CMBS Fresno)

Annual Bible conferences often attracted members of both groups and a new *Allianz* group emerged (calling itself the Evangelical Mennonite Brethren), which sought to bridge the differences between them. Mennonite Brethren continued to be deeply influenced by the Blankenburg Alliance Conference established in 1885. The emphases were on the inner spiritual life, sanctification, fellowship and dispensational eschatology. Jacob W. Reimer, an influential Mennonite Brethren itinerant minister, regularly attended the Conference and was influential in bringing Alliance teaching to the church. The writings of Blankenburg people were a major theological resource of Mennonite Brethren ministers.

These factors shaped Russian Mennonite Brethren immigrants who arrived in North American during the 1920s. Positively, the pietistic influence brought new warmth and deepened a commitment to Biblical faithfulness. But the pietistic emphases on personal salvation, the inward experience of God's grace, the fellowship of all true believers, and millennial eschatology, pushed to the periphery the concept of discipleship within a committed community of believers. The emotional emphasis within the salvation experience had a negative result for some. Furthermore, Mennonite Brethren commitment to nonresistance was often seriously eroded.

Despite these influences the Mennonite Brethren Confession of Faith, first adopted in Russia in 1902, continued to reflect Anabaptist beliefs. The confession is filled with biblical language and references. The emphasis lies on the church, Christ, and the Christian life. Articles deal with such Anabaptist issues as baptism, the Lord's Supper, foot washing, oaths, and nonresistance. Although Mennonite Brethren were influenced by pietism and incipient evangelicalism, the confession demonstrates a continued commitment to Anabaptism.

Developments in North America Until Mid-Century

The influence of fundamentalism and dispensationalism was stronger in the United States Mennonite Brethren Church than in Canada. The chief reason for this was the wave of Russian immigrants to Canada between 1924 and 1930. Theologically the experiences of the earlier and later groups of immigrants were in many respects parallel. Both groups had cooperated with Baptists, and both had been influenced by a dispensationalist theology that had undermined some Anabaptist values. But the first generation of 1920s immigrants in Canada were probably protected to a greater degree from some of the distinctive features of North American fundamentalism. They came to Canada speaking German, so the transition to English in Canada was generally delayed by about two decades and insulated the Canadian Mennonite Brethren from much of the fundamentalist influence that was so significant south of the border. They were struggling to establish themselves economically and had closer relationships with other Mennonites from Russia with whom they shared the suffering and trauma of the Russian Revolution and Civil War. Nevertheless many leading ministers, itinerant evangelists, and instructors at the Bible institutes that were established in the first decades after the new wave of immigration taught a dispensationalist eschatology.

Other leaders and institutions embarked on a different course. Abraham H. Unruh was among the leaders who emerged after the 1920s migration. He preached widely and taught at Winkler Bible School and later at Mennonite Brethren Bible College in Winnipeg. Unruh was highly regarded as a Bible expositor. On one occasion, after attending a lecture in which Bestvater used a large canvas chart to expound the plan of dispensational eschatology, Unruh approached the speaker and asked in Low German, "Brother Bestvater, do you think that God will be guided by your rag?"

Abraham E. Janzen as a young professor at Tabor College.
(CMBS Fresno)

Reshaping Mennonite Brethren Identity

Several factors in the 1940s and 1950s precipitated a shift to an intentional Anabaptist Mennonite Brethren identity. The world wars forced Mennonite Brethren to grapple with the issue of military service. Though a staunch dispensationalist, A. E. Janzen of Tabor College became a strong advocate of nonresistance and alternative service. General Conference sessions were devoted to articulating the Mennonite Brethren peace position both within and beyond the church. During World War II, many Mennonite Brethren served in the Civilian Public Service system in the United States or in the Alternative Service program in Canada. In these camps Mennonite Brethren met other Mennonites and often found that they too were committed followers of Christ. The fellowship and the instruction they received often strengthened their interest in Anabaptist ties.

In 1943 Harold S. Bender delivered his well-known address entitled "The Anabaptist Vision." This laid the groundwork for a recovery of the Anabaptist heritage throughout Mennonite circles. At Tabor College as well as at the Mennonite Brethren Bible College in Winnipeg, the impact of new Anabaptist scholarship was felt very strongly. A change in leadership at Tabor reflected this shift. Presidents Peter E. Schellenberg and Frank C. Peters both supported Anabaptism and the conference peace position, as well as participation in relief efforts. The denominational periodicals and other publications began to feature more and more material in support of Anabaptist positions. Finally, Mennonite Brethren participation with Mennonite Central Committee led to a greater awareness of how Anabaptist values could shape the church and its mission.

In Canada the foremost institution that shaped the theological identity of Mennonite Brethren from the mid-1940s until the 1970s was the Mennonite Brethren Bible College. John A. Toews, who taught at the college for over twenty years and who was president for six years, had a strong commitment to evangelical Anabaptism. Similarly Frank C. Peters, and later Henry Krahn,

They're not a new generation of itinerant ministers, but rather members of the Mennonite Brethren Biblical Seminary faculty in 1981. The seminary played an important role in reshaping Mennonite Brethren theology in an Anabaptist context. (l-r): Henry Schmidt, Elmer Martens, John E. Toews, Howard Loewen.
(CMBS Fresno)

sought to reinforce the Anabaptist identity of the school. New Testament professor David Ewert led in the move toward a more critical biblical hermeneutic that had strong bases in new evangelical schools such as Wheaton College and Fuller Theological Seminary. Aside from Mennonite Brethren Bible College there were others like John H. Redekop and Wally Unger who promoted a Mennonite Brethren identity that was both evangelical and Anabaptist.

The Board of Christian Literature and the Historical Commission of the Mennonite Brethren Conference played a major role in the reawakening of the Anabaptist identity of the Mennonite Brethren Church, beginning with the publication of *The Church in Mission* (1967), edited by A. J. Klassen. Another major milestone was the publication of *A History of the Mennonite Brethren Church: Pilgrims and Pioneers* (1975), by John A. Toews.

Perhaps the most important event to set theological direction for the Mennonite Brethren church in the last quarter of the twentieth century was the founding of the Mennonite Brethren Biblical Seminary in Fresno in 1955. In 1975 this seminary was adopted as a joint seminary for the United States and Canada. During J. B. Toews' presidency during the 1960s the faculty shifted its instruction to emphasize Anabaptist theology. Professors D. Edmond Hiebert, David Ewert, John E. Toews, and Tim Geddert in New Testament; Elmer Martens and Allen Guenther in Old Testament; J. B. Toews, A. J. Klassen, and Howard Loewen in theology; and Hans Kasdorf, Henry Schmidt, and Waldo Hiebert in church and mission served the conference as leaders, Bible conference speakers, and instructors of a generation of pastors, teachers, and missionaries.

On the whole, Canadian Mennonite Brethren tended to favor Anabaptism more highly than their American counterparts. Various studies between 1972 and 1989 have consistently indicated that Canadian Mennonite Brethren scored higher in their commitment to Anabaptist values. Gradually, however, many of these values have shown signs of erosion on both sides of the border.

John A. Toews (CMBS Winnipeg)

During the last quarter century the denomination has struggled to define and articulate its theological identity. Evangelical influences have continued to make themselves felt. The impact of educational institutions, alliances with the National Association of Evangelicals, the Evangelical Fellowship of Canada and their associated mission associations, an openness to the Church Growth Movement with its emphasis on practical means to build churches, and in cooperative evangelistic ventures. The tension and attempts to balance between the evangelical and Anabaptist emphases is evident in the topics featured in the study conferences convened by the General Conference Board of Reference and Counsel and later by the Board of Faith and Life. Topics have included the biblical concept of the church and leadership (the topic of not less than twelve different conferences), the Holy Spirit and the charismatic movement, sanctified and separated living, divorce and remarriage, church and state, discipleship, evangelism and social action, eschatology, women in ministry, peacemaking, hermeneutics and inerrancy.

Sin With A Small "s"?

"It was always a problem to know how much of this new culture to accept and how much to reject. The church across the river determined some of the boundaries for those of us living in Blaine Lake [Saskatchewan]. But where the categories were unclear or without precedent, we knew we could establish a case with Mother and engage in the activity without guilt. We never went to movies in the Palace Theatre, but we could go to school movies, shown after school on Fridays for five cents. These were travelogs and early films like *Les Miserables* and similar classics. The teacher selected these movies, and the teacher was always right. So we handed over our hot five-cent pieces and slipped into the full classroom to sit two to a seat to watch black and white films jerk across the screen. The projector frequently broke down.

"We attended the chautauquas set up in a large tent on the ballpark to watch the films there, often cowboy-and-Indian films and 'educational' lectures. We rushed to the Palace Theatre to watch Little Theatre and minstrel and amateur shows. The guiding principle seemed to be that we could attend any place that didn't have soft seats without committing small 's' sin. But one year I did.

"The teacher was taking a choir to the city to sing in the music festival, an all-day affair. The choir would sing, eat in a restaurant—a real one—then in the afternoon attend the matinee performance of Nelson Eddy and Jeanette MacDonald at the Starlight Theatre. But we had to get permission from our parents. That was a Mount Everest undertaking.

"Mother didn't know what to say. We reasoned. It was a good show, no dirty parts. Everyone else was going. The teacher would be with us. Finally, banking on the word of the teacher, we received Mother's permission.

"We sang in the music festival and went flat, terribly flat, in the big auditorium. We heard the judge with an English accent pronounce another chorus as 'bettah' but not because it was from the town of 'Biggah.' Our teacher probably felt worse than we did. Then off to a restaurant —all thirty of us innocents.

"Next came the movie. I crept in with fear in my heart. This was a real theater with wonderfully soft seats and a ceiling that sparkled with stars. Would the world end? Was I saved? Was I committing a sin, and if so what kind? Big 'S'? Little 's'? Had I been wrong to beg Mother so hard to let us go?

"But the fragile beauty of Jeanette MacDonald and the handsomeness of Nelson Eddy made me forget my fears. I watched spellbound as they sang, riding into the sunset. I liked this kind of sin."

—*From* The Storekeeper's Daughter: A Memoir, *by Katie Funk Wiebe (Herald Press, 1997).*

The church today continues to search and seek to own the best elements of its diverse heritage in shaping its theological identity. Mennonite Brethren pietistic roots have sought nurture in charismatic influences through the years, including a strong interest in the Vineyard Movement and the contemporary music currently associated with British and Australian evangelical charismatics. While some Mennonite Brethren find the music compelling, others lament the loss of theological diversity and richness in the music of classical and contemporary hymnody. The Mennonite Brethren evangelical stream continues to seek nurture in the evangelistic success stories of mega-churches with their seeker-sensitive services. As a result, preaching has tended to shift from exegetical to topical, with an emphasis on relevance that may eclipse a concern for costly discipleship in faithfulness to the Jesus of the Gospels. Although the Confession of Faith adopted in 1999 reaffirms Mennonite Brethren commitment to church membership and covenant accountability in the discipling community, congregations allow pastors to practice the signs of baptism and the Lord's Supper without heeding official polity that links these ordinances to the church.

The three-legged stool of Pietism, evangelicalism and Anabaptism served the Mennonite Brethren General Conference throughout its existence. Often the strengths of Pietism and evangelicalism reinforced the Anabaptist core of Mennonite Brethren theology. At other times, the emphasis on private, personal conversion and piety overshadowed the call to discipleship within a covenant community. The last act of the Mennonite Brethren General Conference under the leadership of the Board of Faith and Life offers hope for a united future. The acceptance of the Confession of Faith, which was the result of a decade-long discernment process within the church, continues the legacy of an evangelical-Anabaptist, Bible-centered, missionary movement.

5

Searching for the Right Structures

Paul Toews

*I*n October 1879 twenty-two delegates representing Mennonite Brethren congregations in Kansas, Nebraska and Minnesota met for three days in Henderson, Nebraska. It was the first official meeting of the General Conference of Mennonite Brethren Churches. One year earlier, Peter Regier, elder of the Henderson church, had invited representatives from other congregations to meet on September 28, 1878, to discuss common concerns. Four representatives from Kansas and seven from Nebraska came to this meeting, agreed that the congregations should unite into a conference, and issued the call for the 1879 event.

The Mennonite Brethren Church in 1879 was less than twenty years old, and still struggled with issues of structure and unity. The Document of Secession, signed in January 1860, resulted in the withdrawal of individuals from the existing Mennonite Church in South Russia, but did not create a coherent organization. That would take time to develop. Those who are willing to break the bonds of existing authority frequently find it difficult to submit to, or create, new structures of restraint.

The individuals who drew up the secession document referred to themselves as a "fellowship of believers." A fellowship was hardly a concept common to the mid-nineteenth-century Russian Mennonite world. It seems to have signaled the desire for a new kind of religious grouping. If the intention was for something less formal and organized, the need to achieve recognition from the Russian government and to regulate internal contradictions encouraged structures for consultation.

Several consultative meetings took place during the years immediately following the secession. The "June Reforms" of 1865, an attempt to reign in the excesses of the early movement and to restore fellowship among people who had excommunicated each other, were the result of extensive consultations. The first meeting of representatives from the congregations in a conference format occurred in 1872.

The focus of this 1872 conference in South Russia was replicated in Henderson in 1879. Both events focused on establishing an itinerant ministerial system that would both nurture the existing congregations and assist in evangelism and church extension. The individuals selected were trusted leaders, and their circulation through the congregations helped insure the preservation of both a common faith and common practice.

The early meetings also addressed the question of conference structure. In the history of western Christianity three essential forms of polity (church government) have been practiced: episcopal, congregational and presbyterian. The episcopal form is based on hierarchy, centralized

Delegates at the 1912 General Conference on the steps of the Hillsboro (Kansas) Mennonite Brethren Church.
(CMBS Fresno)

55

authority and top-down governance. On the other end of the spectrum, the congregational form disavows any real authority outside of the local congregation. Each congregation, under the guidance of the spirit, is autonomous in matters of doctrine and practice. The presbyterian model combines elements of the two. Issues of local concern can be brought to assembled deliberative bodies for discernment and response, but once the representative group make a decision it is binding on the local group.

Mennonite Brethren adopted forms of both the congregational and presbyterian polity. In the selection of local leadership congregations were free to exercise their autonomy. On most other things, certainly in matters of theology and ethics, congregations were expected to adhere to positions reached through the process of conference discussion. Those conference discussions were dominated by the leaders selected by congregations. Thus the polity was congregational only on local issues, and presbyterian on transcendent issues. The positions reached by the conference were to be followed by all member congregations. Deviance resulted in conference-appointed investigatory delegations that would recommend, admonish and if necessary even remove leadership unwilling to follow conference positions.

This essentially presbyterian understanding of how the conference would function was already previewed at the unofficial 1878 event in Henderson. Like subsequent events, it heard concerns brought by member congregations. From one congregation came questions about the appropriate relationships with Baptist groups and the Krimmer Mennonite Brethren, and particularly whether sharing communion with members of either group was acceptable. The consensus was that communion with the Krimmer was acceptable but not so with Baptists. For another congregation the question was the practice of the "sister-kiss," which was a contentious issue in the old country. The 1878 meeting offered a compromise: the practice was unacceptable between male and female members of the congregation, but was acceptable for the leading minister when welcoming a sister into church membership. For another congregation the question was whether women were to wear a head covering only at church or also at home. The delegates, while divided, agreed to require it in both places. On another question—whether Mennonite

How Then Shall We Live?

Mennonite Brethren have always emphasized the ethical dimensions of the Christian life. This concern was often expressed through resolutions approved by conference delegates. The following are some early resolutions passed at General Conference sessions.

1878: In case a brother is excommunicated according to 1 Cor. 5:11, even the wife should have nothing to do with him. This, however, has no reference to material eating or to marital relations.

1879: The Conference does not permit its members to have weapons in their houses (reaffirmed in 1890 and 1893).

1883: A father, member of the church, cannot give his blessing to his child that withdraws from the church through marriage (outside of the church).

1887: The Conference wishes that our members do not enter holy matrimony before they reach the age of eighteen years.

1887: Our members should stay away from circuses, theaters, and such other places.

1890: Members of the church should refrain from participation and involvement in the contentions of political parties, but are permitted to vote quietly at elections, and may also vote for prohibition.

1893: A minister should choose as simple a vocation (or business) as possible in order not to have his own spiritual life nor that of others harmed on that account.

1893: Our brethren shall not hold the offices of justice of the peace or constable. A member may be a notary public.

1897: It [is] decided unanimously that our members should not carry life insurance policies. [This decision was reaffirmed in 1927 by a vote of 88 to 37].

1899: The Conference decided unanimously that church members are not allowed to visit the saloon, attend circus, or sell tobacco.

1900: Jesting and joking by our brethren, whether verbal or in writing, in conversation or in published periodicals, should be avoided.

1905: Churches are not to participate in national celebrations, such as Fourth of July celebrations, but to offer the youth something better, like mission or children's festivities.

1909: Although not forbidden in the Word of God, the Conference is opposed to the practice of marrying near relatives, since it is a violation of the natural laws of life, as well as against the constitutional laws of most states.

Abraham Schellenberg: Itinerant Minister

The role that leading itinerants played in providing leadership for the fledgling conference and in safeguarding unity was significant. Elder Abraham Schellenberg was one of the most notable of these ministers. Born in South Russia, he was elected to the ministry in 1869 and as an elder in 1875. Between 1869 and his 1879 departure for North America he visited all of the Mennonite Brethren congregations in Russia. After his arrival in central Kansas he was elected as the presiding elder of the Ebenezer Church in Kansas (subsequently the Buhler Mennonite Brethren Church). Between 1880 and 1900 he was for eighteen years the moderator of the conference. Sixteen of those years he worked as an itinerant minister and evangelist. While the record is inconclusive, it appears that he visited every Mennonite Brethren congregation during those years. He was also the first chair of the foreign mission board and a strong advocate of the emerging publication and educational work of the conference.

Brethren could hold political office of any kind—the delegates were unanimous that such positions were not in keeping with their understanding of citizenship.

Part of what made it so easy for the decisions to be binding was the role of the itinerant ministers who circulated throughout the congregations. In addition to assisting with congregational nurture and evangelism, and helping to establish new congregations as people moved to differing locations, they also served an oversight function. Until the development of regional conferences in 1909 a substantial focus of the annual gatherings was the reports by the itinerant and leading ministers of their work during the previous year, the processing of requests from congregations for visits during the coming year and working out on the conference floor the assignments of these itinerant ministers.

Continental and Regional Structures

From 1879 to 1909 the General Conference met annually, always in the central states or Canadian prairies. In 1897 delegates from the Canadian churches first attended, and the 1898 conference meeting in Winkler, Manitoba, was the first held in Canada. The meeting in Canada symbolized a new reality—Mennonite Brethren were an increasingly geographically dispersed group. From the original settlements in Dakota, Minnesota, Nebraska and Kansas, people were now moving in multiple directions. During the last decade of the nineteenth century and the first two of the

(Right) Participants at the 1927 General Conference meeting in the newly-constructed Henderson (Nebr.) Mennonite Brethren Church. (CMBS Fresno)

Participants at the 1930 General Conference at the Hepburn (Sask.) Mennonite Brethren Church. The large tent in the background was used to provide additional meeting space, and was a fixture at the General Conference sessions for many years. (CMBS Fresno)

Delegates from Manitoba prepare to return home after the 1933 General Conference in Hillsboro, Kansas. (Mennonite Historical Society of B.C.)

> **From Brotherhood to Congregational Autonomy**
>
> "The 1951 conference saw the beginning of a slide away from our historic sense of brotherhood and a rising sense of individualism and autonomy. . . . The conference response was to refer the document 'A Frank Analysis of Our Spiritual Status' to the local churches for review and reaction. By doing so we lost the full intent of the document. The churches had changed and there was a reaction to the central authority of a special conference committee as suggested in the document. The 1954 conference handed more General Conference authority to the provincial conferences in Canada and the regional conferences in the U.S. where implementation of the directive control of the conference was gradually lost. We on the committee of Reference and Counsel during this time felt that the basic principle of central authority was now gone. This accounts for the fragmentation we find in the Mennonite Brethren Church today, with regional conferences and local churches (and their pastors) being increasingly independent of any larger sense of accountability. . . .
>
> "As I reflect on my years in various levels of conference leadership, I continue to grieve over the relentless move toward greater professionalization of the ministry. I believe it has resulted in the institutionalization of the church. From a covenant people—a brotherhood—we have drifted to become a mere association of independent churches."
>
> —*From* JB: A Twentieth-Century Mennonite Pilgrim, *by J. B. Toews (Center for Mennonite Brethren Studies-Fresno, 1995).*

twentieth century Mennonite Brethren congregations were established across most of western North America. That fact argued for a different conference structure than the one annual meeting.

The first discussion about the need for regional conferences appeared at the 1902 conference in Oklahoma. At the 1903 conference a committee was appointed to plan for an "expansion of the conference." The plan presented at the 1904 convention envisioned a southern and northern conference. The next several conferences entertained a variety of proposals for regional sub-units. Some leaders were reticent, for fear that decentralization would also lead to disunity. These fears were addressed by writing a constitution that spelled out the appropriate role for the "Conference of the Mennonite Brethren Church of North America" and its sub-units. The General Conference would deal with things of common interest, such as foreign missions, publication, city missions and higher education. The regional conferences were to assume responsibility for home mission work and activities of more local concern.

The 1909 conference, after seven years of discussion, agreed to move to a triennial convention and three district conferences: a Southern District (Kansas, Oklahoma and southern California), a Central District (Colorado, Michigan, Minnesota, North Dakota, South Dakota, Oregon), and a Northern District (Canada and Rosehill, North Dakota). The Central California congregations were given the option of joining either the Southern or Central District, while Rosehill and the Manitoba congregations were given the option of joining the Central District. Manitoba chose to meet with the Central District for four years before joining the Northern District. In 1912 the California, Oregon and Washington congregations formed the Pacific District Conference. From 1913 to 1954 this pattern of a General Conference and four regional sub-units remained the North American structure.

The Erosion of Conference Authority

The structures created in the late nineteenth and early twentieth centuries seemed adequate until the early 1940s. By that time there was a growing sense that alternative structures were required to meet new realities. The Board of Reference and Counsel (later the Board of Faith and Life) brought to the 1951 sessions one of the most revealing reports and far-reaching recommendations ever considered by the General Conference. The committee, composed of Conference Executive members B. J. Braun, J. B. Toews and H. R. Wiens, Southern District representatives J. W. Vogt and H. H. Flaming, and Canadian representatives B. B. Janz and A. H. Unruh, was as distinguished a cast of Mennonite Brethren leaders as one could imagine for mid-century.

The first section of their report— "A Frank Analysis of our Spiritual Status"—noted the recent "revolutionizing changes" that had come as the consequence of "educational opportunities" and "economic advantages." Those changes had created a pluralism that threatened established church polity, cherished theological understandings and valued ethical practices. Most distressing was a shift in leadership. Formerly both congregational and denominational leaders emerged from "within" local congregations and with direction of the "elder." It was a system that nurtured both "strength and stability." This leadership was "thoroughly indoctrinated with all Scriptural principles of belief and practice." The system maintained unity and consistency.

A newer system of selecting church leaders from Bible institutes and seminaries often made new leaders outsiders to their congregations. Hiring an outside person, furthermore, often meant that the congregation moved from several congregationally-trained persons to a single pastor. These "one man pastorates" compromised both the "organizational and instructional principles" of congregations and threatened to engulf the entire conference.

A latter section of the report made clear the organizational problems. Conference polity historically included contradictory currents. The strong tradition of congregational autonomy was hinged to an equally strong sense of "brotherhood," which implied authority and consensus. It was the latter that was becoming frayed. The denomination had moved from "brotherhood," where the elders in a "collective relationship offered a strong unified leadership," to an "associative" ideal, where congregational freedom threatened the unity and coherence of the conference.

Behind the analysis were objective changes. By 1950 most churches in the United States hired paid pastors from beyond their membership. These pastors had received training from various seminaries and Bible institutes across North America. The 1951 report identified conference leaders with training from Baptist, Lutheran, Presbyterian, Pentecostal and interdenominational schools. From those places they brought differing conceptions of church and conference.

The report was drafted by the California members of the board—Braun, Toews and Wiens. Their location reflected the leading edge of the social revolution that was taking the Mennonite Brethren beyond their relatively bounded communities of the past. Historically their relationship to larger worlds had been hedged by the protective barrier of village isolation, maintenance of the German language, traditionalism and ethnic seclusion. By the 1940s and 1950s, however, the demise of cultural isolation and the reality of accompanying pluralism was felt everywhere. This was felt most acutely in the United States, where most Mennonite Brethren communities had been established for a longer time than in Canada.

The Board of Reference and Counsel, to meet this new reality and the perceived threats, called for new structures of authority and refurbished carriers of Mennonite Brethren historic identity. They proposed the creation of a Board of Elders to safeguard both polity and doctrine. Their function was to be more authoritative than the Board of Reference and Counsel. The limitation of the Board of Reference and Counsel was that it only "advises and aids" congregations "when serious

"Mennonite Hospitality: 300 Families 'Put Up' 3000 Guests"

"Probably in no place on the earth has there been such a demonstration of hospitality, patriotism, and pacifism as is being given in this small western Oklahoma town during the conference of the Mennonite Brethren church of North America.

"Here less than 300 families have taken more than 3,000 visitors into their homes. Figure that out and decide if it can't be done. Well you haven't been in Corn. It's hard to say how the people sleep or where, but every home in Corn and in Bessie and for miles around is entertaining up to a dozen visitors.

"They're feeding them well on zweibach, schnetka, rye bread, beef, and other delicacies that are dear to the hearts of the Mennonites.

"Corn's unpaved main street has been churned into a dust storm by the unusually heavy traffic and the Corn cafe and drug store ran out of carbonated drinks by mid-afternoon.

"There are many branches of the Mennonite church. The Mennonite Brethren church of North America is not marked by the long whiskers or unusual attire of some sects. The delegates could be Methodists, Baptists or chamber of commerce delegates. These are a cheerful people, contrasted to the dour visages of other Mennonite sects, and except for the pall thrown over the conference, held every three years, by a war that already is threatening the conscientious scruples of Canadian members, there is a festival spirit abroad.

"In the huge circus tent where the daily sessions are held, the chorus of 3,500 voices swelled Monday afternoon and night as delegates from California, South Dakota, Minnesota, Michigan, Canada and nearly all other parts of the American continent joined in hymns in the language of their forefathers. The Mennonites conduct nearly half of their services in the German tongue."

—*Adapted from articles by Lawrence Thompson in* The Daily Oklahoman, *23-24 October 1939.*

(Top left) Program at the 1960 General Conference in the Reedley (Calif.) Mennonite Brethren Church. This was the conference at which the Mennonite Brethren and Krimmer Mennonite Churches merged into a single conference. (CMBS Fresno)

(Bottom left) Delegates at the 1963 General Conference, held in the Mennonite Brethren Collegiate Institute Auditorium, Winnipeg, Manitoba. (CMBS Fresno)

questions arise concerning doctrine and church polity." That was adequate when "our church leadership was still largely a product from within the church; and our congregations were more isolated." Now more was needed. The proposed Board of Elders would provide "strong unified leadership." Its rulings would be "considered final," subject only to the review and change by the conference itself. To further reinforce the consensus and authority of the proposed new structure, four volumes were to be written on Mennonite Brethren polity, doctrine, history and missions.

The proposed Board of Elders, however, was too far-reaching to be accepted at the convention. It was sent to the regional conferences for discussion and there was rejected by all. Of the four proposed volumes only the historical one was written. Abraham H. Unruh's *Die Geschichte der Mennoniten-Brüdergemeinde, 1860-1954*, was completed, but in a language that limited its role as a carrier of identity for the coming decades. The missions history turned out to be a multi-volume project that was partially completed during the 1970s and 1980s. The volumes on polity and doctrine were never completed.

The rejection of the Board of Elders proposal and the inability to complete the four volumes had consequences. The report of the Board of Reference and Counsel said that the historic balance between a congregational and presbyterian polity had shifted during the decades prior to the 1951 conference. That analysis was surely right. The conference's reluctance to restore that balance meant that Mennonite Brethren conference polity would become less presbyterian and more congregational. That reality is now apparent at Mennonite Brethren conferences of all levels. One of the more telling comments frequently heard in the corridor of conventions is "let the conference decide what it wishes, we will go back home and do what we think is best."

The newly-elected General Conference Executive officers converse outside the delegate hall at the 1969 General Conference in Vancouver, B.C. Left to right: Chairman John A. Toews, Vice-Chairman Marvin Hein, and Secretary H.H. Voth.
(CMBS Fresno)

National or Continental Structures

The 1954 General Conference convention, meeting in Hillsboro, Kansas, made the most significant structural change following the 1909 decision to move toward regional sub-units. The convention set in motion a process whereby national rather than continental structures would come to dominate Mennonite Brethren organization in North America. The specific issue that drove what J. A. Toews described as the "constitutional crisis of 1954" was the program of higher education. Tabor College had been adopted as a General Conference school in 1934 but continued disproportionately to serve the United States population. The emergence in 1944 of both Mennonite Brethren Bible College (Winnipeg), as a Canadian Conference school, and Pacific Bible Institute (Fresno), as a school of the Pacific District Conference, and the perceived needs of the United States for a seminary raised questions as to the appropriate relationships of these schools to conferences. Various parties from the United States suggested that both Pacific Bible Institute and the proposed seminary should be General Conference schools. Canada brought forward no such proposal regarding the Mennonite Brethren Bible College. Furthermore, the Canadian delegation declined to vote on the question of the appropriate conference linkages of Tabor, Pacific Bible Institute and the seminary. That declension was in fact a statement that higher education would be a matter for the two nations to decide. Canada had in place a national conference to deal with their school. Their withdrawal of support from Tabor College as a General

Behind the scenes at every General Conference were local volunteers, who helped the events run smoothly. Shown here is the kitchen staff at the 1966 General Conference in Corn, Oklahoma.
(CMBS Fresno)

(Right) Missionary presentations were a significant part of most General Conference programs. Here, a group of missionaries in native costume pose for a group portrait at the 1966 General Conference in Corn, Oklahoma.
(CMBS Fresno)

Conference school and the unwillingness to decide the fate of institutions south of the border necessitated the creation of a United States national conference.

In 1954 education was the specific issue that focused larger unspoken realities. The Canadian Conference, by then larger than the three United States district conferences combined, received a membership allotment on conference boards and committees as though it were simply another regional unit. Furthermore, the Canadian Conference (formerly the Northern Conference) was already functioning as a national conference with subsidiary provincial conferences.

The Canadian Conference had evolved into an identifiable national conference for multiple reasons. All of the offices and institutions (Tabor College, mission headquarters, Board of Trustees office, Publishing House) of the General Conference were south of the US-Canadian border. The United States constituency had a sense of ownership and investment in them that the Canadians did not share. Those institutions and agencies all began before the major influx of Mennonite Brethren into Canada and their leadership remained predominantly American. Canadian leaders often felt their voices and concerns were not adequately heard. Partly from the differing needs than those in the south and partly from a sense of exclusion, parallel institutions had emerged—the school in Winnipeg, the *Afrika Missions-Verein*, the production of separate hymnals, the creation of Christian Press in Winnipeg. These were responses to the perceived or real americanization of the General Conference.

The large influx of Mennonite Brethren into Canada during the 1920s and 1940s meant that they were largely preoccupied with issues of resettlement, initial adaptation

(Above) Delegates at the 1999 General Conference in Wichita, Kansas.
(CMBS Fresno)

and finding a footing in the new society. Preservation of inherited patterns, common to new immigrant generations, was stronger in Canada than in the United States. The rapid acculturation that occurred during the 1940s and 1950s in the United States produced a North American Mennonite Brethren population with two differing cultural orientations. Continentalism could easily become frayed as national differences increasingly shaped the two populations.

Continental or Global Structures

The mid-twentieth-century discussion of appropriate conference structures was not limited to redefining relationships between Canada and the United States. In 1948 the South American churches became a fifth district entity within the General Conference and ever since then Mennonite Brethren have held visions of a global Mennonite Brethren Conference. The 1960s witnessed a more sustained discussion about the possibilities of a global structure. The Board of Reference and Counsel brought to the 1960 centennial convention a proposal to change the conference name from "The General Conference of the Mennonite Brethren Church of North America" to "The General Conference of Mennonite Brethren Churches." The recommendation no doubt reflected the delight and even satisfaction from having several representatives from churches around the world attending the centennial celebrations. In this heady atmosphere it was easy to think that the continental boundaries were limiting. Other voices cautioned that the move from "church" to "churches" opened the door to less uniformity. The 1963 conference sanctioned the name change following assurances from the Board that change would permit bringing other national conferences into affiliation without in any way lessening the historic "voluntary interdependence" on all matters "of common spiritual heritage and mission."

The 1966 conference, with the new name in place, considered a detailed proposal for a World Conference of Mennonite Brethren Churches. The proposal called for a structure that looked very much like the more ecumenical Mennonite World Conference. While calling for this new international body, the proposal simultaneously recognized that the United States and Canadian conferences would continue to have a special relationship and work together in ways analogous to the past. The proposal in essence wished to preserve what was and simultaneously open the door to new possibilities. The proposal met an ironic fate. It was sent out to each national Mennonite Brethren conference, all of whom responded favorably. Simultaneously, the South American churches withdrew their membership in the North American conference in favor of a stronger South American Conference between the churches of Brazil and Paraguay. Just as North America dreamed of global partnerships, South America opted for continental partnerships.

Global, Continental, National or Local

If the North Americans after 1960 dreamed of globalism, the reality is that localism has become more dominant. Following the failed 1966 plan for a global Mennonite Brethren structure, the most comprehensive discussion of conference structures occurred in 1986 and 1987. An early draft of the "General Conference Visions/Goals" statement occupied the central place in an October 1986 meeting of the Board of Reference and Counsel. The draft could not have been more prescient: "There will be increased fragmentation and autonomy due to growing individualism, localism, nationalism, regionalism and theological pluralism." The report further predicted growing fragmentation between Canada and the United States, between the Midwest and West Coast regions and "re-alignments . . . by 2000." The 1999 General Conference convention decision to disband itself would seem to be a prophetic fulfillment.

The trend toward growing fragmentation and autonomy is echoed in other denominations. Modern Western culture drives those social realities with speed and persistence. Conscious effort is required to retain historic bonds or replace them with new ones that have sufficient strength to have consequences. Those larger cultural forces are even more evident in a denomination with a long history of mixing congregational and presbyterian polities. The degree of conference attachment has greatly varied among Mennonite Brethren congregations. Some have found the attachment very important, others less so. Some congregations seek to uphold conference positions, others feel no such obligations. Some congregations meet requests for financial support, others do not. Some congregations are persuaded that local units of the church of Jesus Christ need a close association with other like-minded churches, others do not.

If the Mennonite Brethren wish to reclaim the promise of their strong heritage and make a collective witness to the modern world then a renewed commitment to the structures of collective decision making will be required. Finding the appropriate structural forms for working together—regionally, nationally and globally—becomes an imperative. The early developments of the International Conference of Mennonite Brethren (ICOMB) seem to offer that hope. ICOMB, however, remains more of an idea and a forum for leaders to discuss issues than a working conference. The future will determine whether it becomes a functioning conference entity able to speak with a single voice.

In the cacophony of modern noise, Christians speaking with one voice are more apt to be heard than those speaking in multiple voices. In a culture growing ever more post-Christian the work of the Christian community requires ever more cooperation and unity.

6

From Foreign Mission to Global Partnership

James Pankratz

Mission is at the center of Mennonite Brethren identity. It was an impulse in the formation of the denomination in 1860. It was the dominant theme in the work and meetings of the General Conference for 120 years. From 1880 to 1948 the first item of business on the conference agenda was always mission (evangelism, home mission and foreign mission). Mission always received a greater amount of financial support from Mennonite Brethren churches than any other cause. Since the 1880s, most of the major Mennonite Brethren leaders in North America have at some time in their public ministry been missionaries, evangelists, church planters or mission board members.

When a dozen Mennonite Brethren leaders and an audience of about one hundred met informally in Hamilton County, Nebraska, in 1878, one of the first topics they discussed was "missions." At that time "missions" meant sending traveling preachers to areas in which Mennonites had settled. When the conference met formally for the first time in 1879, organizing and funding these preaching tours was again a major topic.

But already at that conference a delegate reminded the assembly that it was necessary to send a missionary "to the distant lost heathen." The following year the delegates agreed to split the offering of $52.72 evenly between "foreign" and "home" missions. At that time they had no "foreign" projects or missionaries, so the money was given to the deacons from York County, Nebraska, for safekeeping until the conference decided how to allocate it.

During the next two decades, cross-cultural and global mission became a priority for the emerging conference. Offerings from churches and at conference events were used to fund mission projects. By 1897 the conference was supporting work among the Telugu of India and the Comanches of Oklahoma, and provided scholarship support for Peter Wedel, a Mennonite Brethren student at Rochester Baptist Seminary preparing for mission service in Cameroon. A standing "Foreign Mission" Committee oversaw these various projects.

The Meaning and Scope of Mission

Since the founding of the Mennonite Brethren Church, there has been a consistent theological understanding of mission and mission priorities, even though the language used to describe these priorities and the focus of mission programs has changed. These priorities are evangelism and church planting, leadership development, and social ministries.

Peter and Martha Wedel, who served for two years in Cameroon, were some of the earliest North American Mennonite Brethren missionaries to go overseas. Here, Peter is seated with some of his students in Cameroon, ca. 1895-1897.
(CMBS Fresno)

An evangelistic tent used by Mennonite Brethren missionaries in Osaka, Japan, 1956. (CMBS Fresno)

Evangelism and Church Planting

Mennonite Brethren have consistently defined mission by referring to the "Great Commission" texts (Matthew 28:18-20; Mark 16:15-16; Luke 24:46-49; John 20:21; Acts 1:8). In many early mission reports to the Conference the emphasis was on preaching, conversion and baptism. Where were evangelistic meetings held? How many sermons were preached? Who were the preachers? How many conversions were recorded? How many were baptized? As N. N. Hiebert, American missionary to India, wrote in a letter dated 25 January 1901, "What India needs is not money, but the gospel, light and conversion."

During the twentieth century the focus shifted from individual conversion to evangelism and church planting. In the *Guiding Principles and Policies of Mennonite Brethren Church Missions*, first published in 1947, mission was defined as "the response to the command of our Lord to preach and teach the Gospel to every creature. The objective of evangelism is the calling out of a church. . . .

Early Mennonite Brethren missionaries often worked with the colonial officials who governed the regions in which they served. Here several missionaries are seated with British officers in India. Standing in the back row are Anna Suderman (2nd from left), J.H. Pankratz (3rd from right), and Henry H. Unruh (2nd from right). Seated in the center row are Abraham J. Friesen (2nd from left), Mary Friesen (3rd from right) and Maria Pankratz (2nd from right). Seated on the ground is Elisabeth Neufeld (center in dark dress). (CMBS Fresno)

Mission in the Midst of Turmoil

Mennonite Brethren missionaries often found themselves carrying out their work amidst the upheaval of international political events. One such event was the struggle for Indian independence in the late 1940s. In excerpts from letters written in 1948 to Jack W. Enns of Reedley, California, missionary J. N. C. Hiebert describes conditions in India immediately after independence:

31 January 1948: "India is excited these days. I have been in Bombay for a few days. I have been through three mobs of rioters already and don't know just what else to expect. Last night I was on a double decker bus, upstairs, when a mob stopped the bus, pounded the windows and shouted. Most people got off, but I did not like the mob and sat down on the floor of the bus so that I could not be seen. The driver put off the lights. Stones fly often at such times . . . and so we made our way to the bus depot. There I sat awhile and then took courage to walk to the Baptist church where I am staying with friends. They came home an hour later . . . and had a shower of stones on their Jeep when they met a crowd. Gandhi's assassination excited them. . . . These are exciting days in India, believe me."

20 April 1948: "The people are listening to the Gospel . . . as never before. I think the reason for this is that there are so many changes going on in India that they feel their religion is also beginning to shake. . . . We hope that many of the higher caste people will soon turn to Christ."

18 September 1948: "We were asked to take advantage of the evacuation plans made for those in Hyderabad City and near by. It was feared that lawless bands might run loose and that these might endanger the lives of Europeans and Americans. . . . We really expected severe fighting around Hyderabad, including our station of Shamshabad. However, today we hear that the Hyderabad forces have surrendered and the Indian Union army will march peacefully into the city. That is an unexpected turn of events. Now it looks as if I will be able to return to the station very soon. We are glad that the bloodshed is over and that no further disorders have broken out. We hope it will remain quiet now. . . . We were living under suspense for months, never knowing what the next day would bring. This gets rather trying when it goes on for weeks or months. . . . We also now have hopes that the blockade will be lifted from Hyderabad and that we will soon be able to get gasoline and kerosene and other supplies again. Life was getting quite difficult of late without all these supplies."

—*From original letters in CMBS Fresno.*

The planting of local churches as agents of evangelism is thus the central objective of the missionary program." When these policies were restated in 1978, the highest priority of Mennonite Brethren mission was establishing "Christlike, self-propagating churches." In 2002 the goal was "to participate in making disciples of all people groups, sharing the Gospel of Jesus Christ cross-culturally and globally, in Spirit-empowered obedience to Christ's Commission and in partnership with local Mennonite Brethren churches." The first priority was to build "Christ honoring, indigenous churches" by sending out missionaries to evangelize.

This commitment has had remarkable results. In 1900 nearly all Mennonite Brethren were in North America or Russia. In 2002 there are over 266,000 members of the global Mennonite Brethren church family, two-thirds of whom are in Africa and Asia.

Leadership Development

When Abraham and Maria Friesen, the first Mennonite Brethren missionaries to India, returned to Russia on a furlough in 1897, Abraham reported that he had left behind an organized church of about seven hundred members supporting their own pastor. From the very outset of Mennonite Brethren missions it was clear that once a church was established, it should have local pastors, evangelists and Bible teachers.

When the first *Foreign Missions: Guiding Principles and Field Policies* was published in 1947, the focus was on the missionary. There was a short section on developing the indigenous leadership of the local church, which stated that "discovering such men, helping them to stir up the gift that is in them, and training them for effective service for Christ, comes within the sphere of a missionary's blessed service." Even after the indigenous church became self-sustaining it was clear that the missionary would have a continued role in evangelism, preaching, teaching, pastoral care, and intercessory prayer.

By 1963 these guiding principles and policies gave a much higher profile to the local church and to local leaders: "The permanent aspect of the mission program rests in the national church. . . . The missionaries and the mission program are a means to an end and must be looked upon as temporary in the building of a national church."

Since the 1980s leadership development has become more prominent, and its link to church planting has been emphasized. This has involved discipleship training in churches through Bible teaching and training seminars. It has included support for local and regional Bible institutes, seminaries, and theological education by extension. Literature for discipleship and leadership training has been produced or translated. Scholarships have been provided for leaders to train in their countries and internationally. Many

P.C. Hiebert and the Grand Cross of the Order of Merit

Peter C. Hiebert (CMBS Hillsboro)

On June 30, 1953, a small collection of friends gathered at the home of Peter C. Hiebert in Hillsboro, Kansas, to witness Hiebert receiving the Grand Cross of the Order of Merit from the Federal Republic of Germany. The following resolution was read by the Honorable Hans P. Schweigemann, representing the German Consulate in Kansas City:

"Dear Dr. Hiebert and friends. It is indeed an honor and a privilege for me to be able to come here and present personally this declaration that the German government has bestowed upon Dr. Hiebert. The comparatively small community of Mennonites has done a tremendous amount of relief work in Germany and the relief has been received with gratitude. Many a family, as recipient of these activities has gotten new hope instead of utter despair after [World War II]. In recognition of the activities of the Mennonites and as a symbol of the gratitude of the German government, the President of the Republic has bestowed upon you, dear Dr. Hiebert, the Grand Cross of the Order of Merit."

The resolution passed by the German *Reichstag* and signed by President Heuss and Konrad Adenauer, the Prime Minister, came to Hiebert because he was the Chairman of Mennonite Central Committee (MCC) from 1920-1953. It was MCC that led the North American Mennonite effort to assist the German people in their great hour of need. And it was Peter C. Hiebert, more than anyone else, who galvanized the Mennonite Brethren participation in this relief effort. The Mennonite Brethren agency that directly worked with MCC in this relief effort was The Board of Welfare and Public Relations. Hiebert was not only chair of MCC but also a member of the Board of Welfare from 1924 to 1957 and its chair from 1927 to the end of his tenure.

—*Adapted from Wesley J. Prieb, "Peter (P. C.) Hiebert," in* Something Meaningful for God, *edited by Cornelius J. Dyck (Herald Press, 1981).*

Mennonite Brethren leaders from around the world have studied at the Mennonite Brethren Biblical Seminary in Fresno, California.

Social Ministries

Mennonite Brethren mission has always included social ministries. Minutes from the early conferences record frequent expressions of concern for those in need of "relief." Offerings were collected for this cause. At the 1912 convention, for example, an offering of $1,184.50 was received and $1,000 was allocated for foreign mission. Eighteen people voted against this allocation because they wanted at least $100 to go toward the "suffering of the world." The conference agreed that the remaining $184.50 should be sent to the missionaries to help the poor in their regions.

These Mennonites identified with hardship and suffering. The conference minutes of 1943 acknowledged the famine conditions in the countries in which their missionaries worked, and said:

> The suffering of people of other colors and other languages move us to deep sympathy and produce in us a willingness to send relief. The board wishes to remind the churches that this has always been an integral part of our work, and desires that relief funds intended for the sufferers on those mission fields be sent to their destination through our treasury for foreign missions for final distribution by our own brethren and sisters.

The primary reason for establishing clinics, hospitals and schools for medical mission work was to provide opportunities for evangelism. The 1943 Conference expressed it this way: "Our missionaries also have sought access to the hearts of men through channels that were most accessible to them,

Mennonites in the Reedley, California, area pack "Raisins for Relief," 1948. West Coast Mennonite Central Committee sent these rations to European refugees in the aftermath of World War II. The bucket in the foreground to the right is labeled, "Reedley M. B. Gemeinde," suggesting the high level of Mennonite Brethren participation in this MCC project.
(CMBS Fresno)

Magdelena Becker and her husband Abraham worked for many years among the Comanches of Oklahoma. Here she poses (third from right, back row) with members of her canning, sewing and quilting class at the Post Oak Mission, ca. 1920. (CMBS Fresno)

Baptism of Chulupie Indians in Paraguay, 1964. (CMBS Fresno)

namely: The children through instruction in schools, the sick through the channels of medical care in hospitals and the others through contacts on the streets and in the homes."

Hospitals, medical programs and schools helped hundreds of thousands of people, usually in regions poorly served by national or regional governments. Public health programs significantly reduced infant mortality and mitigated the impact of diseases. Schools, established so that students would be exposed to Christian teaching and learn to read the Bible, became incubators for local and national leaders.

There was another Mennonite Brethren Conference program that dealt specifically with these social ministries. The Board of General Welfare and Public Relations was created in 1936 with a mandate that included relief, relations with the Mennonite communities in South America, and peace education and advocacy. It was also the vehicle through which Mennonite Central Committee (MCC) was linked to the Mennonite Brethren Church.

When this board was eliminated and its mandate merged with the Mission Board in 1966, the new board was called the "Board of Missions and Services." According to the conference resolution, "proclamation and welfare ministries ought to be integrated, since our Lord and the early Church were concerned with such a total ministry. Such integration makes relief and welfare concerns, however necessary, subsidiary to the major task of proclamation."

The merger had an immediate impact, consistent with these priorities. Peace-related issues were shifted to the Board of Reference and Counsel, which dealt with them as theological questions. Peace advocacy almost completely disappeared. The partnership projects with South American Mennonites were scarcely heard from again. Mennonite Central Committee reported to the conference as a fraternal agency, and was not connected to the mission report. Many innovative and effective "social ministries" programs continued within Mennonite Brethren mission, but evangelism, church planting and leadership training were always higher priorities and received greatest prominence in reports to the constituency.

The Geography of Mission

The vision for mission in the General Conference was always global. Mission activities in North America and around the world were wide-ranging. In the last years of the nineteenth century evangelistic tours were organized to Mennonite communities throughout the American Midwest. Heinrich Voth was sent to preach and eventually to live among recent Mennonite immigrants in Manitoba. Mission work was established among both Comanches and Mexicans in Oklahoma. Mennonite Brethren students in Baptist seminaries were supported financially as they prepared for mission service. Funds were sent to Baptist missionaries in India and Cameroon; then American Mennonite Brethren missionaries were placed in those countries.

By the mid-nineteenth century the conference had investigated the potential for mission among the Chinese in Los Angeles and San Francisco. It sponsored Russian mission work in several Canadian locations. The Western Children's Mission in Canada was recommended to the churches for their support. A Jewish mission was started in Winnipeg. Mission work in the Belgian Congo was established. Missionaries were sent to Colombia and Panama. The mission initiatives of Mennonites in Brazil and Paraguay

Adjusting to a New Culture

"On September 28, 1934, at 11 a.m. we arrived in Chotzeshan. . . . In the afternoon, the Chinese Christians gave us a reception in the church. Although unable to understand what was said, we felt a bond of love with them.

"Our first encounter with culture was traveling together with the [John S. and Tina] Dick family on a horse cart to Bethany, an outstation close to Chotzeshan. . . . When we arrived at Bethany in the early afternoon, evangelist Chu served us refreshments. The Chinese, who have a unique gift of making guests feel at home in a strange land, invited us to sit on the *kang* (brick bed). The cross-legged posture, however, resulted in aching bones and muscle spasms, cramping limbs not trained to bend at will. The food, cooked in hemp oil, was known to cause acute indigestion in stomachs not conditioned to eat it. We decided therefore, that whenever the host turned his back, we would transfer food to Dick's plate or slip it into his large coat pockets. By the time the meal was finished, Dick's coat pockets bulged with food that otherwise might have played havoc with our digestive systems. The unsuspecting host, satisfied that he had served well, had initiated the newcomers into his culture."

—From Shadowed by the Great Wall, by A. K. and Gertrude Wiens (Board of Christian Literature, 1979).

Missionary Mary Richert (center back) with students in China, ca.1921-1925. (CMBS Fresno)

were supported. In the last half of the twentieth century Mennonite Brethren mission expanded to Japan, Indonesia, Pakistan, Peru, Mexico, Austria, Germany, Portugal, Spain, Thailand, Lithuania and Angola.

Sometimes Mennonite Brethren church members established missions on their own or through other mission agencies, and the conference later assumed responsibility. This happened in China between 1906 and 1919. Similarly, mission in the Congo was under consideration for more than twenty years after 1922 because of independent missions established by Mennonite Brethren missionaries and supported by many members of the constituency. In 1943 the Conference adopted the work there as its own. In the 1990s, after some Mennonite Brethren initiated ministries in Lithuania, the conference began to place missionaries and support projects there.

The Mennonite Brethren mission to Japan started as a cooperative project with MCC. Some missionaries and mission projects, including those in Peru, became Mennonite Brethren with the merger of the Mennonite Brethren and the Krimmer Mennonite Brethren Conference in 1960. Amid all of the planning and conference deliberations, there was also much of what one mission leader called "spontaneous" expansion of the mission program.

As early as the 1880s there were separate conference committees and reports for "home" mission, "city" mission and "foreign" mission. As district, provincial and national conferences developed, they assumed responsibility for "home" and "city" mission, and gradually the General Conference mandate focused on "foreign" mission.

This present division of mission responsibilities may be practical, but North American reality is a daily reminder that the distinction between "home," "city" and "foreign" is even more blurred today than in earlier decades. It was, after all, French-speaking Canadian Mennonite Brethren missionaries who fled from Congo in the early 1960s, returned to Canada, and planted the first Mennonite Brethren churches in Quebec. Dozens of "returned and retired" Mennonite Brethren missionaries have befriended and evangelized university students and immigrants from various cultures who have come to North America. People of Ethiopian, Indian, Chinese, Vietnamese, Mexican, Russian,

Geographic Expansion of North American Mennonite Brethren Missions

1896: Oklahoma
1899: India

1900: North Carolina (KMB)
1901: China (KMB)
1906: China (MB)

1921: Mongolia (KMB)
1922: Congo

1945: Colombia
1945: Paraguay
1949: Brazil

1950: Japan
1950: Peru (KMB)
1950: Mexico
1952: Germany
1953: Austria
1953: Ecuador
1956: Panama

1968: Uruguay
1968: Afghanistan

1974: Bangladesh
1975: Indonesia
1976: Spain

1986: Portugal
1988: Pakistan

1990: Angola
1992: Guatemala
1992: Thailand
1994: Russia
1994: Lithuania
1994: Burkina Faso

—Adapted primarily from Witness magazine, July-October 2000. Additional information taken from C. F. Plett, The Story of the Krimmer Mennonite Brethren Church (Kindred Press, 1985). This list does not include all MB and KMB missionaries who have served under other mission agencies.

Korean, Laotian and Arabic ancestry have established Mennonite Brethren congregations in North America. Some members of these congregations return to their former homelands to strengthen churches there. Today, MBMSI works in partnership with many of these North American congregations to assist them in their mission.

Whose mission is it?

During most of the past 120 years mission seemed to belong to the missionaries, mission board, and church members of the North American Mennonite Brethren Conference. Year after year, missionaries told their stories at conferences, in churches and in homes. Their names became legends. They were the spiritual heroes of the denomination. Their stories were told in a 1946 Sunday school series for children by Mrs. H. T. Esau entitled, *The Story of our Church and the Beginning of Our Missions*. Their pictures were on prayer calendars. When news came that John Wiebe had drowned in India in 1963 it seemed as though a beloved uncle had died, even though most church members did not know him personally. John and Mary Dyck's death in a plane crash in Colombia in 1957 was a tragedy and loss for the whole conference. Kornelius Isaak, speared to death in Paraguay in 1958, was a contemporary Mennonite Brethren martyr.

North Americans who have had the privilege of visiting Mennonite Brethren churches in other countries, have quickly learned how strongly the legacy of missionaries endures. As they were guided through a church or school or hospital they were asked if they knew the missionaries who helped establish it. If they admitted that they had never even heard of the missionary, their ignorance was met with incomprehension. How could they not know such important people who came from their country and their churches? The living memory of missionaries among Mennonite Brethren around the world is an immense tribute to their character and their accomplishments.

Even so, most missionaries and mission leaders in North America recognized that Mennonite Brethren mission would only be successful if it met the goal articulated clearly in the *Guiding Principles and Field Policies*, first published in 1947: "It shall ever be the endeavor of all of our foreign mission activities. . . to unite the local churches into an organized conference or convention, which shall become a church that continues the propagation of the Gospel in its area, directs and regulates its own church affairs, and meets its own financial requirements." Mennonite Brethren have been officially committed to this goal for many decades, and it was expressed in mission correspondence and reports for more than a century.

Today there has been significant progress toward that goal. There are autonomous Mennonite Brethren conferences in fifteen countries. These national conferences plan and implement evangelism and church planting programs. There is a shared commitment to mission among Mennonite Brethren conferences worldwide. Mission belongs to everyone.

But even today the goal of partnership has not been reached. The compelling vision of self-governing, self-propagating and self-financing churches could only be fulfilled if missionaries, mission

Aaron A. and Ernestine Janzen were the first Mennonite Brethren missionaries to serve in Belgian Congo. The Janzens built the Kafumba mission station out of the jungle from the ground up. Here Aaron Janzen and a Congolese assistant are tending to the ovens in which bricks were made for station construction, 1936. (CMBS Fresno)

administrators and the General Conference let go of authority, property, institutions, programs and money. That was, and continues to be, a demanding and painful process.

It is a process often identified with J. B. Toews, General Secretary of the Board of Missions from 1953 to 1963, and with the 1957 General Conference held in Yarrow, B.C. That conference decided essentially to shift control of mission from field-based missionaries to the Board of Missions. The rationale was to centralize coordination and evaluation and to give more authority to the "indigenous church." In 1962, in a "Statement to the Brotherhood from the Board of Missions," some of the implications of the decisions at Yarrow were spelled out:

> From here on all work must be planned with the conference [of the country of ministry]; all workers must be called and approved by and integrated into this conference; all finances, except the personal allowances of missionaries, must be channeled through this conference; and all institutions must be staffed, maintained and directed by this conference. Complete partnership must be accomplished in every area.

The powerful Missionary Councils, which had supervised mission work in each country, lost their administrative authority and became Missionary Fellowships that were supportive but not directive. These changes were intended to foster both local autonomy and a greater sense of partnership between missionaries and the local church. Initially they mostly caused uncertainty and suspicion among missionaries, national church leaders and mission administrators. A substantial and heated debate ensued over the manner in which these policy changes were enacted. Even today that debate continues. The sudden changes also generated difficulties within national conferences, which resulted in incomplete and inadequate transfers of vision and authority, harmful competition for power, and even lawsuits.

But one fundamental message was clear: mission belongs to all who are members of the worldwide body of Christ. Whose mission is it? It is God's mission. Whose mission is it? It is our mission. All of us, worldwide.

Partnership in Mission

The language of "partnership" became prominent in mission as a way to express this shared mission. In fact in 1960 it became the reason for changing the name of the Board from "Board of Foreign Mission" to "Board of Missions." It was an acknowledgment that there was now a global "co-labor relationship of the Mennonite Brethren Church of North America with the Mennonite Brethren Churches in other lands." As J. B. Toews put it in his report to the Conference that year, We have passed from a mission-centered program of world evangelism to an international church-fellowship program. . . . The emphasis falls not on the individual missionary and his labors, but on the younger churches and our relationship to them. . . . From this point the missionary arm of the M. B. Conference becomes an agency to assist the national church to evangelize the people of its own country.

The most recent change of name of the General Conference mission agency in 1998 added the word "International" to signify that it works as a mission partner with Mennonite Brethren congregations, conferences, and mission agencies worldwide.

Partnership also has other implications. In recent years MBMSI has helped congregations establish mission partnerships with congregations in other countries. It has joined other mission agencies for joint projects. It has engaged in mission partnerships in Indonesia, Botswana, and Lithuania to establish or strengthen churches that are not related to the Mennonite Brethren Church.

Partnership in mission has proven to be creative and productive, but also difficult and humbling. The resources and power of MBMSI are limited, but they are still often vastly greater than those of its partners. The dynamics of partnership are complicated when one partner has the capacity to provide or withhold essential resources. Some Mennonite Brethren leaders are reluctant to use the word "partnership" to describe present global relationships among Mennonite Brethren, because in their experience, partnership has not been reciprocal. Yet "partnering internationally in global mission" continues to be the goal.

A New Direction in Missions

In the aftermath of World War II the European colonial empires came tumbling down. J. B. Toews, mission administrator in the 1950s, reflected on what that meant for the Mennonite Brethren global mission program.

"My visits abroad and my consultations with many other mission agencies in various countries gave insight into the radical changes we would need in mission relationship, theology, methods and structure. . . . From 1955 to 1957 I shared openly with the constituent churches the need for major readjustments in our worldwide ministry. Some found these views hard to accept. In the mid-1950s the Mennonite Brethren Church had nearly 200 missionaries in foreign lands. Their motives were genuine. The support from the churches had been amazing. It had been the golden age of Mennonite Brethren missions. Why change now?

"Some of our older missionaries found the new direction very difficult to accept. They were products of a time that had passed. . . . As recently as 1947 their relationship with the national churches had been officially defined as one of parent and child. The new approach anticipated their removal from the churches as early as was feasible to give national liberty for self-identity in the context of their native culture. For some missionaries this implied the end of what they had understood to be a lifelong relationship to the national churches. Their struggle was somewhat like parents having to separate from their children. . . . National governing councils were created for each field to take over decision-making. The missionaries were asked to serve only in advisory capacities. The missionary council, formerly the legislative body, was now to function as a fellowship. The implementation of the new policies was difficult."

—From JB: A Twentieth-Century Mennonite Pilgrim, *by J. B. Toews (Center for Mennonite Brethren Studies-Fresno (1995).*

A Mennonite Brethren congregation meets in Medellin, Colombia, 1982. (CMBS Fresno)

A longer view of how the global Mennonite Brethren partnership in mission has matured is instructive. For about eighty years mission reports were about North American missionaries. The stories of their "passion for the lost," their industriousness, their adventures and their successes provided the only perspective on mission. Only two or three times during those years did the names of local co-workers appear in the official conference records. When mission pictures were published the missionaries were named and those who were with them were unnamed.

In 1960 Kyoichi Kitano from Japan, M. B. John from India, and G. B. Giesbrecht from Paraguay reported to the General Conference in person as part of the mission report. This signaled a change. These other churches and conferences now had faces and voices. In subsequent years such reports became more common and their content changed. The first reports were mostly tributes to missionaries. Later reports focused on work by local Mennonite Brethren in these countries.

A Global Commitment to World Mission

In 1988 Mennonite Brethren leaders from around the world met in Brazil to discuss their common commitment to world mission. They laid the groundwork for the International Committee of Mennonite Brethren (ICOMB), which has met several times since then. The vision for a global Mennonite Brethren fellowship that was expressed again and again through the twentieth century is now a reality.

It may seem that the high water mark for Mennonite Brethren mission was in 1960, when there were 256 long term missionaries, or in 1969, when the short-term Christian Service program was established, and there were 224 long-term and ninety-two short term mission workers. By comparison, at the beginning of 2002 there were 117 long-term missionaries supported by MBMSI.

Worldwide Mennonite Brethren Church Membership, 2000

Country	Members	Congregations
Congo	84,000	345
India	72,000	813
Canada	33,426	210
United States	26,219	162
Germany	14,030	67
Paraguay	6810	158
Angola	4600	25
former Soviet Union	4000	15
Brazil	3720	37
Japan	1890	29
Colombia	1800	36
Panama	860	15
Uruguay	190	7
Mexico	175	8
Venezuela	60	2
Argentina	40	1
Portugal	35	2
Spain	10	1
Total	253,865	1,933

—*Figures for North America from the* 2001/2002 Planner Directory *(Kindred Productions, 2001); figures for outside of North America provided by the International Committee of Mennonite Brethren Churches, 1999-2000. All figures are approximate.*

But that is only part of the story. At least nine hundred North Americans were involved in mission projects through MBMSI and its partner agencies in 2001. In addition, thousands of Mennonite Brethren from fifteen countries were engaged in local, national or international cross-cultural mission through other conferences and mission organizations, serving in sixty-five countries.

Mission, indeed, remains at the center of Mennonite Brethren identity.

7

The Printed Path to Unity

Wally Kroeker

Visit a Mennonite Brethren editor today and you won't see much shuffling of paper. You're more apt to see computer screens, zip disks, photo scanners and spell checkers.

A century ago you would have found the editor doing double-duty in a backroom world of simmering lead and hand-cranked presses, where typesetters hunched over wooden mazes of metal alphabets to assemble words, paragraphs and headlines.

Techniques can change with breathtaking speed, but the yearn to communicate with one another, by page or by pixel, has been constant. For 117 years Mennonite Brethren editors and publishers have been there to make it happen.

Late start in Russia

Mennonite Brethren in Russia were slow to engage the power of the press. Their larger Mennonite world was not known for literary or educational attentions. Nor was the restrictive Russian environment fertile soil for publishing. It was simpler to import reading material from Europe. Other than songbooks, little Mennonite publishing took place in nineteenth-century Russia. When traction finally was gained, Mennonite Brethren led the way.

Abraham J. Kroeker was the "father" of Mennonite Brethren publications in Russia, a partner in the noted Raduga (Rainbow) Press. In 1897 he began producing the daily devotional *Christlicher Familienkalendar*, followed two years later by the *Christlicher Abreisskalendar*, a wall calendar of tear-off devotionals.

In 1903 Kroeker launched *Friedensstimme*, the first Mennonite periodical in Russia. It became the semi-official organ of the Russian Mennonite Brethren, reaching a circulation of 5,800. Shortly after World War I it fell victim to anti-German sentiment and was discontinued.

These were private initiatives, as publishing was not seen as a conference responsibility in Russia. Only a confession of faith in 1902 and the German publication of P. M. Friesen's long-awaited history were initiated by the Mennonite Brethren Conference. In 1910, the conference did provide funds for *Erntefeld*, a missionary publication produced in India by Abraham Friesen.

Mennonite Brethren Publishing House, Hillsboro, Kansas, during the 1950s.
(CMBS Fresno)

Pioneer publishers

North American Mennonite Brethren were faster off the press. In 1884, only a decade after they first set foot on prairie soil, conference leaders decided they needed a periodical to communicate with their scattered churches. They hoped to preserve unity, a goal that would be shared by subsequent

The wandering editor: John F. Harms

John F. Harms was born in Russia in 1855. He migrated to the United States with his wife, Margaretha, in 1878. They settled in Mountain Lake, Minnesota.

In 1880 Harms was offered an opportunity to become the editor of a new German publication that John F. Funk, the Mennonite Church publisher at Elkhart, Indiana, was establishing. Harms accepted the job and moved with his family to Elkhart. This periodical, known as the *Mennonitische Rundschau* (Mennonite Observer), was intended to serve all Mennonite settlers in the newly-established Russian Mennonite communities of the Midwest.

Harms soon realized that he needed more biblical and theological training. With Funk's consent he attended the Evangelical Bible Institute in Naperville, Illinois, from 1882 to 1884 while continuing to edit the *Rundschau* in absentia.

Instead of returning to Elkhart after the 1884 school year, John and Margaretha moved to central Kansas and settled in the small village of Canada. There John managed a lumber business while still editing the *Rundschau* until 1885. When the lumber business was sold, he conducted German school in his home.

In 1884 John and Margaretha were baptized by immersion and joined the Mennonite Brethren Church. The following year he became the first publisher of the *Zionsbote*, the first official publication of the Mennonite Brethren Church in North America.

In 1886 the Harms family moved to the nearby town of Lehigh, Kansas. They stayed there only a short time before moving to the larger city of McPherson. There Harms established a printing plant in which he produced the *Zionsbote*, the *Marion County Anzeiger* (which he also published), and did other printing job work. Harms stayed in McPherson only two years, when he moved the printing plant operation to Hillsboro.

In 1899 Harms was caught up in the search for new land, and moved with his family to Medford, Oklahoma. His type cases and meager printing equipment went with him to Medford. A small lean-to was added to their house, which constituted the printing plant where the *Zionsbote* was produced.

In 1906 Harms resigned as editor of the *Zionsbote* and moved to Canada. Margaretha, who suffered from severe headaches, had been told by a doctor to seek out a colder climate, and so the family moved to Edmonton, Alberta, for a short time before settling in Herbert, Saskatchewan. There Harms homesteaded and became involved in itinerant ministry among Russian immigrants. He later became administrator of the Herbert Bible School.

In 1918 Harms decided to leave Canada. Hoping to visit relatives in Russia, John and Margaretha traveled to Seattle, Washington, where they planned to take a ship to Vladivostok. In Seattle, Harms met M. B. Fast of Reedley, California, who was preparing a relief shipment for Mennonites in Russia. Harms stayed in Seattle for several months, helping Fast prepare the shipments.

Before they were able to leave for Russia, however, Margaretha's health began to deteriorate. They returned to Edmonton, where Margaretha was diagnosed with stomach cancer. Soon thereafter, John and Margaretha headed for California, where they hoped the mild climate would help ease her suffering. They settled in Reedley and purchased a house there in 1919.

When it became clear that Margaretha's end was near, she and John decided to return to Hillsboro in 1921, where she died only a few weeks later. Following Margaretha's death, John stopped his wandering, and lived in Hillsboro until his own death in 1945. He remained active in publishing and writing activities for the rest of his life.

—*Adapted from* Pioneer Publisher: The Life and Times of J. F. Harms, *by Orlando Harms (Center for Mennonite Brethren Studies-Hillsboro, 1984).*

Mennonite Brethren publishers. At this point the emerging obstacle to unity was geographic, as the new German-speaking immigrants were widely dispersed. For later editors the defining dispersions would be language, ethnicity, education, urbanization and modernity.

Attending the 1884 conference was a newly-minted Mennonite Brethren who had joined the church only a few months earlier after moving from Elkhart, Indiana, to Kansas. John F. Harms, a teacher, was already well acquainted with religious publishing. He had worked earlier with the noted Mennonite Church publisher John F. Funk, becoming the first editor of the *Mennonitische Rundschau*, a publication for Russian Mennonites that began in 1880 and would later be owned by the Mennonite Brethren Church. Now the twenty-nine-year-old Harms was chosen by the Mennonite Brethren to direct their new publication, *Zionsbote* (Messenger of Zion). He would dominate Mennonite Brethren publications for decades.

The *Zionsbote* began as a four-page quarterly sent in bulk to churches. It soon came out monthly and by 1889, weekly. It would be the official organ of the Mennonite Brethren until 1951, and would exist until 1964.

Mennonite Brethren Publishing House, McPherson, Kansas, ca. 1908. (CMBS Hillsboro)

Don Ratzlaff as editor of The Christian Leader. *(CMBS Hillsboro)*

Giving Youth a Chance

Conference roles were often the preserve of seasoned elders, but not when it came to publications. For more than a century, Mennonite Brethren had a tradition of handing the reins of conference periodicals over to people below the age of thirty.

John F. Harms, later known as "the father of Mennonite Brethren publishing," was twenty-nine when he was given the task of launching the *Zionsbote*. Other editors of Mennonite Brethren periodicals who began their assignments while in their twenties: Leslie Stobbe (*Mennonite Observer*), Rudy Wiebe and Harold Jantz (*Mennonite Brethren Herald*), and Wally Kroeker and Don Ratzlaff (*The Christian Leader*).

—Wally Kroeker

A caricature of Christian Leader *editor Wally Kroeker as published in the* Leader *in 1981.*

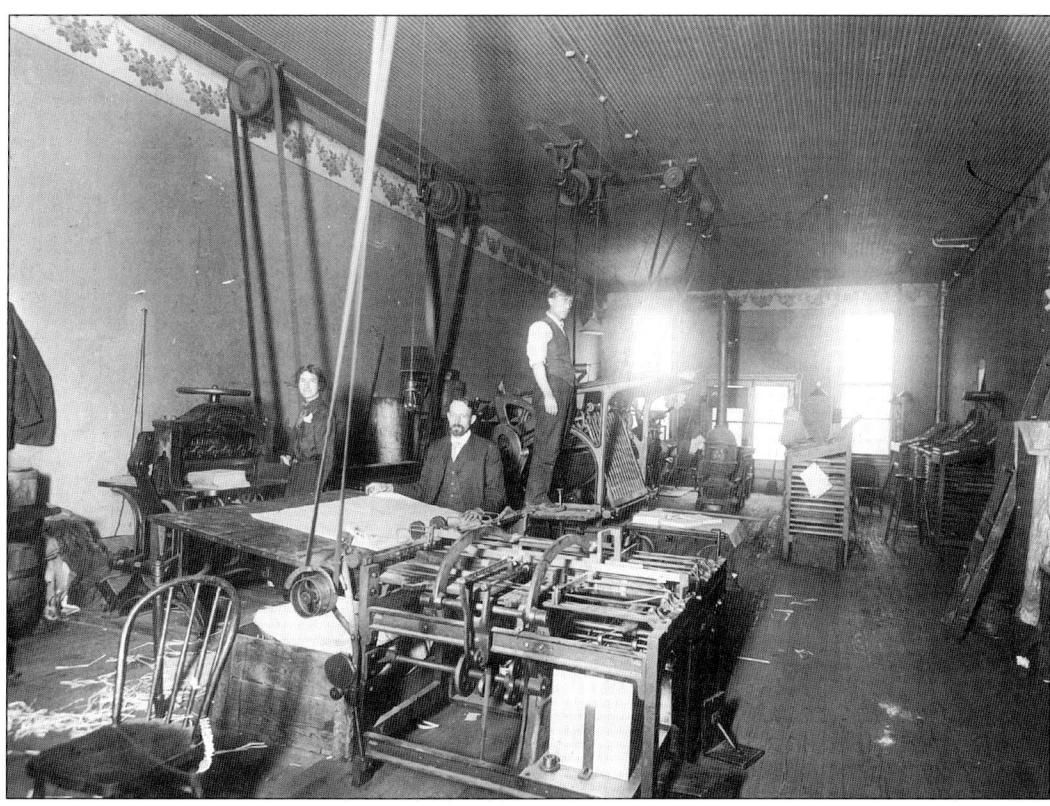

Interior of Mennonite Brethren Publishing House, date unknown. Editor A. L. Schellenberg is seated in foreground.
(CMBS Hillsboro)

The Editor Who Always Spoke His Mind

Abraham L. Schellenberg, while editor of the Mennonite Brethren paper *Zionsbote*, was never one to mince words. Schellenberg was known to insert parenthetical rebuttals into *Zionsbote* reports when he disagreed with the ideas expressed there.

One issue that particularly offended Schellenberg was the widespread migration of Mennonite Brethren settlers across the western regions of North America. He apparently feared that this dispersal of members would weaken the existing Midwestern congregations, and frequently provided a dissenting opinion when these migratory members wrote in to the *Zionsbote*. In a report from Hollywood, California, in 1909, Anna Janzen commented that "I don't know why we must live so alone, but I am sure God has a reason." To which Schellenberg parenthetically replied, "Is it really God's will that you are there or mostly your own wills?" In 1912, Mrs. F. F. Becker wrote from El Modena in Orange County, California, "We are renting here, until the Lord shows us his will for us." Schellenberg retorted in print, "The Lord has something for you, but it is in Oklahoma."

A goal of this 25-cent-a-year paper was to hold the church together. It carried missions news, conversion experiences, correspondence from churches, and scriptural exposition and interpretation. "In the far-flung constituency of the Mennonite Brethren in North America it would have been impossible to 'maintain the unity of the spirit in the bond of peace' without a church periodical," writes historian J. A. Toews.

Harms was paid $50 one year, $25 the next. Some years he received only a word of thanks and a pat on the back. He earned extra money with job printing, part-time teaching and farming.

One of his many relocations took him to a farm near Medford, Oklahoma, where he set up his printing press in a small lean-to. It was a meager operation, with cast-off equipment. He farmed by day and did editorial work by night. His daughters set the type, and he ran the press by hand.

A crisp new look

The overworked Harms grew discouraged. The conference stepped in and took over Harm's operation in Medford. Thus was born the Mennonite Brethren Publishing House, with Harms as editor and manager. Money was raised for equipment, including a folder, paper cutter and stitcher. The results were immediate. The issue of the *Zionsbote* that came off the new press on 25 May 1904 had crisp, clean type and pictures from zinc etchings. Mennonite Brethren publishing had entered a new era.

In 1906, however, Harms resigned to move to Canada for his wife's health. The "Harms era" came to an end, though the "father of

Martin B. Fast and the unmoveable earth

Martin B. Fast was an influential Krimmer Mennonite Brethren author and editor. Born in 1858 in South Russia, he migrated to Nebraska in 1877 with his parents. He was baptized and joined the Jansen (Nebr.) KMB Church in 1880. Fast served as editor of the inter-Mennonite newspaper, *Mennonitische Rundschau,* from 1903 to 1910, and became the first editor of the KMB periodical *Der Wahrheitsfreund* in 1915, a position he held until 1917.

Fast was very involved in efforts to provide relief for suffering Mennonites in Russia following the 1917 revolution, and even made a trip to deliver relief materials to Siberia in 1919. From 1929 to 1933 he served as chairman of the KMB Board of Foreign Missions. He died in Reedley, California, in 1949.

Fast published several books, most on Mennonite history or descriptions of his travels. One of his lesser known—and more unusual—publications was a small pamphlet entitled *Ein biblischer Beweis, dass die Sonne auf und unter geht und die Erde auf ein von Gott gebautes Fundament steht* ("A Biblical Proof that the Sun Rises and Sets, and that the Earth Stands on a Foundation Built by God"). The following passages are taken from this 1944 pamphlet:

"I was asked to publish a pamphlet about my idea that the earth stands and the sun moves. . . . Everything I am going to write, I will try to prove with God's Word. I do not want to attack the teachings of astronomers and professors, and will try to stay on biblical ground. . . .

"We read in Isaiah 66:1, 'Heaven is my throne and the earth is my footstool.' If heaven stands and the earth spins, this is impossible! So, heaven and earth stand. The earth stood two days in the water, and on the third day the water was gone. There is no place in the Bible that says that the earth started spinning after [God] told the grass and plants to grow.

"We read in Proverbs 8:29, 'when he marked out the foundations of the earth.' Psalm 104:5 says 'Thou didst set the earth on its foundations, so that it should never be shaken.'

"Many readers might have seen the Balancing Rock in Colorado Springs. The foundation of this rock is very small, but the rock has stood there for thousands of years. I walked around it and thought, 'this is how the earth stands. I don't know what God created the foundation from, but it is there. It is God's business.' . . .

"I think of a story that I once read, in which a professor told his class that the earth spins around the sun. . . . He then asked a student, 'Peter, how do we know that the earth spins?' Peter stood up and answered, 'Professor, I haven't noticed that it does.' It is the same for me as for Peter—I haven't noticed that it does.

"To conclude I invite you to read Isaiah 24:18-'For the windows of heaven are opened, and the foundations of the earth tremble.' . . .

"I have written many times in the *Newton Herold* that the earth stands and that the sun rises and sets. Professor Goertz once replied, 'Brother Fast, the earth stands!' That was good to hear. Others also wrote me with the same message, but other dear readers still fly around the sun with the earth—or at least think they do."

Martin B. Fast, with his wife Elizabeth Fast (seated) and daughter Agnes (standing). This portrait was taken while Fast served as editor of the Mennonitische Rundschau *in Elkhart, Indiana, ca. 1903-1908.*
(CMBS Fresno)

Mennonite Brethren publications" would return to the fold in 1921 to serve another long stint as assistant editor of the *Zionsbote* and other periodicals.

With Harms's departure the conference decided to transfer the publishing house from Medford to McPherson, Kansas, where commercial printing opportunities beckoned. Soon it would move once again to more ethnically familiar Hillsboro, twenty-five miles east, where it would remain until being sold in the 1980s.

Succeeding Harms as editor-manager was A. L. Schellenberg, an outspoken progressive who favored women's suffrage, a minimum wage and labor legislation, as well as pro-German causes. Colorful and volatile, he enlivened the Mennonite Brethren publishing landscape.

Conference publishing had grown under the Harms influence. Various kinds of Sunday school literature were produced. From 1905 to 1912 a monthly Russian language publication, *Golos* (Voice) was published for Russian-speaking immigrants in Saskatchewan and North Dakota.

Non-religious periodicals were printed. One was the *Vorwärts* (Forward), a weekly German family paper that had been purchased when the publishing house moved to Hillsboro. Schellenberg was happy to become its editor, for it coincided with his pro-German leanings.

Schellenberg was a shrewd business manager, and both the *Zionsbote* and *Vorwärts* prospered under his hand. But his pugnacious editorial spirit raised hackles. During an editorial fray in 1919 he resigned and moved to Texas to farm. His competence and business acumen could not easily be matched, however, and in a few years he was invited back. In 1930 he again resigned amid an editorial scuffle, this time for good.

With Schellenberg gone, the 1930s were quieter, if less lively. In 1937 *The Christian Leader* came into being as a youth publication to serve a constituency that was fast switching from German to English. It became the official periodical of the General Conference in 1951 but never caught on among Canadians, who were beginning to feel less like the Northern District of the General Conference and more like a separate national conference with their own identity.

Orlando Harms, editor of the *Leader* from 1953 to the mid 1970s, was a stabilizing influence who brought the Mennonite Brethren Publishing House to consistent profitability. A tireless conference servant, he presided over the eventual demise of the *Zionsbote* and the demotion of the *Leader* from a General Conference to a United States Conference publication.

In 1968 he was taken to task at the United States Conference for giving readers too much controversial material. Did the *Leader* really need to report on racial ferment, campus unrest and the Vietnam War? Six years later the pendulum swung the other way when the United States Conference suggested he had gone too far to placate readers. He was, as he would later describe it, "censured for not having more controversial material."

Lack of controversial content would not be a charge leveled at the next two *Leader* editors, Wally Kroeker (1975-1985) and Don Ratzlaff (1985-1998). They would periodically be admonished for their handling of issues ranging from materialism and militarism to the Moral Majority and Promise Keepers.

When Ratzlaff left in 1998 the *Leader* crossed the editorial gender barrier. Assistant editor Connie Faber served as interim editor until Carmen Andres was appointed editor late that year.

Publications unfold in Canada

A surge of Russian immigrants redefined Mennonite Brethren life on the Canadian prairies in the 1920s. Readership demographics were in flux. The newcomers embraced the *Mennonitische Rundschau*, which J. F. Harms had edited in Indiana in the 1880s and that still functioned as an inter-Mennonite weekly for Russian Mennonites. In 1923 it was moved to Winnipeg, Manitoba,

by Hermann H. Neufeld as the flagship of his new Rundschau Publishing House, which would later become the Christian Press and be owned by the Canadian Mennonite Brethren Conference.

Christian Press, Winnipeg, 1951. (CMBS Winnipeg)

North American Mennonite Brethren now had two publishing centers—the Christian Press in Winnipeg, and the Mennonite Brethren Publishing House in Hillsboro. This would continue until the United States Conference decided to sell its publishing house in the 1980s.

The *Mennonitische Rundschau* went on serving the larger Mennonite family while achieving semi-official status in the hearts of Canadians. When it finally became fully adopted by the Canadian Conference, the *Zionsbote's* days were numbered. The *Zionsbote* folded in 1964, yielding the field—and a list of unexpired subscriptions—to its victorious competitor to the north. The *Rundschau*, today more than 120 years old, is still published, but its German audience keeps shrinking.

Although *The Christian Leader* was the official English periodical of North American Mennonite Brethren, Canadian readers chafed under its American tone and lack of attention to Canadian matters. They wanted a publication of their own. In 1955 Canadians launched the *Mennonite Observer*, a "younger companion" to the inter-Mennonite *Mennonitische Rundschau*, with Leslie Stobbe as editor. Stobbe worked feverishly, without the benefit of secretarial help, to produce the twelve-page weekly, which was thoroughly Mennonite Brethren in flavor but not explicitly a conference paper. From the outset it faced stiff competition from another weekly, *The Canadian Mennonite*, edited by Frank H. Epp, which had the benefit of a two-year head start plus a more aggressive editorial policy that appealed to a growing segment of young urban readers. The *Observer* lasted until the end of 1961, when it was suspended to make way for a new magazine.

Harold Jantz, long-time editor of the Mennonite Brethren Herald. (CMBS Winnipeg)

The *Mennonite Brethren Herald* appeared in January 1962 as the official periodical of the Canadian Mennonite Brethren Conference. Its editor was Rudy Wiebe, a bold and creative writer with theological training. He treated readers to stimulating articles, profound editorials and a new column, "Petronius and his pew pals," which took a lighthearted look at congregational life.

With quirky timing, the magazine's debut issue announced Wiebe's first novel, *Peace Shall Destroy Many*, which explored life in a small Mennonite community during World War II. The novel irked many Mennonite Brethren (even those who didn't bother to read it), who were unaccustomed to seeing their beliefs and behavior put to public and not necessarily flattering scrutiny. A firestorm ensued, more over the novel than Wiebe's editing of the *Herald*. He stepped down from the editorship in 1963 and went on to a brilliant career as one of Canada's top novelists and winner of two prestigious Governor General's Literary Awards.

The *Herald's* next full-time editor was Harold Jantz, who would serve with distinction from 1964 to 1985. He would manage to achieve a high level of conference trust while still being able to pose tough conference questions when necessary. Later editors would be Herb Kopp, Ron Geddert and Jim Coggins.

Merged magazines?

While the notion of separate church periodicals made regional and journalistic sense, it did not sit well with some leaders who were concerned with what this said about church unity. Over the years there were repeated conversations about unifying publication efforts, or at least merging the magazines. These discussions never went far, however. Both the *Herald* and the *Leader* had a life of their own, and there was no putting the genie back in the bottle.

The editors of the two magazines (then Harold Jantz and Wally Kroeker) worked together on numerous projects, and on one occasion joked in print about merging and opening a joint office in Aberdeen, South Dakota—the geographic midpoint between Winnipeg and Hillsboro. But there was no mistaking their goals. "Both of us intend to create the strongest publications we are capable of within our areas," they wrote in a joint report in 1977.

"Of making many books there is no end"

General Conference publishing leapt ahead in 1966 with the formation of the Board of Christian Literature (BCL) to publish, coordinate and encourage Christian writing. It produced a new devotional booklet, *Worship Together* (later to become *Rejoice!*), various membership and ministers' manuals, and a congregational handout, *Introducing the Mennonite Brethren Church*.

It also moved ambitiously into book publishing. As if to signal new literary energy, the board in 1967 produced a 417-page hardcover book, *The Church in Mission*, honoring the ministry of J. B. Toews as a teacher, pastor and missions administrator.

Over the next two decades the BCL stimulated a flurry of publishing activity, much of it to catch up telling the Mennonite Brethren story. Moody Press book editor Leslie Stobbe, serving as the Board's literature consultant, urged the conference to publicize its illustrious history lest Mennonite Brethren think only Baptists had heroes of the faith.

By the early 1970s very little of the Mennonite Brethren story had been published in English. The task of writing a new history was assigned to John A. Toews, a respected minister, teacher and former president of the Mennonite Brethren Bible College in Winnipeg. *A History of the Mennonite Brethren Church* came out under the BCL's imprint in 1975. The 513-page book, combining scholarship and readability, would sell out and be re-printed in 1982.

Another volume of history was soon on its way. A monumental work of over a thousand pages, the translation of the German version of P. M. Friesen's *The Mennonite Brotherhood in Russia (1789-1910)*, came out in 1978. Friesen himself became the subject of the first "Trailblazer," a series of short readable biographies of pivotal people in the Mennonite Brethren Conference. This was followed in the mid-1970s by volumes on Paulina Foote, H. H. Voth and A. H. Unruh. Longer biographies would chronicle the contributions of Johann Classen and B. B. Janz.

Missions was also a subject of interest, though perhaps more to conference officials than to book buyers. In the late 1970s the BCL published *The Mennonite Brethren Church in Zaire* by J. B. Toews, *The Latin American Mennonite Brethren Church* by J. J. Toews, and *Shadowed by the Great Wall* by A. K. and Gertrude Wiens.

In 1980 the board signaled a new direction. *Conversion: Doorway to Discipleship*, edited by Henry J. Schmidt, linked the Mennonite Brethren emphasis on spiritual rebirth with another Anabaptist theme, following Christ in daily life.

Elmer Martens (right), Chairman of the Board of Christian Literature, presents a copy of P. M. Friesen's Mennonite Brotherhood in Russia *to editor J. B. Toews (center). Peter J. Klassen (left), a member of the book's translation and editorial committee, looks on. The completed book was unveiled at this event in Fresno, California, in 1978. (CMBS Fresno)*

Publishing took on a new glow. Book ideas and manuscripts began to flow, pushing the need for editorial diplomacy to new heights. How, after all, did you tell a venerated church leader that his writing was dull?

Professional designers were employed to improve the face of BCL books. Yet production glitches persisted. One board member, after finding forty typographical errors in a new release, wrote, "It is a shame that such otherwise good work by the author and the artist is shorn of much excellence by shoddy production work."

Pricing could be contentious. BCL typically set retail prices at double the cost of production. This left room for a standard bookstore discount of 40 percent, plus 10 percent for promotion and distribution. (Authors received a modest stipend instead of royalties.) One author, complaining that the high retail price of his book would discourage sales, threatened to take future manuscripts elsewhere.

The bane of publishing is deciding how many copies to print. Front-end costs of editing, typesetting, proofreading, design and layout remain the same regardless of quantity. Printing more copies cuts the per-unit cost, but the saving is illusory if the additional books gather dust in the warehouse. Many BCL press runs were small (seven hundred to a thousand copies), thus the cost per book was relatively high. "We have the books in our warehouses, but we haven't always been able to get them into the hands of the prospective readers," noted literature coordinator Katie Funk Wiebe.

The BCL yearned for a trade name of its own, not only to bolster its image on bookstore shelves but also to bring coherence to Mennonite Brethren publishing. It didn't help that Mennonite Brethren books were being produced with a variety of imprints. Even conference leaders didn't know the difference between the various publishing entities.

Both the Canadian and US publishing boards hired book editors and were moving forward along with BCL. The US board had devised its own trade name, Kindred Press, and was trying to market books beyond denominational lines. It produced four titles in its first year.

The BCL asked if it could share the Kindred name. At first the US board declined, but later relented. Henceforth, Mennonite Brethren books on both sides of the border would carry the Kindred Press logo.

By the late 1980s it was time to expand the literature mandate to cover other forms of communication, and BCL was replaced by the Board of Resource Ministries. In 1993 the name Kindred Press became Kindred Productions as the agency widened its mandate to include Sunday school, video and music resources.

During the 1990s Kindred ventured into provocative fare like *Your Daughters Shall Prophesy: Women in Ministry in the Church*, edited by John E. Toews, Valerie Rempel and Katie Funk Wiebe, and *All Are Witnesses: A Collection of Sermons by Mennonite Brethren Women*, edited by Delores Friesen.

As the twentieth century ended Kindred was producing three to four books a year, though its finances were faltering. It brought out a new line of inspirational books such as *Rogues, Rascals and Rare Gems* by Dan Unrau and *Remember, Dad?* by Lorlie Barkman. As well, there were youth devotionals such as *A Walk on the Wild Side* by Dave Ens and *Take the Plunge* by Brad Huebert.

Reaching out to youth

The BCL had also played a role with youth periodicals. In 1971 it started *Bridge*, a newspaper for high school students. To keep costs low, the bi-monthly tabloid was shipped in bulk to Mennonite Brethren congregations. Distribution could depend on how local leaders felt about the contents. *Bridge* was discontinued in 1974.

In 1976 a different youth emphasis came into being as part of BCL's efforts to stimulate greater cooperation between the *Mennonite Brethren Herald* in Canada and *The Christian Leader* in the United States. *Sonkist*, an occasional insert in the periodicals, was produced under BCL's auspices by a group of fun-loving young Mennonite Brethren in British Columbia. Its tone and graphic style, more like *The Wittenburg Door* than *Campus Life*, were not universally appreciated by adult readers, though a fervent minority applauded its courage and vigor. It ceased publication in 1978.

Inter-Mennonite publishing

Mennonite Brethren were not always eager to publish cooperatively with other Mennonites, partly due to a perception that the larger Mennonite groups were less evangelical and preoccupied with peace and social issues. Mennonite Brethren remained cool to joint ventures such as the youth publication *With*, the Foundation Series Sunday school curriculum and a joint hymnal project.

A notable exception was the devotional book, *Rejoice!*, which evolved from the Mennonite Brethren *Worship Together* to an inter-Mennonite publication in 1972. Despite heavy promotion, Mennonite Brethren acceptance of *Rejoice!* remained tepid. Not all appreciated the inter-Mennonite flavor; some objected to the use of women writers. Many Mennonite Brethren who practiced daily devotions preferred the more pietistic *Our Daily Bread*, which came to them free.

Mennonite Brethren Broadcasting

Unlike print, broadcasting never built up a head of steam among Mennonite Brethren. The airwaves were initially distrusted, even regarded as evil. Some leaders feared radios (and later television) would reduce family music making and diminish the role of the church. Still, some in the church saw broadcasting as a promising new ally in proclaiming the gospel. As early as 1940 a Mennonite Brethren program called *Gospel Tidings* aired in Saskatoon. Numerous congregations, like Winkler, Manitoba, and Kitchener, Ontario, produced their own programs for local use. Other churches followed, and by 1955 there were radio programs in every province with a Mennonite Brethren presence.

In 1947 three students from the Mennonite Brethren Bible College in Winnipeg began a new program called *Gospel Light Hour*. It grew into a ministry of the Manitoba Mennonite Brethren Conference and developed a following in several provinces. High German, Low German and Russian programs were added in the 1950s and to this day have a significant ministry in numerous countries. More recently, Spanish and Arabic programs have been added. A Christian open-line show, *God Talk*, is broadcast on a major Winnipeg radio station. Over the years the name of the ministry was changed to MB Communications, and now Family Life Network.

In the United States, broadcasts were first initiated by local churches, such as Buhler, Kansas, and Delft, Minnesota. Tabor College and Pacific Bible Institute also had programs. *Words of the Gospel* broadcast was launched by the Pacific District Conference in 1960 and eventually came under US Conference sponsorship. Ambitious perhaps to a fault, the ministry became extensively involved in radio, cassette, studio and audio-visual ministries, and even some television and film projects. *Words of the Gospel* radio program, broadcast widely over myriad stations across the United States, was also beamed to Central and South America via Trans World Radio. The Words of the Gospel Singers had an extensive touring ministry. *Words of the Gospel* continued under US Conference support until 1983.

Mennonite Brethren lay people made notable contributions in private broadcasting ventures. Brothers Egon and Dave Hofer, members of the Zion KMB Church in Dinuba, California, launched KRDU in 1946 and later the first FM stereo station in the Fresno market. Dave Hofer went on to prominent leadership of the prestigious National Religious Broadcasters. Entrepreneur and churchman Edward J. Peters operated a radio station in Wasco, California. In Manitoba, Mennonite Brethren lay people were part of a group that launched CFAM in 1957. Specializing in community, religious and agricultural broadcasting, it grew into a chain of stations across Canada's Prairie Provinces.

The Mennonite Brethren profile in television was more modest. In 1954, the Canadian Committee of Reference and Counsel warned against television, concluding that "the terrible damage which through this invention is inflicted on the church, cannot be rectified by an occasional religious program."

Some local churches and agencies nonetheless dabbled in television, but the medium was too expensive for sustained conference use. During the 1970s the First Mennonite Brethren Church of Wichita, along with the Inter-Mennonite Media Group, produced *Back Seat*, a docu-drama film dealing with loneliness and alienation. In 1976 Words of the Gospel appointed Louis Paul Lehman as its director of television. In 1977, Manitoba's MB Communications entered the TV world with *The Third Story*, a thirteen-week series that presented a Christian message to unchurched children.

In central Canada a weekly church music program called *Hymn Sing* became regular Sunday afternoon TV fare, starting in 1964. Though not explicitly a Mennonite Brethren production, it was started by renowned Mennonite musicologist Ben Horch during his time with the Canadian Broadcasting Corporation and employed numerous Mennonite Brethren singers over the years. It lasted until 1997, becoming one of the CBC's longest-running programs.

—Wally Kroeker

David and Egon Hofer preparing to turn on the transmitter at radio station KRDU in Dinuba, California. (CMBS Fresno)

Mennonite Brethren also cooperated in the four-volume *Mennonite Encyclopedia* (published in the 1950s) and the more recent *Believers Church Bible Commentary.*

A stew called unity

Mennonite Brethren pens and presses were far from idle throughout the twentieth century. Common to this activity was a desire for the Holy Grail of "unity," and the hope that publishing would help attain it. Most Mennonite Brethren publications at some point avowed their pursuit of unity. Alas, the act of publishing can complicate this quest by highlighting diverse perceptions of reality, itself a fragmenting influence. But genuine unity eludes if diversity is suppressed rather than celebrated. As the founding editor of one paper said, "We wanted to create a sense of unity, and to do this we needed freewheeling exchange and honest interaction." This caused dissonance for conference leaders who wanted editors to be recording secretaries and cheerleaders rather than partners in shaping a vision.

Mennonite Brethren publications have always functioned best when they dared to go beyond narrow piety, when they saw their task as not merely an act of collection but as an act of assertion, when they scoured the strewn reaches of the priesthood of believers for the blessing of diversity, when they sought to forge consensus rather than timidly report some official imitation of it.

Reading Mennonite Brethren publications at their best is like dining on soup that is neither anemic consomme nor bland puree, but rather a zesty, populist stew with different shapes and colors of vegetables, assorted chunks of meat, plenty of herbs and spices, and maybe even a chili pepper or two. To an editor, that is something like the stuff of Scripture, where rulers are brought low and sinners become saints.

BOOK NEWS

Kindred Productions

169 Riverton Ave., Winnipeg MB R2L 2E5
Phone: 800 545-7322 Fax: 204 654-1865
Email: custserv@kindredproductions.com
315 S Lincoln, Box 220, Hillsboro KS 67063
Phone: 800 545-7322   Fax 620 947-3266
Website: www.kindredproductions.com

For Everything a Season

Mennonite Brethren in North America, 1874-2002

An Informal History
Paul Toews, Kevin Enns-Rempel

Commissioned by the Mennonite Brethren General Conference Executive, compiled by the Historical Commission, and published by Kindred Productions, *For Everything a Season* is an informal history of the birth of the General Conference (Canada and the US) structure, the ministries that were carried out under its umbrella and the ways God used these ministries and his people to further his kingdom.

The demise of the General Conference in the summer of 2002 as an active entity became the impetus for this book of reflection, thanksgiving and challenge. The fourteen essays look at the early beginnings, the migration from Russia to the US and Canada, music in the churches, publishing, mission efforts, educational endeavors, and how the church is positioning itself for the future.

A coffee table type book, many black and white pictures help to tell the story.

Price: $35.99 CDN; $26.99 US
ISBN: 0-921788-84-3
Pages: 188, hardcover
Dealer Discount: 40%
Library Discount: 15%

Check our website at www.kindredproductions.com for order information
or
Email: custserv@kindredproductions.com
or
Call: 1 800-545-7322

8

Embodying the Vision: Higher Education

Paul Toews & Abe Dueck

*I*t is hard to exaggerate the Mennonite Brethren commitment to education. The decision in 1857 by some members of the Mennonite church in the village of Gnadenfeld, South Russia, to establish a private Christian school was one of the early acts in the drama that led to the formation of the Mennonite Brethren Church. Teachers, furthermore, were disproportionately represented among those who joined the early Mennonite Brethren Church.

Discussion regarding schools was one of the recurring topics of Mennonite Brethren conferences at virtually all levels. The 1881 sessions of the General Conference already raised the need for private education. The minutes, in a statement echoed by many subsequent conventions, noted that "the brothers had such different ideas and the possibility of a Church-school caused tremendous pressure." The solution was to ask each church to select someone who would investigate the requirements for establishing local private schools. Many communities and local leaders took the 1881 conference advice seriously and began local schools. By 1902 there were at least seven Mennonite Brethren schools in Kansas, Nebraska and Oklahoma. Some were elementary, some also included preparatory programs. A favorite means for establishing these schools was the creation of a *Schulverein* (school society).

In the early 1880s some Mennonite Brethren in Kansas fashioned such a society whose aspirations were more than just another local school. They hoped to establish a school for training denominational young people to serve as teachers both in the elementary schools and in mission settings. In 1884 the General Conference offered its commendation for the work. To achieve their goal the society sent Peter Wedel to the Baptist seminary in Rochester, New York, with hopes that he would return and develop a school. Wedel did return, but the conference then asked the society for his services as a Conference evangelist and reimbursed the society five hundred dollars for his education. John F. Harms, editor of the *Zionsbote*, was dismayed at the turn of events. He asked Wedel, "Why have you done this to us?" Wedel responded: "What can you expect? . . . You send me to a seminary and make a preacher out of me—small wonder that I am no longer a teacher."

With or without Wedel, there was growing momentum in Kansas for a higher educational institution. In 1896 several Mennonite Brethren individuals responded to overtures from McPherson College, a liberal arts school operated by the Church of the Brethren in McPherson, Kansas, to establish a "German Department" there. The purpose of the rather misnamed department was to provide a context in which German-speaking Mennonite students could

The Tabor College administration building, constructed in 1920.
(CMBS Fresno)

"Tabor College Still Lives!"

Tabor College on fire, 30 April 1918. (CMBS Fresno)

April 30, 1918, dawned beautiful, quiet and unsuspecting. It was an ideal spring morning on the Kansas plains. In the serenity of that quiet morning stood Tabor College, "tried and true," as the college song says, in the small village of Hillsboro. At 7:00 in the morning, the cry of "Fire! Fire!" awakened the villagers. Everyone nearby rushed to the scene of the spectacular fire. By 7:20 the roof of the Tabor College building had collapsed and by 8:00 there were only smoldering ruins. Everything was lost: the building, the library, records, equipment, the museum. Students, faculty and townspeople stood speechless and overcome by grief. But a word soon filtered through the crowd: "Tabor College still lives!" Who had the courage to proclaim that is still unknown. The oral tradition attributes the phrase to Henry W. Lohrenz, the founding president of the college. But it was more than a phrase. At 10:00 in the morning the students, faculty and friends of the college gathered for a meeting in the Hillsboro Mennonite Brethren Church. They sought to understand what had happened. The college, though only ten years old, had prospered. Now it was gone. They did what Mennonite Brethren have frequently done in the face of danger and despair. They turned to God in prayer. After a two-hour prayer meeting, they committed themselves to the rebuilding of Tabor College and pledged $10,000 toward reconstruction. Their prayers were answered, and soon a new and more glorious structure was built. Tabor College did indeed still live.

John F. Duerksen (with full beard) and students of the McPherson College German Department, 1903-1904. Future Tabor College president H.W. Lohrenz is standing in the back row, third from right. (CMBS Fresno)

Reflections on Education in Canada

"In 1939 . . . I entered the Coaldale Bible School at age sixteen. Here I spent three wonderful years under the tutelage of men such as Jacob H. Quiring, John A. Toews, and Bernhard W. Sawatzky.

"Sawatzky took a personal interest in me and helped me to regain some self-confidence. Since humility was seen as the epitome of piety in those days . . . , we had been duly knocked down in our youth. Some of us needed to be delivered from despising ourselves . . .

"Higher education was generally suspect when I grew up. It was often equated with 'the wisdom of the world' of which Paul speaks in 1 Corinthians. However, I rejected that attitude and earned a B.A. at . . . the University of British Columbia. On one occasion when my father-in-law saw some of my textbooks he could only exclaim: *'Gefährlich, gefährlich!'* ('Dangerous, dangerous!')."

—Adapted from David Ewert's "Theological Autobiography" in Bridging Troubled Waters: The Mennonite Brethren at Mid-Twentieth Century *(Kindred Productions, 1995).*

receive training both for church ministries and for teaching in their parochial schools.

The Kansas initiative for an advanced school soon came under the purview of the General Conference and achieved a quasi-denominational status. In 1898 McPherson College offered the Conference "full control of the German department." The conference was at first unwilling to accept the responsibility, but in 1899 it encouraged all congregations to help pay the salary of John F. Duerksen, the newly-designated Mennonite Brethren teacher and leader of the department.

Each General Conference session between 1899 and 1904 heard reports from the German Department, encouraged its financial support and simultaneously refused to adopt the program. They repeatedly noted the need for "our own school," but continued to favor its development through a society rather than its own action.

The opening of Tabor College in Hillsboro, Kansas, in the fall of 1908 fulfilled that goal. It was the result of a society, largely based in Kansas. Society chairman J. K. Hiebert, together with Henry W. Lohrenz and Peter C. Hiebert, both young graduates of the McPherson program, led the initiative. While the leaders wanted General Conference sponsorship they knew that was unattainable and so asked for its "good will and . . . recognition."

Bestvater and a class at Herbert Bible School, date unknown. (CMBS Fresno)

The reluctance to accept Tabor as a General Conference school was rooted in various factors. The far-flung geographical dispersal of the Mennonite Brethren by the early twentieth century made establishment of a central school more difficult. The 1909 decision by the General Conference to meet triennially instead of annually, and to establish district conferences that met annually was an acknowledgment that some tasks were better carried out in smaller regional units than on a continent-wide basis.

The move toward district conferences also reflected that Mennonites in different parts of the continent were on differing acculturation paths. Those differences would become more pronounced with time. Furthermore, as clusters of congregations grew and a critical mass of Mennonite Brethren emerged in differing regions, they felt the need for their own local school. The second meeting of the Northern District (later the Canadian Conference) in 1911 appointed a committee to explore the establishment of its own school. The Pacific District Conference, at its inaugural meetings in 1912, pledged its commitment to Tabor College. By 1916, however, the Pacific District was also discussing the creation of its own school.

The hesitancy for the General Conference to commit to Tabor College was not only geographical. Tabor also reflected a particular form of education—one that was to be a training ground for ministers, but also combined training in the classics with religious studies. A striking symbol of this expansive quality was the building Tabor erected in 1920, with its classical Greek facade. By 1920 Tabor graduates were attending the finest universities in the country. More sought training in divinity at Yale University than at any other place. That intellectual progressivism was a source of unease to some Mennonite Brethren constituents.

Why a Bible College?

"The Mennonite Brethren Bible College is being founded in response to a longfelt [sic] want. Official expression of this need was given by Rev. Joh. A Toews' report to our Canadian Conference in July 1939 in Coaldale, Alberta. This report stressed the acute problems of obtaining properly qualified teachers for our numerous Bible Schools. Advanced theological training and a broad general education will be required of our Bible School teachers, if these Schools are to survive and to progress. Wherever spiritual young men are adequately prepared and show teaching ability, our local Churches should help them to attend higher Bible Colleges and Seminaries. But there exists the danger of choosing the wrong College, and some have returned to us with ideals and interpretations foreign to our Mennonite Brethren conceptions and doctrines in the light of the Scripture. 'Watch and pray' lest Satan would succeed in undermining the foundation of faith in which our Church and our Bible Schools are based."

—*From the first catalog of Mennonite Brethren Bible College (1944).*

Even so, the General Conference conventions from 1909 to 1933 invariably included reports from committees recommending financial support for Tabor. Some conference sessions included strong endorsements of Tabor by significant leaders, but the school remained under the control of the *Schulverein* rather than the General Conference.

Development of Bible schools in Canada

While the United States was casting its lot with the liberal arts college, Mennonite Brethren in Canada were moving in a different direction. For them, the preferred educational institution was the Bible school.

By the early twentieth century, there were already several Mennonite educational institutions on the prairies: Mennonite Collegiate Institute in Gretna, Manitoba (1889); Rosthern Junior College in Saskatchewan (1905); and Mennonite Educational Institute in Altona, Manitoba (1905). None of these were sponsored by the Mennonite Brethren Church, although its members were among the teachers as well as students. These institutions were essentially high schools, although they also functioned to some degree as teacher-training institutions and to provide instruction in Bible and the Mennonite faith.

The first Mennonite Brethren Bible school in Canada opened at Herbert, Saskatchewan, in 1913. Herbert Bible School began as a school of the Northern District under the leadership of John F. Harms, although from 1916 to 1921 it operated as a local society school. In 1921 William J. Bestvater began a new initiative for the school, once again sponsored by the Mennonite Brethren Conference.

Mennonite Brethren Bible College, Winnipeg, Manitoba. (CMBS Fresno)

École de Théologie Évangélique de Montréal. (CMBS Winnipeg)

Bethany Bible Institute, date unknown.

The Canadian prairies became fertile soil for the establishment of dozens of Bible schools, and at least nineteen were established by Mennonite Brethren between 1925 and 1947. Two others were founded in Ontario. Many of these schools survived only a few years, whereas others prospered for a time but encountered difficulties that forced them to close by the 1960s. The three schools that survived into the final decades of the twentieth century were Winkler Bible School in Manitoba, Bethany Bible School in Hepburn, Saskatchewan, and Columbia Bible College in Abbotsford, British Columbia. Winkler Bible School was the first school established by the

Winkler Bible Institute, date unknown.

Russländer in 1925, but encountered difficulties both because of competition from other Bible schools and because the Mennonite Brethren Bible College was also located in Manitoba. It closed in 1997.

Bethany Bible School, founded in 1927, was able to survive despite some difficult years and in 1965 became a joint institution of the Alberta and Saskatchewan Mennonite Brethren Conferences. In 1995 the Evangelical Mennonite Mission Conference of Saskatchewan became another sponsoring body.

Columbia Bible College developed after a series of closures and mergers of local Bible schools, including the Mennonite Brethren Bible Institute of British Columbia. In 1970 the Mennonite Brethren Bible Institute merged with Bethel Bible Institute of the United Mennonites of British Columbia to form Columbia Bible Institute, later renamed Columbia Bible College. It has experienced the most remarkable growth of all the Mennonite Brethren schools in Canada and draws from Mennonites and others in the lower Fraser Valley and beyond.

Still another educational institution began as a by-product of Mennonite Brethren mission work in Quebec beginning in the 1960s. In 1976 Institute Biblique Laval was begun by the Canadian Conference to train leaders for the Quebec churches. Today it is know as École de Théologie Évangélique de Montréal.

Tabor becomes a General Conference school

The 1933 General Conference sessions, coming at the depths of the Great Depression, heard reports regarding various Mennonite Brethren schools. Given Tabor's unique role as a quasi-denominational school, its economic plight dominated the educational discussions. The 1930 convention had revisited the question of ownership and declined because of a lack "of general agreement in the conference to accept and assume the school," but did agree to a $10,000 annual contribution for the next three years. More was needed, however, if Tabor was to remain open.

This time the conference agreed to refer the matter to the churches for a vote as to whether Tabor should become a General Conference school. The committee overseeing the balloting met in January 1934 and reported a favorable vote. The meaning of their report remains unclear, however, as the extant tally sheets do not confirm the same result. Whatever the final count, the General Conference was now the owner and sponsor of a school of higher education.

Establishment of new liberal arts institutions

Tabor's status, however, was soon challenged by new educational developments. In 1944 two new institutions of higher learning came into existence: Mennonite Brethren Bible College (MBBC) in Winnipeg and Pacific Bible Institute (PBI) in Fresno. Both of these new schools, in contrast to the liberal arts quality of Tabor, began more like "higher Bible schools," concerned with the reinforcement of biblical understanding and training for churchly vocations. With time both moved toward Bible college status and offered a religious baccalaureate degree. Eventually both further transformed themselves into liberal arts institutions.

The first formal calls for a Canadian national school had come in 1939, but war and other factors delayed implementation of this vision until the creation of Mennonite Brethren Bible College in 1944. The college was intended to prepare young people for missions and church ministries at home. In this respect its purpose overlapped with that of Tabor College, which many Canadians had attended in the earlier years and continued attending for some years. But various issues, including the fact that Canadians had not yet made the transition to the English language, led Mennonite Brethren in Canada to create their own school. Even though it was a Bible college, it offered several courses that were more akin to a liberal arts curriculum.

The Pacific District Conference began serious discussions about establishing its own school in 1916, but did not achieve that goal until 1944. The delay can be attributed to various causes—the trauma of being Germanic through two world wars, the economics of the Great Depression, and the need to absorb countless migrants from the Midwest. But the more serious reasons for the delay were theological. The period from the 1920s to the 1940s was a time of uncertainty for West Coast Mennonite Brethren. Some were drawn to the Bible Institute of Los Angeles with its vigorous fundamentalism. Others found a new freedom and expressiveness in the Pentecostal-Holiness movement, which contrasted with their more restrained forms of religious expression. Wartime concern for passing on distinctive values bridged some of these differing theological emphases, however, and the school opened in 1944 with solid district support and a traditional American Bible institute curriculum.

A unified approach to education

Between 1944 and 1954 there were repeated discussions about a unified or coordinated approach to higher education. For the most part the discussions involved representatives from the General Conference Education Committee, which governed Tabor, and representatives of the three schools. Little coordination was achieved, however, as each school had keen supporters. The prospect for a unified program further dimmed as the two new schools found their footing and growing regional support.

The 1954 General Conference was a watershed moment for shaping Mennonite Brethren higher education. The issues were multiple: Could one General Conference school adequately serve such a geographically dispersed constituency? What would be the relationship between Tabor, PBI and MBBC? Should the church support a liberal arts education or a more Bible-centered education? Was a Mennonite Brethren seminary needed or not?

The United States Conference Board of Education, 1958.
(CMBS Fresno)

Answers to these questions divided largely along national lines. The United States was past the transition from German to English and many of its young men were attending various denominational seminaries. The language transition helped to introduce the professional pastorate. Canadian churches, with the more recent immigrant infusions of the 1920s and 1940s, largely retained the German language into the 1960s. Retention of the German language and the continuation of the multiple lay ministry were linked.

Representatives from the two United States schools and district conferences called for Pacific Bible Institute to become a General Conference school under a unified Educational Board. The Canadians were opposed and came with no similar recommendation regarding Mennonite Brethren Bible College. The consequence was that in 1954 Tabor College and Pacific Bible Institute came under the governance of a United States Conference Board of Education. Tabor retained its liberal arts orientation and in the early 1960s gained full accreditation. Pacific Bible Institute added a junior college curriculum, renamed itself Pacific College and in the mid-1960s became a fully-accredited liberal arts baccalaureate-level institution. Beginning in the 1970s it added numerous Masters degree programs, and eventually became known as Fresno Pacific University.

Mennonite Brethren Bible College in time also broadened its purpose and added more liberal arts courses to its curriculum. An agreement with Waterloo Lutheran University (now Wilfrid Laurier University) allowed transfer of credit into a general liberal arts degree program. By 1970 an arrangement with the University of Winnipeg allowed students to enroll concurrently in a university program while attending MBBC.

By the 1970s, however, MBBC found it increasingly difficult to attract students from across Canada, particularly British Columbia. Columbia Bible Institute became a viable alternative as it matured into a baccalaureate-level college. By the late 1980s it was clear that MBBC was no longer viable as a Canadian Conference school, and in 1992 it became Concord College, spon-

Mennonite Brethren Biblical Seminary, Fresno, California.
(CMBS Fresno)

sored by the Manitoba Conference. Eventually it became one of the founding colleges of the Canadian Mennonite University, an inter-Mennonite university in Winnipeg.

Establishing a General Conference seminary

The first General Conference discussion of the need for a seminary came at the 1948 convention, when the Educational Committee recommended that the conference consider making the Tabor Bible School a seminary. Behind that recommendation was not only the need for pastors with greater training but also the recognition that receiving such training at other seminaries carried risks to denominational unity. The Seminary Commission, established at the 1948 conference, reported in 1951 that "present church workers" had received their training at sixteen different seminaries. The list included Lutheran, Baptist, Pentecostal, Presbyterian and interdenominational schools.

The professionalizing of the ministry had proceeded faster in the United States than in Canada. It was to this need that the United States Board of Education responded when it decided to establish a seminary without Canadian participation. By combining members of the Tabor College and Pacific Bible Institute faculties, the school opened in Fresno in the fall of 1955.

Virtually every General Conference convention from 1954 to 1975 reviewed the development of the seminary and raised the question of it becoming a binational institution. Several study com-

Reshaping the Seminary

"In the spring of 1955 the Board of Education approached me to accept the presidency of the new seminary. I declined for several reasons: First, the seminary program was considered only provisional, subject to ongoing negotiations toward a joint sponsorship by the U.S. and Canadian conferences. Second, the Fresno location for the seminary was also considered provisional; the permanent location was to be selected by the two conferences when agreement was reached with Canada. Third, the faculty already appointed from the Bible departments of Tabor College and Pacific Bible Institute did not project an Anabaptist character for the seminary. It was to be known as an evangelical seminary, and all publicity identified it as such. With the rising religious pluralism and individualism of the 1950s I could not see myself leading a program that did not project a distinct Anabaptist identity."

—From JB: A Twentieth-Century Mennonite Pilgrim, by J. B. Toews (Center for Mennonite Brethren Studies-Fresno, 1995).

missions investigated a unified seminary program. Throughout these years the United States was ready for such a joint program, but the Canadians questioned whether it would best serve their interests.

Canadian reluctance to join the Americans was based on several factors. Because most had arrived in North America about fifty years after the Americans, they found it difficult to place their own stamp on already-established institutions. Although their numbers soon almost equaled the Americans, they were under-represented on most boards. Cultural and linguistic differences also remained. Canadians held firmly to the German language until beyond mid-century, and their institutions were the main instruments to retain the language. In more general terms they also often felt that the Americans did not adequately understand their needs.

As late as 1968 the General Conference Board of Reference and Counsel suggested that both national conferences consider establishing a joint seminary in the Vancouver area. The United States Conference responded favorably, but the Canadians rejected the proposal. Yet six years later, at the 1975 convention, the seminary came under the ownership of the General Conference.

Several developments during the 1960s and early 1970s made this possible. When the seminary opened in 1955, it did so under the theological shadow of American fundamentalism. While that movement was attractive to some Mennonite Brethren in the United States, it was less so to Canadian Mennonite Brethren. J. B. Toews, upon assuming the presidency of the seminary in 1964, broke with these fundamentalist moorings and reoriented the school toward Anabaptism. In the coming years a new faculty not only theologically re-centered the seminary but made it central to the denomination's recovery of its Anabaptist heritage. During the 1970s and 1980s the school played an important role in several General Conference boards, particularly the Board of Reference and Counsel, the Board of Christian Literature and the Historical Commission.

Developments in Canada in the early 1970s argued for joining with the Americans in a seminary program. The Mennonite Brethren Bible College, which had been central in training leaders for thirty-five years, was facing a crisis caused by low enrollment, loss of confidence within the constituency and increasing strength of provincial schools. In 1971 the conference discontinued the B.D. program that MBBC had offered for several years. That same year the conference appointed a commission to study the future of post-graduate theological education and to examine various alternatives.

The theological reorientation of the seminary plus the fact that most of the new faculty were Canadians surely made the school more acceptable to the Canadian conference. The language shift in Canada and the accompanying professionalization of the ministry also called for education beyond what the Bible institutes and the Bible college in Winnipeg could provide. So in 1975 the Seminary became the second officially-sponsored school of the General Conference.

Conclusion

The General Conference's official sponsorship of Tabor lasted twenty years. The Conference's decision to disband in 2002 means that its sponsorship of the seminary will be twenty-seven years. These realities reflect the larger pattern of uncertainty in the educational focus, governance and

The Resource Centre at Columbia Bible College, Abbotsford, British Columbia.
(Columbia Bible College)

ownership of Mennonite Brethren higher educational institutions. The story of Fresno Pacific University is the most graphic illustration. In its short history since 1944 it has undergone more fundamental shifts than many schools with longer histories: from a Bible institute, to a junior college, to a senior college, to a university with undergraduate and graduate programs; from ownership by the Pacific District Conference to ownership by the United States Conference and then back to the Pacific District in 1979; from training students primarily for churchly vocations to educating them primarily for vocations in the world; and from a college designed to foster distinctive Mennonite Brethren identity to one that is religiously ecumenical. This story is repeated in varying degrees with virtually all of the Mennonite Brethren schools of higher learning.

These transitions reflect growth and maturation. They also reflect differing impulses in the history of the Mennonite Brethren. The impulse to build these schools was rooted in the need to insure that Mennonite Brethren young people would receive appropriate denominational understandings. Denominational schools are typically nurseries of denominational identity. They shelter students from the impact of alien ways. But the question of what is to be mediated to the next generation sometimes becomes unclear. Should schools be established to train people for churchly vocations or should they see their mission to train people for many diverse vocations? Should schools offer some liberal arts courses within an essentially religious studies program or should they offer religious studies courses within an essentially liberal arts program? Denominational schools need denominational support and governance. But the best structure for that support has been unclear. Is leadership preparation for the Mennonite Brethren best done in a denominational setting or in an ecumenical setting? Is it best provided by local societies, districts or provinces, the national conferences, or the unified General Conference?

These uncertainties notwithstanding, the story of the Mennonite Brethren commitment to higher education is astonishing. Seldom have so few people developed so many institutions of

McDonald Hall, Fresno Pacific University. (CMBS Frsno)

learning. Seldom have institutions with so few resources accomplished so much. Their capacity to do so in the future largely rests with the church. Christopher Jenks and David Riesman, American commentators on distinctive institutions, noted some years ago that the survival of distinctive institutions of learning depends on "the survival within the larger society of . . . enclaves whose members believe passionately in a way of life radically different from that of the majority, and who are both willing and able to pay for a brand of higher education that embodies their vision." Mennonite Brethren schools, with their concern for passing on the strengths of the Anabaptist-Mennonite tradition, have believed passionately in a different way of life. Their ability to survive with that distinctive voice will be possible only so long as the denomination wishes to retain those distinctive elements.

IN HIS FIRST NOVEL
RUDY WIEBE
A YOUNG THEOLOGIAN
WRITES OF PREJUDICE
AND BIGOTRY ERUPTING
TO DESTROY THE PEOPLE
OF A SMALL CANADIAN
COMMUNITY
PEACE
SHALL DESTROY
MANY

9

The Dilemma of the Mennonite Brethren Writer: Having One Soul or Two?

Katie Funk Wiebe

In his history of the Mennonite Brethren Church, respected minister and teacher A. H. Unruh lamented the dearth of writers in the Mennonite Brethren Church in Russia. Why did Mennonite Brethren not have a literature of their own? The church had competent preachers and evangelists but few writers. Unruh was convinced that some "brethren" had manuscripts lying in their desks but the church was not ready to sacrifice to publish them.

In 1962, at the beginning of his ministry as book editor of the Mennonite Brethren General Conference, Walter Wiebe wrote in *The Christian Leader* that Mennonite Brethren compared favorably with other denominations in missions and education, but the production of literature lagged far behind.

In 1974 the first anthology of Canadian Mennonite literature was published by the Mennonite Historical Society of Manitoba, entitled *Harvest: Anthology of Mennonite Writing in Canada 1874-1974*. In the foreword G. K. Epp comments that for historical reasons, Mennonite literature—the serious product of professional writers—was slow to develop. The anthology includes works by only two Mennonite Brethren writers—Rudy Wiebe and David Waltner-Toews.

The same year Mennonite Brethren Bible College in Winnipeg sponsored a Festival of Fine Arts. It highlighted sculpting by Gathy Falk, musical performances, and oral presentations directed by Esther Wiens. Creative writing was not central to the festival. In some sessions the conflict between the arts and Christian faith was discussed. Are the two compatible? Are the arts generally worldly and thus outside biblical truth? Are literary writing and other art forms a marginal activity for the church?

Fifteen years after the arts festival, in the first anthology of short stories by Mennonite writers, *Liars and Rascals*, editor Hildi Froese Tiessen bemoans Canadian Mennonites' lack of receptivity to the arts during the first half of the century. She applauded, however, the "vigorous minority literary cultures enriching the Canadian mainstream" in the 1970s and 1980s, of which the anthology was a prime example. Again, the number of Mennonite Brethren writers in this anthology is small: Rudy Wiebe, David Waltner-Toews, Katie Funk Wiebe, Sarah Klassen.

What Unruh and Wiebe were thinking of when they lamented the lack of Mennonite Brethren writers was literature that witnessed to the truth of God, that inspired devotion, that explained the Gospel clearly, that invited to salvation. What Tiessen and Epp were thinking of was writing that

The novel Peace Shall Destroy Many, *by Rudy Wiebe, was a landmark in Mennonite Brethren literary development.*

sought to grasp the meaning of life through an imaginative blending of structure and content without stipulated content.

People of ethnic subcultures, as Mennonite Brethren originally were, often begin by writing for their own people to clarify the meaning of their cultural and religious traditions, to comfort and encourage their own people, and to interpret their people to society at large. Mennonite Brethren have turned to each of these purposes at stages in their writing development.

Mennonite Brethren writing can only be discussed as an entity in itself if it has an identifiable ethos like Jewish or Catholic writing. The following emphases characterize the Mennonite Brethren ethos as expressed in writing, especially in the early years until well into the twentieth century.

Elements of pietism and sanctification entered with evangelist Eduard Wuest in Russia, who spoke of sin and salvation, dead forms and orthodoxy. This emphasis allowed members of the newly formed Mennonite Brethren Church to publicly relate their personal conversion, not encouraged openly before.

A separatist attitude coupled with a sense of moral superiority resulted from protests against what the founders saw as immoral living and low spiritual life. Segments of the Mennonite Brethren rejected old leaders, old sermons, old hymns, and old styles of worship and books. Memory of past hurts at the hands of some leaders and members of the Old Church intensified this separatist attitude.

Mennonite Brethren writing also illustrated *a strong concern for evangelism and missions*. This emphasis was present from the beginning of the Mennonite Brethren Church. It grew stronger with time and became a significant emphasis in written works.

Laying the groundwork for a literary tradition

Novelists and poets were slow to develop in the North American Mennonite community. They lacked a comfortable language with which to clothe their thoughts, in part because Mennonites had so often moved from country to country. In each new setting, when they reached a level of economic and social stability, and could begin to invest energy in creative thought, political upheaval forced them to look to survival once again, not the needs of the creative soul.

Despite these limitations, Mennonite creative writing owes much to the storytellers and poets who came to Canada from Russia in the 1920s. They prepared the literary soil by writing and publishing poetry, novels and plays—often at their own expense—in German.

When Canadian Mennonites began writing in English, they took giant strides ahead of Americans in developing creative writing. This Mennonite renaissance occurred in western Canada beginning in the 1960s, primarily Winnipeg. Why did writing among Mennonites, especially Mennonite Brethren, not take off with as much vigor in the United States? Because there a national literature had already been strongly established for several centuries, not for mere decades as in Canada. As Canadian Mennonite literary critic Al Reimer has noted, Mennonite writers in the United States were anonymous voices within a larger and more mature national literature.

"The End Times"

The old sow, she'd have to go.

Prom pulled at the thin wisp of white hair puffing irregularly out from the sides of his bald head like the white matter out of a bullrush. I'm going to seed, he thought, so old am I. That old sow, can't even remember when I got her.

"Didn't I get her for preaching at the Klopfen Church?" he asked out loud. "Vic Reimer, he's a pig man."

Rachel, her thin black hair greying at the edges, stood at the counter pinching out the balls of dough for zwieback. She was, by now, becoming used to being admitted to Prom's thoughts part way through. It took her a few moments to make the connection from Reimer to the appropriate church to the "her" in question: the old sow of course. Hadn't had a litter for a year.

"Yes," she sighed. "It was those folks. I think they were trying to tell you in as subtle a way as they are capable of what they thought of your preaching."

"Well I think I better take her over to Thiessen's and get some ham out of her. No use feeding her through another winter."

Rachel looked out the kitchen window. Large flakes of snow were settling softly from the grey sky, as if the clouds were feather-filled quilts that had come undone. "Today?" she asked, simply.

Prom set his teacup down on the white wooden kitchen table. "For everything there is a season and winter is the season for butchering."

—From "The End Times", by David Waltner-Toews. Previously published in Liars and Rascals: Mennonite Short Stories, *edited by Hildi Froese Tiessen (University of Waterloo Press, 1989).*

Peter M. Friesen, the preeminent historian of the Mennonite Brethren Church in Russia.

Furthermore, American Mennonite Brethren did not generally have the soul-searing experiences of the Russian Revolution, the Stalinist years, World War II and its aftermath in Siberia that compelled so many Canadian Mennonite Brethren authors to write.

Obstacles to creating a Mennonite Brethren literary tradition

The literary pilgrimage of the Mennonite Brethren, like that of many other religious denominations, was skewed away from works of the imagination, such as poetry and fiction, toward historical and theological tomes. This occurred for several reasons.

Facts over fiction

Mennonite Brethren leaders knew it was important to nail down the history of the new movement and to clarify doctrine and polity for a fast-growing church open to unsettling influences from the outside. Invented truth was not acceptable. Historical accounts were considered the better source of reality.

Furthermore, historians were more likely than novelists to present a positive picture of the developing church, without raising troublesome questions. Historians shaped the Mennonite Brethren profile by looking at its systems and institutions from the outside. They examined written sources, both published and unpublished, so that their work could be documented. Often historical writings were commissioned by church boards and agencies, beginning with P. M. Friesen's extensive history of the Mennonite Brethren church in Russia.

Early church leaders did not grasp that the truest picture of a people comes from writers who are free to imaginatively articulate human experience in their own language. Creative writers look within their world to find the soul of a people. They hold that God functions in ordinary situations and in story. While doctrine is codified truth and allows no room for the imagination, creative writers see the imagination as a gift from God. Early Mennonite Brethren leaders understandably did not sense that to discourage the creative writer was to silence the prophetic voice in their midst.

Consequently, the Mennonite Brethren Church seemed limiting rather than freeing to many novelists and poets. Writers who grew up in Mennonite Brethren congregations spoke of soul-saving pressures. This perception became more powerful than the reality, limiting anything but church-endorsed writing within the community.

What fiction existed in the Mennonite Brethren community in America at first came in the form of "Christian" fiction with upbeat endings and a heavy sprinkling of religious language. It also appeared as historical fiction, attached to some news peg, such as an escape from Russia or a missionary experience, to give the story validity. Writers were encouraged to produce such material because it introduced readers to heroes of the faith and provided a role model, a legitimate purpose. What would it have been like if the Mennonite Brethren profile in its early years had been shaped by poets and novelists and not by historians? What if half a dozen Mennonite Brethren fiction writers had been able to write passionately and honestly about the view from the inside during the schism from the Old Church?

Poetry doesn't pay the bills

Poet Don Marquis writes that "Poetry is like dropping a rose petal into the Grand Canyon and waiting for the echo." Waiting for silent echoes has not appealed to Mennonite Brethren. They much preferred the full rich tones of a preacher thundering the Word of God in hard-hitting cadences, loud enough to awaken the soundest pew-sleeper. A loud preacher was a good preacher.

Mennonite Brethren propensity for doing all things "decently and in order" has on occasion given rise to great preaching but seldom allowed for the ecstasy of hearing bread dough rise or snow falling on haystacks. Their ears were tuned to the whirr of a cream separator or roar of a threshing machine—sounds that indicated forward movement in the new land. It was more important to put *Borscht* and *Zwieback* on the table than to encourage a child to line up words, one after another, in a poem. For many religious groups at the time, literature and other fine arts were seen as frivolous compared to the real work of the church—spreading the Gospel. Editors stayed away from publishing stories and especially poetry that did not use religious language.

The Bible is the sole source of truth

An understanding of the Bible as the sole source of truth and taking a serious stance toward faith and moral issues combined to make Mennonite communities unfruitful ground for any art form except music in worship. Mennonites have traditionally had a passion for plain speaking. Faith was expressed in propositional theological statements and forthright living. When some writers did write fiction, their stories were expected to identify moral and spiritual issues and strengthen the reader's inner life. Any other kind of fictional writing was wrong, even sinful. Light-hearted writing, fictional or true, did not fit the Mennonite Brethren image of sincerity and seriousness.

To live and create in the Mennonite Brethren community was like having two masters, or two souls, each demanding allegiance. The two seemed irreconcilable.

Accepted outlets for written expression

Within the limitations of this worldview, however, certain forms of written expression did exist among the Mennonite Brethren. Though not all are "literary" writing in the fullest sense of that word, they nonetheless provided a limited outlet for Mennonite Brethren writers.

Obituaries: The Story of a Life

"Jacob C. Willems, our beloved husband and father, was born September 15, 1890, at Inman, Kansas. At the age of 10 he suffered the loss of his mother, Sarah Klassen Willems, after which his father George D. Willems united in marriage to Anna Block Willems, whose motherly devotion was a great source of comfort and a guiding Christian influence in his early life. His father preceded him in death in 1947.

"At the age of 16 he accepted Christ as his personal Savior, and upon confession of faith was baptized and confirmed to membership in the Zoar [Krimmer Mennonite Brethren] Church at Inman, Kansas, March 31, 1907, where he remained a faithful member to his end. . . .

"His life was characterized and motivated by Christian ideals. He constantly gave primacy to the spiritual values of life over the material things. In his earlier years he taught a Sunday school class in the different churches he attended. He often expressed his hope and trust in his Master by personal service in contacting wayward souls wherever he was.

"The nature of his illness was lengthy with a full measure of suffering. . . . He endured it calmly, and with an undying faith in God. . . . His last message to us was, 'I'm going home now. Good-bye old world, I'm through with you. I'm going home.' . . .

"Why should our tears in sorrow flow
When God recalls His own,
And bids them leave a world of woe
For an immortal crown?

"Is not even death a gain to those
Whose life to God was given?
Gladly to earth their eyes they close,
To open them in heaven.

"Their toils are spent; their work is done;
And they are fully blest,
They fought the fight, the victory won,
And entered into rest.

"Then let our sorrow cease to flow,
God has recalled His own."

—*Originally printed in the* Zionsbote, *14 June 1950, p. 11.*

Conversion narratives

A special kind of spiritual autobiography expressing a Mennonite Brethren ethos is the conversion narrative, a simple story that tells how the individual became a believer. Mennonite Brethren pietism gave people freedom to articulate this spiritual experience in the first person, an important detail for a Mennonite people cautioned against self-pride.

In the 1890s the *Zionsbote* published 150 of these accounts under the headings of *Meine Errettung von meinen Sünden* (My salvation from sin), *Meine Bekehrung* (My conversion) and *Meine Erfahrung* (My experience). Others appeared in little booklets. Every believer was expected to have such a conversion story. Some people wrote theirs down to be used at future testimony meetings.

The testimonies followed a pattern that began with inner conflict over one's sinful state, going behind the barn to weep over specific sins, followed by much crying and repentance, reading of Scripture and prayer. The climax was an understanding of God's plan of salvation followed by assurance and joy at being able to be baptized by immersion.

These conversion narratives were an explicit invitation to other Mennonites to duplicate the pattern and a subtle judgment of the spiritual lack in the Old Church. In time the writers developed a stereotyped vocabulary to describe this experience.

This coded writing declined when crisis conversions could not always be substantiated in real life. Early Mennonite Brethren in Russia had been adults when the new emphasis on conversion took place. Later adherents were also mature men and women; joining this renegade group meant possible ostracism.

The next generations in America were nurtured in Christian homes from birth. Young converts did not necessarily have a life of gross sin to refer to, but were expected to relate one in their testimonies. The drift toward speaking and writing about an experience one did not have was rejected by creative writers. Younger writers trained in creative writing and analytical thinking recognized that not all spiritual experience follows a set pattern. Poets and fiction writers rebelled against letting other people's language write their works for them.

Obituaries

The lowly obituary was one of the most-read sections of early Mennonite Brethren publications. It clearly incorporated the Mennonite Brethren ethos. At first obituaries were written by family members of the deceased in great detail, showing how he or she lived out Mennonite Brethren ideals. They followed a pattern, giving important biographical information, including date of conversion and baptism. Language was often stylized, using evangelical phrases such as "gave their hearts to the Lord," and "the Lord called him home." Today they are often much condensed to include only vital details.

Biographies

Conversion narratives and obituaries became the model for telling life stories in the form of biographies and, later, autobiographies. Russian-born Abram Kroeker was successful in popularizing both autobiography and biography among Canadian Mennonites in the 1920s because he had an altruistic goal—to arouse sympathy among American Mennonites for the desperate needs of those left behind in Russia. Peter M. Friesen includes several biographies of ministers in his lengthy history. The Board of Christian Literature commissioned many biographies of Mennonite Brethren leaders during the 1960s and thereafter.

It remained difficult for Mennonite Brethren to write their own story, using the first person, about anything other than their spiritual experience because it might be seen as pride. With the flourishing of the family history phenomenon begun by Alex Haley in the book *Roots*, autobiography and family history became more popular among Mennonite Brethren.

Devotional/inspirational poems/prose

Devotional and inspirational writing has always been a large part of Mennonite Brethren writing and has had full acceptance within the church. Such literature aims to encourage and strengthen the believers. Its precursor was the hymn, originally written to be read.

Russian Mennonites brought to Canada a well-defined ethnic culture and the rudiments of German literary tradition. In Canada and the United States, a Christian version came to life in the form of the much-beloved *Jugendverein* (later called Christian Endeavor) where young people sang, recited poetry, and performed oratorical pieces.

Inspirational poetry was popular at such events, sometimes created by a local poet. Poems that were especially appealing were passed from congregation to congregation. Poets who could write occasional verse for a wedding, birthday or other special event had strong acceptance in the local congregation. However, for poets to find their own voices in poetry or fiction that was not specifically Christian was a difficult process.

For decades devotional poetry was used as filler in denominational publications rather than for its own sake. The message, niceties of rhyme, and the right number of lines often were more important than the excellence of poetic skills.

(Left) Many Mennonite Brethren, including Anna Reimer Dyck, have turned to the memoir as a way of telling not only their own stories, but the story of an entire people.

(Below) An example of a poem from Peter Wiebe's book, Gott grüsse dich!

Vögleins Gotterhöhn.

Vöglein, komm herbeigeflogen,
Setz dich auf den Brückenbogen,
Sitze dann ein Weilchen still, —
Hör' was ich dir sagen will.

Sanggenosse, sorglos Wesen,
In der Tonkunst auserlesen, —
Du beseelst auf Gottes Spur
Die gefall'ne Kreatur.

Ja, mit deiner süßen Kehle,
Rührst du meine kalte Seele, —
Denn aus deiner Sängerbrust
Quillt ein Lied von Lieb und Lust.

Darum ist mir wert und teuer
Deine heil'ge Sangesfeier,
Weil du dankend sie gebracht,
Gott, der Schöpfer, „Amen" sagt.

So, nun fliege fröhlich weiter
Und sing' deine Weisen heiter!
Gott mit dir! Und Dankeschön
Für dein hehres Gotterhöhn!

> **Mennonite Music**
>
> Shutting out
> the jazz of the world
> we made our own music
>
> a strained choral tone
> like a taut rope
> pulling us through
>
> getting our pitches
> from those who know
> breaking into harmonies
>
> and dissonance
> and those outside rarely
> heard us in our closed places
>
> our tones flattening
> into our lives, or did they
> now and then perceive
>
> melodies escaping
> the ones with wings
> flapping softly upward
>
> —*Reprinted from* Words for the Silence, *by Jean Janzen (Center for Mennonite Brethren Studies-Fresno 1984).*

Despite lack of direct encouragement from editors, some Mennonite Brethren poets, mostly men, published their own writings in simple form. In 1947 self-taught Mennonite Brethren poet Peter P. Wiebe, of Coaldale, Alberta, and later Yarrow, British Columbia, published his own book of poetry, *Gott Grüsse Dich*, patterned after the German romantic writers. In it he asks whether, among the songbirds, does only the nightingale have the right to sing? Among humankind, do only the most brilliant have the right to give voice to songs and poems? Unlike the accepted poetry of the time, which was expected to follow religious lines, his small book includes a section on nature and another on "The Song of Creation" in ten sections. It is likely there were many such unrecognized poets and fiction writers in the Mennonite Brethren during the early years whose material did not fit the then-acceptable mold.

Women were outsiders in the Mennonite Brethren literary world for many decades, other than as devotional writers. Their subject matter was restricted to the world of home and children. Their work as wives and mothers was expected to provide avenues of creativity. The essence of Christian womanhood was submission to God and others, and a spirit of humility. Their contribution came mostly in the form of inspirational and devotional writing or correspondence in Mennonite publications like the *Zionsbote*.

Tracts and pamphlets

Tracts and pamphlets often function to clarify current issues and specific doctrines. They were cheap to publish and easy to distribute. Mennonite Brethren published scores of these little booklets. Sometimes a sermon series preached at a special occasion found its way into print in this way.

Written Sermons

Written sermons have never reached the full art form among Mennonite Brethren because of the emphasis on accepted, codified truth. The emphasis in homiletics at Mennonite Brethren Bible schools and colleges in the 1940s and 1950s was on three-point alliterative sermons. Such teaching casts a long shadow. Yet the elements that make a sermon a work of art rather than a treatise are unpredictability, a joining of form and content to surprise and delight the listener with new glimpses of truth.

Critical Studies

The development of creative writing with high artistic standards depends on a branch of writing closely akin to it—the literary review. Critical reviews that freely examine literature from all aspects are fundamental to good creative writing. Critical analysis of another's writing was first rejected by Mennonite Brethren because of the biblical admonition not to judge lest one be judged. Even as one did not judge the preacher ("touch not the Lord's anointed"), one did not judge any writing that had spiritual intent.

The earliest literary criticism came in the form of book reviews, more often book summaries or positive endorsements rather than actual analysis. It moved to a new level suddenly in the 1960s with the strong reaction to Rudy Wiebe's *Peace Shall Destroy Many*. Critical essays and letters to the editor of Mennonite Brethren publications showed that readers did not know how to handle a fictional piece that openly admitted that Mennonites might not be all they said they were.

Mennonite Brethren, some of whom saw themselves as the brunt of the book, preferred the public image of the church to be kept shining. Wiebe depicts Deacon Block, the main character, not as an idealized religious leader but as domineering and hypocritical. Wiebe had imposed his own

Correspondence from the *Zionsbote*

Manitoba, Winkler, 2 March 1910.

Last Sunday we were privileged to have a beloved brother from England in our midst. He has visited Russia, Siberia, Turkey and other regions. His name is Broadbent. Some readers of the *Zionsbote* in Russia will recognize him, and it might be interesting for you to learn that our dear brother is currently in America working for the Lord and his Kingdom.

In the morning we heard a blessed message from him on Hebrews 11:23-31. In the evening he had the opportunity to speak sincerely to the youth group. He also shared several things about his work among the Russians in the Far East, how the gospel is making entry there and how the kingdom of God is being built. The evening went by too quickly and again it was time to part.

As far as I know, the dear brother will go back to Russia and continue his work after visiting in America for awhile. We love him dearly and wish him God's richest blessings in his ministry. Brother Broadbent speaks German and Russian in addition to the language of his country.

Sunday, while I was listening to him, the words of Isaiah 52:7 became important to me: "How beautiful upon the mountains are the feet of him who brings good tidings, who publishes peace, who brings good tidings of good, who publishes salvation, who says to Zion, 'Your God reigns.'" May all readers of *Zionsbote* be deeply blessed.
—**J. M. Elias**

Russia, Sparrau, 24 January 1910.

Today Brother Johann Toews of Konteniusfeld died after three months of suffering from jaundice, at the age of 56 years. Sister Toews is my niece.

A hearty greeting to my siblings with their families in Minnesota. Our family is all healthy. I am waiting for a letter.
—**Johann Dueck**

Oklahoma, Korn, 13 March 1910.

Dear brothers and sisters: Today a baptism took place in the Krimmer Mennonite Brethren Church at Weatherford. Many came from the Washita Church, including me. It was a beautiful day. Brother Heinrich Wiebe from Hillsboro, Kansas, came also. In the morning he spoke to the congregation, and especially to the baptismal candidates. He spoke about Moses, the man of God, who preferred to suffer shame with God's people than the temporary enjoyment of sin. In the afternoon we went to the water, where 22 beloved souls were baptized. Yes, the Lord still performs miracles of grace. He calls sinners to him and offers forgiveness of sins. He deserves praise.

In our meeting at Korn, widower Jacob Gorsching and widow Wedel were married by Brother Wohlgemut.

Brother and sister J. J Kroeker from Hillsboro, Kansas, moved back here again. Brother and sister Wiens from Nebraska will move here as well. We welcome them warmly. The J. J. Warkentins went to California this week. The E. G. Kliewers, who moved to Michigan four years ago, are back again.

The people move back and forth,
to see if it's better here or there,
But everywhere they find
endless worries and work;
So let each struggle where we are,
and hold fast to Jesus Christ.

The old brother and sister Aron Warkentin have been sick for a long time, especially Aron. He has had hiccups for nine days, but they are happy in the Lord.

Old brother Heinrich Unruh has also been sick for a long time. There also has been illness here and there among the children.

The oat harvest is finished and we desire rain, since it is becoming dry. Greetings,
—**P. J. Schmidt**

Esther Loewen Vogt, known especially for her "Turkey Red" series of stories, has been one of the leading writers of children's literature among Mennonite Brethren.

structure on his understanding of the church community and dared to reveal it in a novel. This structure in Mennonite Brethren circles had previously always come from the top-preachers, ministers, church councils, and boards.

A leader in literary criticism has been Canadian Harry Loewen. He has written extensively in the *Journal of Mennonite Studies, Conrad Grebel Review,* and other journals and books. *Direction,* the academic journal for Mennonite Brethren schools of higher learning, has not been so aggressive in promoting literary criticism.

Drama, missionary playlets and skits, pageants

Some playlets and skits, usually with a biblical or missionary theme, were published in *The Youth Worker* or self-published. Individuals also have written pageants for special occasions like the celebration of the coming of the Mennonites to Kansas in 1974.

Conclusion

During the 1960s Orlando Harms, editor of *The Christian Leader,* made a serious effort to encourage "Christian" writers, more rightly, Christian journalists. Each year one Sunday was named Publications Sunday to promote the distribution of Christian literature. But Mennonite Brethren writers were few. A panel in 1964 suggested how to improve this situation. They recommended more exchange of opinions in *The Christian Leader,* greater openness to questions, fewer platitudes and more honesty.

Encouragement for creative writing continues to come to Mennonite Brethren from the broader Mennonite writing constituency as well as Mennonite Brethren institutions in the form of creative writing courses, conferences and workshops. Journalists are numerous in Mennonite Brethren institutions and publications, including news writers, columnists, television and radio scriptwriters, publicists, article writers and others.

Many "Mennonite" writers, particularly those in Canada, are no longer members of a Mennonite congregation. They have become disenchanted with Mennonite identity. Their own pilgrimage in search of creative freedom has led them beyond church publications.

Yet some Mennonite Brethren writers have persevered and are recognized in the larger Mennonite constituency and beyond. Such writers include novelists Rudy Wiebe and Dora Dueck, journalists Wally Kroeker and Don Ratzlaff, poets Jean Janzen, Sarah Klassen, literary critic Harry Loewen, children's author Esther L. Vogt, and writers of non-fiction prose such as Katie Funk Wiebe.

Peace Shall Destroy Many: A Review of Rudy Wiebe's Novel

"The book gives an account of a year in the life of a small Mennonite settlement located in an isolated area of Northern Saskatchewan. The pattern of life depicted in the novel could well have been duplicated with minor variations by a great many other Russian-Mennonite communities across Canada. . . .

"Mr. Wiebe knows his Mennonites very well indeed. The description of various details of life so familiar to the first and second generation of Mennonites in Canada will bear the minutest inspection. In this respect alone the book is a valuable compendium of typical Mennonite practices of an age just passing.

"The author is to be commended for his courage in tackling difficult problems. The problems are old ones for Christians and Mennonites—how to live in the world yet not be of the world; how the distinctive patterns of the Mennonite way of life may be retained in our present [age]; how one can avoid the evil influences from without; how one can best [fulfill] the commands of the Lord to evangelize the world. The merit of the novel lies in the clear presentation of the problems involved . . . and the necessity for solving problems of this type realistically and scripturally. . . .

"The central issues of the novel are brought into focus as the characters in the novel become familiar to the reader. A dominant role is played by Peter Block, the deacon of the Wapati Mennonite Church. He is deeply concerned with trying to make out of the community an 'island of holiness in a sea of despair.' The disintegration of his personality under the strain of this attempt is fearful to behold. In young Thom Wiens we have the new church member who tries to find the answer to the many problems that thrust themselves upon him—the Christian who has seen some light and tries to walk in it; who recognizes that his responsibility to the world must be met. . . .

"The novel begins peacefully enough, but soon the conflicts increase in intensity. I believe that many Mennonites will be disturbed to see themselves cast into this mold. On more than one occasion we are forced to ask, 'Lord, is it I?' This novel is sure to be far too 'critical' for some readers. Others will object to certain 'worldly' episodes. Seen in context, they arise naturally enough out of the complex of characters. . . .

"A first novel—and a good one. 'A book that will appeal to all and upset many.' Don't be the last to read it."

—*Excerpts from a review by Peter Klassen, published in* The Mennonite Brethren Herald, *12 October 1962.*

Though most Mennonite Brethren writers have worked with the printed page, others have expressed themselves in different ways, including film making. The film And When They Shall Ask *(1984) brought the story of Mennonites in the Russian Revolution to audiences in a new way. A scene from the filming of that movie is shown here.* (CMBS Winnipeg)

Today the struggle for writers to choose between the Mennonite Brethren Church or their muse is not as acute. Mennonite Brethren have come a long way since Unruh and Wiebe lamented the lack of writers, but they still have a long way to go. We now have patrons of historical and theological research. This is needed also in the fine arts to encourage creative writers of all ethnic backgrounds within the church in North American and overseas to articulate their own experiences. Finally, we need to keep reminding ourselves that unwillingness to raise critical issues freely in our publications is death to prophetic thought.

10

To Improve Congregational Singing: Music in the Church

Doreen Klassen

From its beginnings in Russia in 1860, the Mennonite Brethren Church has been a singing church. For its founding members, joyful congregational song was a necessary expression of their new understanding of faith. Using a livelier musical style and more subjective texts than the traditional chorales of the time, they conveyed the vitality of their conversion and relationship with God. Expressing the faith musically has continued to be a priority for Mennonite Brethren. Over the past 140 years, music has held an important place in worship, spiritual nurture, and outreach. Church minutes, church histories, hymnal prefaces and conference periodicals have echoed a common refrain: the importance of maintaining dynamic congregational singing.

Perspectives on how to keep congregational singing vibrant have varied in their emphases. Some have seen musical education, whether through singing schools, song festivals, college music programs or graded church choirs, as key to improving congregational song. Others have cited a particular form of leadership—such as song leaders, choirs, or contemporary worship bands—as central to achieving that goal. Some have argued that the use of musical instruments—whether keyboard instruments, drums or amplified guitars—would improve participation in congregational song. More frequently, discussions have centered on balancing traditional and contemporary songs or worship styles to ensure universal congregational participation. Finally, some voices emphasize the importance of singing hymns reflective of Mennonite Brethren theology from a conference-produced hymnal.

From borrowed to denominational hymnals

Although congregational song has been at the center of defining conference identity, the Mennonite Brethren Church expressed its identity essentially from borrowed hymns and hymnals for its first ninety years. Throughout its existence, the conference has borrowed both music and worship practices from pietist, fundamentalist and even liturgical traditions. Mennonite Brethren, however, assert that selective borrowing of music has resulted in a distinctively Mennonite Brethren musical identity.

The practice of borrowing church music began in Russia. There, during the late nineteenth century, Mennonite Brethren borrowed their hymnody from the German Baptists, pietists, and more commonly from the spiritual folk song tradition of the German Methodists. The *"Dreiband"* (which included the hymnals *Heimatklänge, Frohe Botschaft in Liedern,* and *Glaubensstimme für die Gemeinden des Herrn*), published in 1890 and used as the first unofficial Mennonite Brethren hymnal in both Russia and America, contained essentially borrowed

The Henderson (Nebr.) Mennonite Brethren Church choir, 1918.
(CMBS Hillsboro)

Ziffern notation: a new way of singing

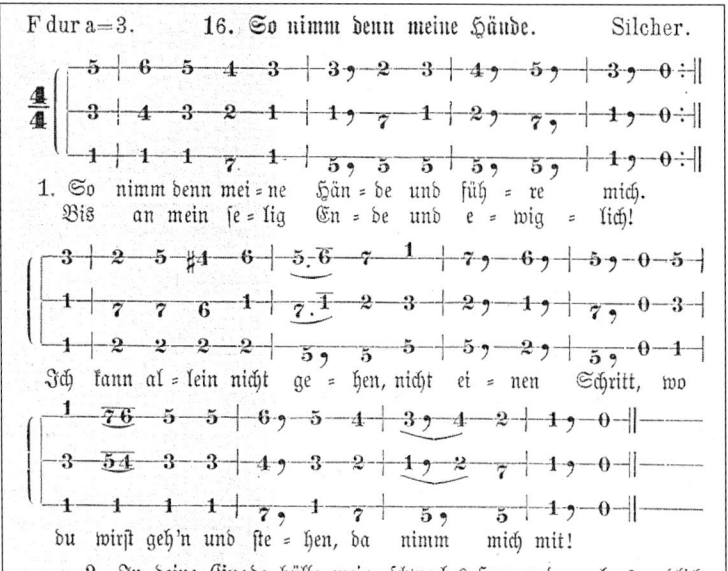

During the mid-nineteenth century the *Ziffern* (cipher) form of musical notation was introduced among Russian Mennonites. It first appeared in Mennonite schools, but was later adopted for use by church choirs and congregations. Rather than placing notes on a staff, *Ziffern* used numbers to represent the pitches of the scale (1=do, 2=re, 3=me, etc.).

The *Ziffern* system marked a fundamental shift in how Mennonites sang. Prior to the middle of the century, Mennonites had sung without musical notation, instead following a *Vorsänger* (song leader). Under the leadership of *Vorsängern*, melodies tended to move slowly, be highly embellished and differ from one leader to the next. Using *Ziffern*, melodies were standardized and could be sung with more precision. Harmonies could also be added, something difficult to do with the older method.

As with most innovations, the use of *Ziffern* was controversial. Many Mennonites opposed it on the grounds that it was overly regimented, and that its precise nature would lead to prideful performances rather than worship experiences.

The new Mennonite Brethren Church, however, quickly embraced the new notation. Church choirs, another innovation introduced by Mennonite Brethren congregations, often used the *Ziffern* arrangements to learn new music, which they then would teach to the congregation. The three-part arrangement of "So nimm denn meine Hände" ("Take Thou My Hand, O Father") illustrated here is an example of one such song popularized by the Mennonite Brethren in the nineteenth century. In other cases, the choir might use *Ziffern* to learn more complex pieces, such as the "Hallelujah Chorus" from Handel's *Messiah*, also shown here.

hymnody. Similarly, the *Zion's Glaubensstimme*, subtitled *Gesangbuch der Mennoniten Brüdergemeinde in Nord America*, was an adaptation of a Baptist hymnal with a Mennonite Brethren imprint. The influence of American revivalism at the turn of the century brought in other gospel songs through the ever-popular *Evangeliums-Lieder 1 und 2*. Such gospel songs were standard fare in many German-speaking Mennonite Brethren congregations until the mid-twentieth century, when English-speaking congregations might substitute books like *Tabernacle Hymns No. 3*. These songs too perpetuated experience-centered evangelical, and, at times, fundamentalist theology, and suited the Mennonite Brethren emphasis on conversion and a personal relationship with God.

The move toward compiling and publishing Mennonite Brethren hymnals since the middle of the twentieth century has been as much a theological and political as a musical venture. Creating denominational hymnals was an attempt to deal with increasing theological pluralism within the conference. Conference leaders and musicians alike repeatedly shared a vision for a hymnody expressive of Mennonite Brethren theological beliefs. An overview of the six books published by Mennonite Brethren conferences in North America offers insight into the realization of this vision.

Interest in creating a conference-wide songbook was first officially considered when the General Conference convened in Dinuba, California, in 1945. Discussions focused on producing a joint, bilingual book, but resulted in a German hymnal for Canada and an English one for the United States. Canadian Mennonite Brethren published the *Gesangbuch der Mennoniten Brüdergemeinde* in 1952, while their American counterparts published the *Mennonite Brethren Church Hymnal* in 1953.

Canadian consideration of a German hymnal centered on various congregational needs: to preserve the soon-to-be-lost chorale, to balance congregational favorites with new songs of musical and textual integrity, and to move beyond the theological confines of the gospel song in

The Tabor College Oratorio Society, 1915. (CMBS Fresno)

Herbert C. Richert

It was September 1958, and I was an insecure freshman at Tabor College. Professor H. C. Richert welcomed me into his studio for an audition. His eyes smiled. His wavy hair swept back from his broad brow in imitation of Paderewski. His resonant baritone voice, which had once earned him a season in the famed Chautauqua concert series, was now, after two decades of vocal teaching, little more than a high-pitched stage whisper. His voice may have weakened, but his personality remained electrifying.

During the next two academic years, as accompanist for the Concert Choir, I watched Richert transform average singers into ensembles of warmth and power. "Relax your jaw as if yawning and breath from the diaphragm," he would instruct his singers. The resultant vocal quality was dark and full, ideally suited for the Romantic literature he preferred. We students seldom thought about the fact that we were studying with a man who had profoundly shaped music in the Mennonite Brethren Church of the United States. Born in 1900 into a musical family, he studied at Tabor Academy, the Bible Institute of Los Angeles, California Christian College, and the University of Southern California. For several years he sang in professional male quartets in southern California.

Following a few years of teaching in public schools, Richert was invited to join the faculty of Tabor College in 1935. He taught voice and directed the choirs at Tabor for twenty-five years. Also during this time, with the assistance of his wife, Mary, he served as editor of the Mennonite Brethren English-language hymnal.

Richert's church music workshops, which included instruction in song leading and vocal production, had a profound effect on Mennonite Brethren churches. The annual tours of the Tabor Choir served as models of new literature and new refinement for local church choirs. Under his direction, the Oratorio Choir at Tabor introduced such classical compositions as Stainer's *Crucifixion*, Handel's *Messiah*, Brahm's *Deutches Requiem*, and Mendelssohn's *Elijah*.

In spring of 1960 "Prof Richert," as he was affectionately called, took the Tabor Choir on a final tour of the West Coast. There he was greeted as a valued and revered mentor. All of us in the choir sensed that we were part of a historic event. One of the final concerts was in the Dinuba Mennonite Brethren Church where, with deep emotion, Richert introduced Paul Wohlgemuth as his replacement at Tabor the following year.

Richert's career did not end at Tabor. From 1966 until 1970 he directed high school choirs in western Kansas. Those who heard his groups in choral competitions were struck with the power of his personality. One year, every student in his high school was enrolled in mixed choir. He was voted teacher of the year by his peers.

Herbert C. Richert's life came to an end in 1992, but his influence continues in the lives of all who knew him.

—*Larry Warkentin*

providing a hymnody that would parallel the seasons, practices, and mission of the church. A committee spent seven years producing a hymnal that could serve "as preacher and teacher." By 1955 the book was in its fourth printing, widely used both by Mennonite Brethren and some other Mennonite denominations.

American Mennonite Brethren, meanwhile, produced the *Mennonite Brethren Church Hymnal* for similar reasons, but added the goals of improving congregational singing and fostering conference unity. Their hymnal contained a broad range of hymns, borrowed predominantly from the gospel song tradition, along with aids to worship. Edited by Herbert C. Richert, long-time Tabor College music professor, it was hailed by *The Christian Leader* as a "characteristically Mennonite Brethren" hymnal. Six printings and the sale of 37,000 copies attest to its acceptance.

The compilation process for this hymnal set the tone for producing future conference hymnals. The process was essentially a collaboration between a committee and various segments of the church constituency. Mennonite Brethren musicians and church workers across the United States recommended hymns for the new book. Edited lists of hymns were then submitted to *The Christian Leader*, enabling all conference members to respond. Next, Mennonite Brethren college choirs, as well as musicians and ministers in selected congregations tested the singability of these hymns. Finally a group of ministers and laymen examined the hymns for theological integrity.

The Canadian Mennonite Brethren Conference lagged behind Americans in producing an English hymnal. The effects of block settlement patterns, a more multicultural government policy, and the influx of German-speaking immigrants from Russia in the 1930s and late 1940s slowed the language transition from German to English by several decades in Canadian churches. When they did publish an English hymnal in 1960, it was a translation of their 1952 *Gesangbuch*,

Members of the General Conference Hymnal Committee at work on the Worship Hymnal. *Left- right: Dietrich Friesen, Peter Klassen, Elmer Martens, Eugene Gerbrandt, Paul Wohlgemuth, Victor Martens. This committee worked together from 1965 to 1970.* (CMBS Fresno)

Aron G. Sawatzky

(CMBS Winnipeg)

The German Gothic letters A. G. Sawatzky come from a distant time. Who was this person? Why does his name appear in nearly every Mennonite Brethren music publication between 1911 and 1929? Was he a musician, was he a minister, or was he both?

Aron G. Sawatzky also appears in the 1971 *Worship Hymnal*. He is listed there as composer and poet for the hymn "Hail, Heavenly Night." Already curious about the name, I became even more intrigued in 1990 when Bruce Evans, a music student at Fresno Pacific University, told me that he was Sawatzky's great-great-grandson.

Fortunately, Sawatzky answered some of the questions about his life in a few autobiographical pages written just months before his death in 1935. He was born into a large family in Andreasfeld, South Russia, in 1871. From early childhood he demonstrated a deep concern for spiritual matters. He accepted Christ and was baptized by the age of twelve, and immediately began witnessing to the unsaved in his neighborhood.

Sawatzky also had a predilection for music. By the age of fourteen he was active in a band and at the age of twenty-two he was elected choir director of the Andreasfeld Mennonite Brethren Church. The church sent Sawatzky to study with Franz Schweiger in Zyrardów near Warsaw, Poland. He continued his training in Łódź, Poland.

In 1903, with his wife, Elizabeth, and their six children, Sawatzky emigrated to Rosthern, Saskatchewan. Within a few years he was receiving invitations to teach choir directing courses in Mennonite Brethren churches in both Canada and the United States. In 1911 he began publication of the music journal, *Sänger-Bote*. Each month for seven years this journal brought music, poetry, drama and other worship information to Mennonite Brethren churches. Many of Sawatzky's hymns and choral pieces first appeared in this journal.

The Aberdeen Mennonite Brethren Church in Saskatchewan called Sawatzky to be a minister in 1912, and thus his passion for music and ministry were united. In 1920 he moved to California, where he lived and worked for one year in Lodi, two years in Livingston, and finally for nine years in Winton. In 1928 he was chosen as the minister of the Winton Mennonite Brethren Church, and was ordained in 1930.

In 1929 Sawatzky revived his music journal under the title *Lieder-Quelle für Kirche und Haus*. Some of his compositions appeared in this journal but the publishing attempt was short-lived. Sawatzky's name has now faded from the hymnal, but his shaping influence on Mennonite Brethren Church music is still evident. The final lines of one of his poems may serve as his epitaph: "And when they shall say, 'He used to live here,' May this memory give them joy."

—*Larry Warkentin*

called *The Hymn Book*. This translation gave continuity to the rich heritage of German hymnody while addressing the growing language problem within the church. It also was hoped that the use of one hymnal (in German and English) would foster spiritual unity in the conference. Some lauded the link, while others criticized both the quality of the translations and the exclusion of many significant English hymns.

Intermittent discussions concerning a joint Canadian-American hymnal resurfaced in the early 1960s. A committee of two musicians and one theologian from each of the national conferences, chaired by music professor Paul Wohlgemuth, was appointed in 1965. Their musical, textual, and theological concerns were similar to those of earlier hymnal committees, as was their process of involving the church constituency. By combining over 400 well-known with 250 lesser or unknown hymns, they created what they called "a Mennonite Brethren hymnal with a denominational emphasis." When *Worship Hymnal* was published in 1971, General Conference Chairman Marvin Hein called it the "first fruitful cooperative effort in hymnal production between our Canadian and United States churches."

The uniqueness of this hymnal lay not only in its reliance on new sources—including Anglican, Lutheran, and Inter-Varsity hymnals—but in the committee's search for new materials written or translated by Mennonite Brethren. They not only encouraged Mennonite Brethren to write hymn texts on theological beliefs such as nonresistance, nonconformity to the world, and service and welfare, but also encouraged the composition of new tunes. The hymnal thus includes translations of German *Kernlieder* (gospel songs) by Mennonites like Esther Bergen, Esther Horch and Peter Klassen, and new texts from the Hymn Society of America set to tunes by Dietrich

The Reedley (Calif.) Mennonite Brethren Church choir with instrumentalists, ca. 1931-1933.
(CMBS Fresno)

The hymn that could not be left out

In 1953 the Mennonite Brethren Church published its first English-language hymnal. The first printing included 500 hymns. But in later printings, the hymnal suddenly contained 501 hymns. There, in the back of the book, following the benedictions, was "What Can Wash Away My Sin?"

No written documents seem to exist that explain this late addition to the 1953 hymnal. Oral tradition and a knowledge of theological issues of the time, however, help to explain what apparently happened.

The song, written by Robert Lowry, was part of the American gospel song tradition that had become very popular in Mennonite Brethren churches beginning already in the late nineteenth century. It appeared in *Evangeliums-Lieder*, a hymnal edited by Walter Rauschenbusch and Ira D. Sankey and used widely in Mennonite Brethren congregations, under the German title "Nur Das Blut des Lammes." It also appeared in the 1952 German hymnal published for the Canadian Conference of Mennonite Brethren Churches, under the title "Was macht mich von Sünden rein?"

We don't know for sure why the editors of the 1953 hymnal committee decided to omit the hymn, though oral tradition suggests that it may have been more a question of musical quality than theological interpretation. Whatever the reason, the decision was roundly criticized. Various conference leaders and congregations demanded that the omission be corrected, and so the committee relented and squeezed the song onto an otherwise blank page toward the back of the hymnal.

Why did this particular song stir up so much passion? Again, we don't have clear evidence. Perhaps it was simply an old favorite of many people, and they missed it in the new hymnal. The issue, however, may have been bigger than simply a question of musical taste. The "blood of Jesus" had become a test point for many evangelicals in the early 1950s, who accused allegedly liberal theologians of downplaying or ignoring the doctrine that Jesus' blood had been paid as a ransom for human sin. This was one of the main evangelical and fundamentalist criticisms of the Revised Standard Version of the Bible, published in 1952. Accusations that the RSV had "taken the blood out" of specific verses were commonplace in the evangelical press of the time, and undoubtedly led to a heightened awareness of this issue within that community. The 1953 hymnal appeared only months after this controversy erupted, and it seems plausible that some Mennonite Brethren might have been particularly sensitive to the removal of a hymn about the "blood of Jesus" under those circumstances.

The story does not end, however, in 1953. The committee in charge of publishing a new hymnal in 1971 again struggled with inclusion of the song, in part because of concerns about the quality of the music. For that reason, the song was included, but with an alternate melody, in *Worship Hymnal*. This compromise was unacceptable to many congregations, and song leaders of the time were sometimes heard to announce, "Let's sing #240 using the old, familiar tune that we know."

The hymn appears—with its original tune—in the 1995 hymnal, *Worship Together*, even though the committee was divided on which tune to use. While they differed on the best melody, the committee had no doubt that the hymn would appear in the new hymnal. A survey of song use among Mennonite Brethren congregations in 1990 indicated that it remained a widely-used and well-loved hymn in many Mennonite Brethren congregations.

Friesen, Peter Klassen, Herbert C. Richert and Larry Warkentin. Additionally, responsive readings allowed for greater congregational involvement, and suggested a growing interest in new forms of worship.

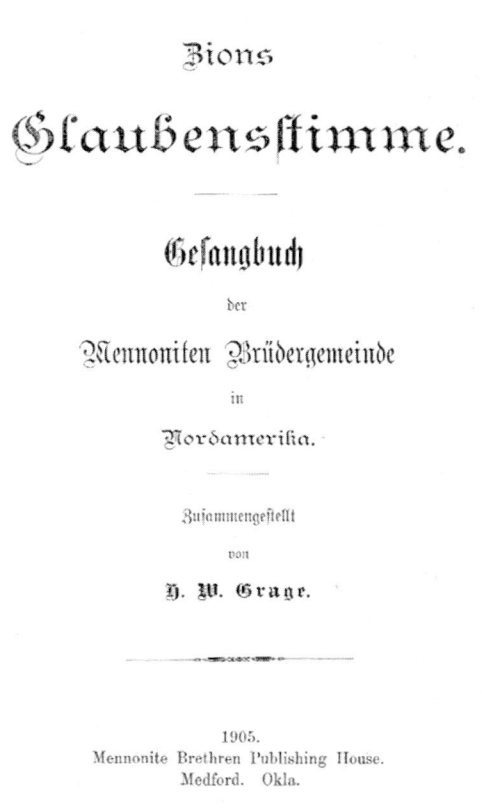

Title pages from early hymnals used in the Mennonite Brethren Church: Zions Glaubensstimme, Evangeliums-Lieder 1 und 2, *and* Sänger-Bote.

To ensure conference-wide use of the hymnal, the Board of Trustees sent Dietrich Friesen to some sixty churches in Canada and the United States during the summer of 1970 to acquaint them with the new hymnal and to encourage pre-publication purchases. About 17,000 of the first 25,000 hymnals printed were sold on this basis. After the hymnal was published, several articles in *The Christian Leader* and *Mennonite Brethren Herald* acquainted the general membership with its contents and new features. Articles ranged from what made this a Mennonite Brethren hymnal to the rationale for including folk hymns.

Within a decade, the need for contemporary worship music was raised again. The folk hymns with guitar chords in *Worship Hymnal* were no longer reflective of the growing trend of using amplified guitars, synthesizers and drums, nor the new textual emphasis on "praise and worship." Recognizing the somewhat temporary nature of the new music, the committee—commissioned by the Board of Christian Literature—prepared a loose-leaf hymnal that allowed for ongoing additions. The new book, *Sing Alleluia* (1985), made no pretense of being a comprehensive hymnal. Instead, it included primarily songs for praise and worship, communion and outreach, arranged in alphabetical order. Along with songs common to the broader evangelical and charismatic traditions, it included texts and tunes by about twenty Mennonite Brethren composers.

At the same time, discussion was beginning about the need for a new church hymnal, possibly a joint hymnal with other Mennonite conferences. This option was plausible because *Worship Hymnal* and *The Mennonite Hymnal* (used by the Mennonite Church and the General Conference Mennonite Church) already shared 185 tunes and 277 texts. Some committee members argued that a joint hymnal would be better stewardship of time and money, and that the distinctive theological emphases of the two groups could complement each other. The Mennonite Brethren Board of Reference and Counsel (BORAC), however, rejected this option. Consequently, when a newly-formed Mennonite Brethren Hymnal Commission convened in August 1989, it met for the purpose of producing a new Mennonite Brethren hymnal and not to participate in a joint hymnal project.

Board of Reference and Counsel directives to the commission stressed the need to address three issues: a Mennonite Brethren theological emphasis, cultural issues, and communication

Combined choirs at a song festival in Reinland, Manitoba, 1942. (CMBS Winnipeg)

issues. In terms of theological emphases, BORAC cited the centrality of Christ and the need for forgiveness, reflective of the conversion emphasis they felt would be lost in a joint effort with other Mennonites. Cultural issues included multi-cultural diversity and the need to reflect the 1990s perspective on worship as experience, while communication issues centered on inclusive language, the use of contemporary metaphors, and the renewed interest in storytelling as a means to understanding truth.

The Hymnal Commission incorporated these directives into the new hymnal, but balanced the essentially evangelical theological framework suggested by BORAC with more distinctively

This band played at Jugendverein *meetings of the Ebenfeld (Kans.) Mennonite Brethren Church, 1915.*
(CMBS Hillsboro)

Anabaptist themes such as discipleship, the church as a covenanting body, peace and reconciliation, and servanthood. In fact, the commission claimed *Worship Together* was an Anabaptist/Mennonite version of the widely used evangelically-oriented *Hymnal for Worship and Celebrations* published by Word in 1986.

New cultural issues, such as the need for experience-centered worship, required both new repertoire and new ways of organizing it. In response, the commission organized the hymnal in chapters relating to their function in worship—such as gathering, praying, and walking with God—rather than by theological focus. Additionally, they grouped songs—whether chorales, hymns, or choruses—thematically, often with written instrumental transitions. Lastly, they integrated Scriptures, prayers and readings into the chapters, rather than placing them in an appendix, to reflect an understanding of worship as moving easily from one genre to another.

Response to the other cultural issue—the representation of multicultural diversity—is evident in the inclusion of international music and European folk worship traditions. International and cross-cultural Mennonite Brethren music, however, is virtually absent and so one gets no sense of how Congolese, Brazilian, or even Chinese-Canadian Mennonite Brethren worship.

As with earlier hymnals, the church constituency was actively involved in the decision-making process. In fact, the *Mennonite Brethren Herald* reported that about 65 percent of the more than 42,000 North American Mennonite Brethren responded in some way. As a result, the Hymnal Commission, which worked together for seven years, could claim *Worship Together* was a truly Mennonite Brethren hymnal.

Choirs and ensembles

Mennonite Brethren first introduced choirs into their worship services in Russia to assist in teaching new music to their congregations. Instituting a choir provided leadership when the fledgling church abandoned the *Vorsänger* (cantor) tradition, prevalent in the larger Mennonite church, and singing by *Ziffern* (a form of numbered staff notation introduced into Russian Mennonite schools in the 1830s), facilitated learning four-part singing. When they moved to North America, Mennonite Brethren transplanted their choral music tradition. Consequently, many American Mennonite Brethren churches started choirs around the turn of the century, often to improve congregational singing but, as in Russia, also to provide a social outlet for young people.

Within the next few decades, the church choir was often complemented by other vocal ensembles formed on the basis of age, gender or interest in a specific musical repertoire. These included children's, youth, and senior citizen's choirs, as well as men's choruses. Smaller ensembles, such as trios, quartets and octets, were likely to sing at Sunday evening services or to focus on outreach through hospital visitation or church-sponsored radio programs.

Although music did not become a conference-wide issue until mid-century, local church choirs emerged in the context of choral festivals organized by regional committees. By the turn of the twentieth century, these festivals, held in conjunction with American Mennonite Brethren Sunday School conventions, were becoming common practice. By about 1930, these festivals were held independently and often featured multiple choirs, each of which sang several selections, but also joined to perform as a mass choir. In the earlier part of the century repertoire came from German gospel song collections like *Evangeliums-Lieder* or *Zionslieder*, but later, English repertoire moved in the direction of anthems and oratorio choruses. When the repertoire became more challenging, local church choirs began rehearsing the music in advance and abandoned performances by individual choirs in favor of the mass choir. Several American Mennonite Brethren song festivals continued as late as the mid-1970s. In the last two decades, the church choir itself has, in some churches, become a festival choir that performs primarily for special occasions such as Christmas and Easter.

In addition to its musical and social function, the song festival tradition also served a distinctively educational function. A choral society formed by Mennonite Brethren in Saskatchewan in 1906 fostered not only *Sängerfeste* (song festivals), but also the *Dirigentenkurse* (conductors' seminars) tradition. Serving members both in Saskatchewan and Manitoba, as well as in states from Minnesota to California until 1923, the society published a periodical and a collection of hymns (both entitled *Sängerbote*), many by Aron G. Sawatzky (1871-1935), a noted Mennonite Brethren conductor in Russia, Canada, and the United States. Through the periodical and conductors' workshops with choral leaders like Nicolai Fehderau (Ontario), Benjamin Horch (Manitoba), C. D. Toews (British Columbia) and Herbert C. Richert (Kansas), church choir conductors received a new impetus for using and developing their gifts. Bible schools, often opened in the 1930s, began offering music programs—and sometimes mandatory music courses—as well. Conductors' workshops organized by the Canadian Mennonite Brethren Conference after 1944 continued until the 1950s when college music programs began fulfilling that educational role. A biennial week-long church music seminar, begun in 1975 and sponsored by the Mennonite colleges in Winnipeg, continues to serve a similar function.

Increasing urbanism and formal education have influenced the musical life of the church as well. Receiving a Master of Music degree was not the norm for church musicians when David P. Unruh, of Henderson, Nebraska, received his degree in about 1917. This level of training was unusual for Mennonite Brethren church musicians, and often even for music instructors in church-sponsored institutions. Currently, formal musical training is a prerequisite not only for teaching, but for the increasing number of salaried Minister of Music positions that have emerged

The Mennonite Oratorio Choir and Symphony at Grace United Church, Winnipeg, ca. early 1950s. Ben Horch is the conductor. Performance groups such as these provided an outlet for musical expression among Mennonite Brethren and other Mennonites beyond the congregational setting.
(CMBS Winnipeg)

since the mid-1970s. Salaries, too, are well beyond that of Herbert C. Richert, who received fifty dollars in 1938 and three dollars per week in 1939 for conducting the church choir in Hillsboro, Kansas. Increasingly too, ministers of music have become more transient than the three generations of the Suderman family at the Ebenfeld Mennonite Brethren Church near Hillsboro, Kansas, who provided musical leadership there for seventy years, or the three members of the Enns family who successively directed the church choirs over a period of fifty years in Reedley, California.

The professionalization of musical leadership has allowed for an expanded musical program in many churches. Special occasions in the church year such as Christmas and Easter were often marked by the performance of larger choral works like cantatas or children's musicals. Churches in urban centers or those who could draw on trained singers from institutions like Tabor College usually performed these works several decades before their more rural counterparts. Local Mennonite Brethren church histories provide ample details of these and other changes in repertoire since the early twentieth century.

The Mennonite Brethren choral tradition, however, is changing in level of involvement, performance style, manner of dress, and choice of repertoire. In the earlier part of the century, singing in a church choir was almost a rite of passage for young people. Canadian conference yearbooks

The Messengers Quartet, from St. Catharines Ontario, 1973: John Block, Bill Schroeder, Menno Kroeker, Abe Block.
(CMBS Winnipeg)

refer to 1148 singers in 51 choirs in 1938 and 2500 singers in 63 church choirs by 1950. American church histories also document Mennonite Brethren churches with multiple choirs, often totaling 300-400 singers, by the late 1960s. Some churches still maintain this tradition, while others have replaced or supplemented choirs with praise and worship ensembles of only four to eight musicians. As a result, choirs seated in pews on the platform have often been replaced by small ensembles standing on a platform with microphones in hand. The "Sunday dress" worn by choir members in the earlier part of the century and the choir robes of the mid-century have often given way to more casual dress. The sacred anthems and cantatas of choirs have frequently been replaced by "packages" of contemporary music, though, an increased use of arts like drama, poetry, and even liturgical dance has accompanied the narrower range of musical repertoire. At the heart of these changes has been the motivation to involve the congregation in worshiping in a spiritually dynamic and culturally-relevant manner, but there have been those in every era who have questioned whether these changes are sacrificing congregational involvement for a performance orientation.

From *a capella* singing to praise and worship bands

In some North American Mennonite Brethren congregations, musical instruments were initially viewed with distrust because of their association with dance music and "worldly entertainment" in Russia. Even by 1919, the purchase of a reed organ, reportedly used in a Wichita, Kansas, theater, was still so controversial that it remained on the Ebenfeld Mennonite Brethren Church porch for three weeks until an elder's resistance was overruled. In early Canadian Mennonite Brethren churches the presence or absence of musical instruments was as often a matter of economics.

Initial resistance to musical instruments eventually gave way to their increasing use in Mennonite Brethren churches. Occasionally congregations were introduced to keyboard (piano or reed organ) accompaniment by bringing a borrowed family instrument to the church for special services.

The progression of keyboard instruments at Reedley, California, was typical of many Mennonite Brethren churches. A reed organ, purchased in 1912, was replaced by a Hammond organ in 1946, which, in turn, was retired when the congregation purchased an Allen organ in 1974. Similarly, in Hillsboro, Kansas, a reed organ was introduced in 1906 to help raise the musical standard of the congregation, but by 1975 the installation of a $48,000 Reuters pipe organ was celebrated with two full-fledged organ recitals, one by hymnologist and organist Don Hustad of Louisville, Kentucky. Typically, organists and pianists in Mennonite Brethren churches have been women, one of their few opportunities for public ministry in the earlier part of the century.

Since the early 1980s, Mennonite Brethren churches across North America have increasingly come to incorporate praise and worship bands, sometimes in addition to, and sometimes in lieu of traditional keyboard instruments and choirs. These bands generally consist of amplified guitars, electronic keyboard instruments, and drums, in addition to a small group of singers with microphones who lead the congregation in contemporary praise and worship music. Often, the congregation sings these texts from overhead screens, and in some churches, accompanies them with clapping or some form of movement, not unlike the exuberant music of the first Mennonite Brethren in Russia as they expressed a new-found faith.

The singing church

The impetus for changes in Mennonite Brethren music-making—whether in the creation of hymnals, the formation of choirs and vocal ensembles, or the use of musical instruments—has perpetually been that of involving a church community in its own worship practices. An overview of 140 years of Mennonite Brethren musical involvement can only hint at the joy and breadth of this rich musical tradition. It cannot capture the tune that gets whistled at a construction site, the text that comes to mind in the midst of a crisis, the resonance of a clear soprano or rich bass voice, much less the sense of belonging to a community of believers. But, an overview offers insight into the conference structures, the local church dynamics, and the essentially communal processes involved in creating a singing conference.

These efforts "to improve congregational song" have rarely been essentially musical issues, but rather, concerns about fostering community, theological integrity, contemporary relevance, and spiritual vitality.

11

The Life of the Congregation

Valerie Rempel

*F*aith is nurtured and expressed through the life of local congregations and Mennonite Brethren churches have had a rich congregational life. In the early immigrant days the local congregation served as the primary community for both social and religious activities. Because of that, congregations and the events of the church community often assumed a central role in the life of individuals and families. Even as early immigrants assimilated into the wider North American society and other people joined to become part of the Mennonite Brethren church, local congregations continued to assume the central importance of a wide range of activities designed to nurture faith and community life. The shared rituals of these local congregations helped form identity both within particular congregations but also between the like-minded congregations of the Mennonite Brethren Conference.

Immigrants arriving on the high plains of Kansas, Nebraska, Dakota and Minnesota in the 1870s and 1880s regularly gathered in homes for fellowship and prayer, as did later immigrants who moved into the Canadian provinces. As immigrants settled and became established, they organized into local congregations. They continued meeting in homes, or even hay barns, and then in school buildings until enough money could be gathered to build a meeting house. The first buildings were simple sod or wood frame construction, often with double entrance ways, one for the men and one for the women. They were called "meeting houses," a term deliberately chosen as a reminder that the church was made up of people and was not simply a building. As congregations became financially stable and grew numerically, these early buildings were replaced with solid white frame church buildings, still with double entrance-ways but now with towers and more imposing facades.

In Russia, Mennonite Brethren had frequently gathered in homes for fellowship, and their worship services were characterized by exuberant singing and a warm piety that found expression in the frequent use of the Low German dialect rather than the more formal High German. Low German lent itself to a more informal atmosphere and allowed for greater participation in the service, thus shaping the way worship services developed. Early worship services, like those today, frequently included times of congregational sharing and praying together. Members called each other "sister" and "brother"—terms of endearment that continued for a century and reflected the believers' understanding of themselves as brothers and sisters in the Lord.

The first immigrants from Russia brought these habits with them, as well as the regular practice of foot washing and communion, and, in some communities, the continuing custom of the fellowship kiss. That kiss, a simple form of greeting taken from a literal reading of the Apostle Paul's frequent instruction to the New Testament believers "to greet one another with a holy kiss," proved contentious. In most congregations this ritual greeting took place between men or between women, but in a few congregations it was deemed appropriate for both men and women

Members of the Reedley (California) MB Church gather for a congregational photo during the dedication of their new sanctuary on 13 September 1919.
(CMBS Fresno)

Many Mennonite Brethren churches participated in inter-denominational revival meetings. Pictured here is the audience for a George R. Brunk revival meeting in Chilliwack, British Columbia, in 1958.
(CMBS Fresno)

to exchange the kiss of fellowship. Not wanting to be accused of any impropriety, the "sister kiss" as it was often called, was strongly discouraged by the Conference and eventually fell from practice, and even the more circumspect fellowship kiss was eventually replaced by warm handshakes. The communion service itself was a time of great solemnity as members examined themselves for unconfessed sin before partaking of the bread and wine.

During the early years of the Conference, ministers were regularly called out from the congregations they served and were self-supporting. Together with elders and deacons, they served to guide the church through preaching and pastoral care. Though referred to as lay ministers, they were often men who had extensive biblical and even in some cases formal theological training. They served as local leaders and were ordained to the ministry but they were not granted sole authority over the congregation. Local congregations took seriously their responsibility for the ordering of their fellowships and for decision making.

The role of the elder in early Mennonite Brethren church life was somewhat unique in that it required an ordination beyond that of the ministry. Elders, while considered part of the multiple ministry of a congregation, were often strong leaders whose authority reached beyond any particular local congregation, especially as they were the ones who officiated over the ordination of teaching ministers. Over the years, this became a point of tension within the Conference. Some understood the role of elder to be separate from that of minister and wanted the elder to function as a sort of bishop; others read the Bible to mean that elder, teacher and shepherd were interchangeable names for the same role. Eventually, it was agreed that any minister called out by the congregation was to be viewed as an elder and after 1935, the Conference no longer ordained special elders.

Though there was debate about the precise nature of these various ministerial roles, there was widespread agreement on the importance of a shared ministry and of shared leadership.

Mennonite Brethren congregations thought of themselves as brotherhoods, and while recognizing the need for good leaders, they were convinced that the Bible was the sole authority for faith and practice within the church. "What does the Word say?" was the question most frequently posed when issues arose within the congregation. A model of shared leadership was understood to protect the congregation from the singular influence of any one leader. Gradually, a system of church organization developed that relied on an elected church council that met and gave leadership to the congregation, made decisions on matters of church discipline, and addressed theological concerns. Congregations met in regular business sessions to hear reports, elect deacons and council members, and also to discuss issues related to church governance, discipline, theological direction and mission. As a reminder that congregations were dependent on God for their well-being, they regularly set aside the first week in January as a special time of prayer.

The vast open territories of the Canadian and American West, and the diversity of those who were settling there, were a challenge to people used to living in tightly-knit ethnic and family

A Sunday school class in Mountain Lake, Minnesota, date unknown. The teacher is Anna Hiebert.
(CMBS Fresno)

groups. Some from Mennonite Brethren backgrounds chose to join other denominational groups such as the Baptists or Seventh-day Adventists. Others formed small house fellowships and looked to the day when they could establish a formal congregation. The Conference frequently sponsored preaching tours by established ministers for those living at considerable distance from the main Mennonite Brethren settlements. A visit from these teams of traveling ministers were occasions for weddings and baptisms, as well as the celebration of the Lord's Supper. Over time, the practice of special preaching services spread to all the congregations. A gifted minister or a Bible teacher from one of the Conference schools would be invited to give a series of sermons and congregations would gather together in meetings that were part Bible study and part revival service. Meetings such as these were occasions to see the Holy Spirit at work convicting sinners of their need for salvation, or feuding church members of their need for reconciliation. In addition, the

Sunday school class at Swift Current, Saskatchewan, ca. 1950s.
(CMBS Winnipeg)

practice of inviting teachers or ministers from within the Conference helped to nurture theological identity and unity, a particularly important issue given the far-flung nature of the churches and the diversity of theological emphases to be found in Canada and the United States.

From the beginning, Mennonite Brethren church members have had a passion for mission and evangelism, and the support of mission activity has been the impetus for many gatherings within the congregation. As an alternative to the celebration of Independence Day on July 4 in the United States, congregations were encouraged to hold mission festivals, thereby celebrating the freedom offered to all through belief in Christ Jesus. More than just preaching services, some of these early festivals quickly grew to include picnics and mission sales which auctioned off the handiwork of women in the church. The celebratory aspect of these events with their fellowship meals, missionary preaching and the good-natured competition of the auction, proved an attractive alternative to traditional Fourth of July celebrations. The practice of holding a church picnic on that date lasted for many years in some locations. Mission sales also became an annual event in many congregations, though not all of them were held on July 4. The tradition of auctioning off homemade goods as a way to raise money for missions dates back at least to the 1880s and lasted as late as the 1970s in some congregations. A few church leaders were unsure of the wisdom of these sales, fearing that the competitive nature of the auction was not suitable for mission fundraising, but these voices were generally drowned out by the determination of women to participate in the work of the Conference, the enjoyment of those participating in the events and the success of the events in raising considerable monies for missions!

Nearly all congregations held an annual thanksgiving festival in the fall and these became mission events, too. The Harvest Thanksgiving Mission Festival, as it came to be known in many churches, was another occasion to combine fellowship, inspiration and giving for missions. Missionaries home on furlough were in great demand for these occasions, and their stories of work among the peoples of Africa, India and China held their audiences enthralled, particularly once electricity made possible the use of pictures and slide projectors. The shared thanksgiving meal with its bountiful menu (a menu which might vary from congregation to congregation but was always the same from year to year), the harvest-theme decorations, the exotic displays of goods brought back from the mission field, all lent an air of excitement to the festival. Ritual celebrations such as these nurtured an ongoing interest in missions and spurred the joint work of the Conference mission agency. They also served to gather the local congregation together in

Quilting groups, such as this one in Harvey, North Dakota, have provided Mennonite Brethren women an opportunity to express their creativity while also raising funds for mission and relief projects.
(CMBS Hillsboro)

Baptism at Borden, Saskatchewan, ca. 1950s. Nick Willms is the officiating minister. (CMBS Winnipeg)

Ebenfeld Mennonite Brethren Church, Hillsboro, Kansas, Sunday school class, ca. 1917.
(CMBS Hillsboro)

celebration of God's physical provisions and reminded people of their responsibility to share with others in need.

Mission interest and support were also a motivating factor in the development of local mission societies. The earliest societies provided occasions for fellowship for both men and women who gathered together at someone's farmstead. While the women sewed, the men would meet for Bible study and prayer. As cars replaced horses and buggies these meetings were increasingly made up of women only and gradually became formally organized. From the beginning, these mission societies were influential in both the nurturing of mission awareness and support, and in the provision of goods and monies for support of missionaries. Donations from women's missionary societies appear in Conference minutes as early as 1881 and throughout the life of the Conference it has been rare for any congregation to be without a women's society of some kind. Often referred to as simply the Sewing Circle, or the Ladies Aid, or in many congregations as the Women's Missionary Service, these societies were an integral part of congregational life. Many congregations had several; as younger

Low German

Even before adopting the English language in the twentieth century, Mennonite Brethren were a "bilingual" people. While the language of church and school was German (often called "High German"), their language of everyday life was *Plautdietsch*, or "Low German."

Plautdietsch was the language generally spoken in the Vistula Delta region of Poland where Mennonites first migrated from the Netherlands in the 1530s. Because *Plautdietsch* was very similar to Dutch, it was fairly easy for these first migrants to adopt this new language. As other Mennonites came to Poland from other parts of Europe, they generally also adopted *Plautdietsch* as their daily language.

Though once an official language of politics and commerce, *Plautdietsch* had already ceased to be a written language by the time Mennonites adopted it. When Mennonites spoke among themselves, they did so in *Plautdietsch*; but when they wrote, read or worshiped, they did so in "High German." *Plautdietsch* thus tended to be a "common" and even "earthy" language, concerned mainly with the stuff of everyday life. It did not generally have words for abstract concepts and theology, which were most often expressed in German.

From Poland, Mennonites carried *Plautdietsch* with them to South Russia and later to new homes in North and South America. Today, the dialect is still heard in many Mennonite Brethren communities. In the United States it is limited mostly to older community members, and is close to dying out there. It remains more common in Canada and South America, where the influx of *Plautdietsch* speakers from Russia in the 1940s has kept the language alive. There also has been a renewed effort to document and preserve the language, particularly in Canada. *Plautdietsch* today can more easily be found in written form than was formerly the case. The creation of *Plautdietsch* dictionaries and published collections of stories, sayings and poems offer hope that this unique language will survive in some form even as the number of people who speak it declines.

women began to be active in church work, they would often start a new group. Their projects ranged widely; they helped furnish new church buildings, outfitted missionary families, aided city mission projects, helped provide for those involved in alternative service during times of war, and engaged in numerous fund-raising projects in order to contribute money to missions. But beyond the money raised for projects, these women's organizations served as places to gather and share the concerns of the members' lives, a particularly important aspect when Mennonite Brethren congregations were primarily rural and women often lived at some distance from each other. Meetings fostered a sense of community and shared purpose and provided ways for women to engage in the work of the church. Societies helped women develop leadership skills as they organized and ran their meetings, managed budgets, studied the Bible together, and participated in prayer services.

Women's missionary societies were not the only specialized groups that developed within congregations. Young people's associations also became widely popular throughout the Conference. The earliest groups appear to have been modeled after the Christian Endeavor societies that were popular in North America in the late 1800s and early 1900s. They seem to have sprung up under private sponsorship but gradually moved to church sponsorship. Often meeting on Sunday afternoon before the evening service, these young people's societies encouraged Bible verse memorization, devotional study of the Bible, singing and Christian fellowship. They provided opportunities to address the special concerns of young people, though "young" was a designation with wide boundaries and often included both single and married adults from their late teens to late thirties. Gradually, these meetings were incorporated into the regular program of Sunday evening

Church picnic, Springfield KMB Church, Marion County, Kansas, ca. 1918. (CMBS Fresno)

143

The Christmas Program

Participants in the children's Christmas program at Butler Avenue MB Church, Fresno, California, ca. 1980s.
(CMBS Fresno)

The evening of December 24 was an important event in the life of every Mennonite Brethren congregation. This was the night of the children's Christmas program, in which all children from pre-school through the elementary grades participated by re-enacting the nativity story, singing songs, or individually reciting a "piece." The event usually began with the youngest children, proceeding through the grade levels until the oldest children concluded the program.

The evening always ended with the distribution of the *Weihnachte's Tüte*, or "Christmas bags," to each child who participated in the program. The tradition of distributing brown paper bags full of Christmas treats was already practiced by Mennonite Brethren churches in Russia, and continues in many congregations even today. The contents of these bags has remained remarkably consistent over the years—an orange or perhaps an apple, hard candy, and peanuts still in their shells. Though children were typically instructed not to open their *Tüte* until they got home, many church custodians over the decades likely found themselves sweeping up peanut shells from the church floor in the days following Christmas.

worship services and given the name "Christian Endeavor." One or two Sundays a month the evening service would be given over to the Christian Endeavor meeting. These popular services were a bit like a variety show—someone might read or recite a poem or a passage of scripture, there would be small musical groups such as trios or quartets, church members who played musical instruments might favor the congregation with a special song, and the congregational singing often included popular gospel songs and choruses.

Strongly conversionist groups such as the Mennonite Brethren have taken seriously their responsibility to nurture and pass on an active faith in Jesus Christ, and young people's societies were places where this could happen. Like the women's groups, these young peoples' societies were an important part of leadership development within the local congregation and helped assimilate young people into adult roles within the church. Christian Endeavor meetings provided places for a young person to practice preaching or praying aloud, and to polish and display musical skills. In addition to concerns for the spiritual well-being of their young people, congregations were eager

Sunday School picnic on the Ewert farm near Coaldale, Alberta, ca. 1930s. (CMBS Winnipeg)

to have young people marry within the church and these early societies provided opportunities for young men and women to meet each other and socialize.

As Christian Endeavor meetings gradually evolved into a regular Sunday evening service some congregations began to look for new ways to minister to their youth, particularly since many young people felt more at home with the English language than the German and, until World War II, most services were still conducted primarily in German. In the 1930s and 1940s, many began to establish more narrowly defined Youth Fellowships with programs geared specifically for teens and young adults. Focusing on Christian fellowship, Bible study and prayer, these groups were the forerunners of today's MBY (Mennonite Brethren Youth) groups. During the next decades, the increasing mobility of American and Canadian youth, as well as the growing youth culture in the wider society, frequently challenged congregations to provide creative ways of reaching and keeping their young people.

From the beginning, Christian education was an important part of congregational life. The importance of knowing what the Bible says, and believing it, spurred the development of Sunday

Representatives of the Pacific District Conference Women's Missionary Service present a donation to Mennonite Brethren Board of Foreign Missions Secretary-Treasurer A.E. Janzen in 1955. Left to right: Maria Litke, Sophie Enns, A.E. Janzen, Lydia Martens, Marie Leppke. (CMBS Fresno)

school classes for all ages as a wide range of biblical and topical studies were developed for adults as well as children. Adult classes, in particular, became a significant way to nurture a sense of community among church members. Many classes met together for years, sharing and praying together, as well as socializing outside of the classroom. An annual Christmas program put on by the children's Sunday school department also became a tradition in many Mennonite Brethren congregations. Often held on Christmas Eve, the programs were a mix of songs, recitations and a retelling of the Christmas story. The packed sanctuary full of proud parents and grandparents, the anticipation of Christmas packages waiting at home and the nervousness of having to say a Christmas piece were all a part of the excitement of the evening. In the late spring or summer many congregations celebrated the activities of the Sunday school department with an annual picnic where the three-legged race, relays, softball and volleyball games provided activities for all ages.

Volunteers dismantling the old country church at Henderson, Nebraska, 1926. (CMBS Fresno)

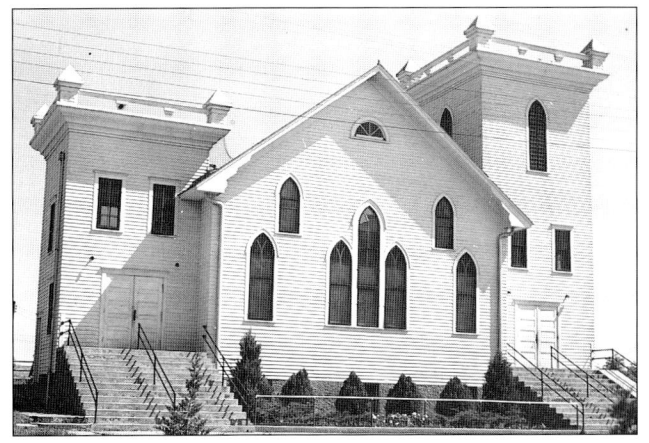

Many Mennonite congregations during the early 20th century built meeting houses with imposing, squared towers. Variations on this theme can be seen in the buildings at Buhler, Kansas (upper left); East Chilliwack, B.C. (upper right); Bingham Lake, Minnesota (middle); and Elm Creek, Manitoba (bottom).
(CMBS Fresno)

For many years, Wednesday nights had been the other church night. Wednesdays had traditionally been set aside for congregational prayer meetings, and so it was natural to add choir practice and special club programs for children on this night. Boy's Brigade, Pioneer Girl's and AWANA programs, and MBY meetings meant something for everyone and many congregations found their facilities stretched to maximum capacity on Wednesday evenings. The increasing segmentation of ages and interests required a host of volunteers, and increasingly, specialized staff. During the later part of the twentieth century, some congregations found themselves returning to a multiple ministry model, though on a paid, professional basis as youth pastors, music ministers, children's ministers and pastoral care staff were added. Large programs often meant more space needs, and many congregations built gyms or family life centers. Facilities and specialized programs were seen as necessary in order to effectively minister to congregations whose members were increasingly involved in the activities of the wider society. At the same time, this move toward multiple ministries directed at all ages and stages of life continued to be informed by an understanding of the local congregation as the central institution for both the social and religious life of its members.

As Mennonite Brethren congregations became increasingly urban, they found themselves having to become more intentional about nurturing the community aspect of the congregational life. Small fellowship groups, Sunday potlucks and even Wednesday night suppers were initiated as ways to encourage fellowship among members. With more women entering the workforce, many sewing circles struggled to stay active. New ministries with more specialized focus on the needs of women were begun. Programs for stay-at-home moms and Bible study groups often replaced the traditional mission-focused sewing circles. Many congregations also began to focus on the needs of senior members and began to sponsor special activities for this age group. Men's breakfast and Bible study groups, family activity nights, church retreats and camp-outs were other ways of gathering church members for fellowship and inspiration.

The mission emphasis that has been so present among Mennonite Brethren has also expressed itself in the outreach ministries of local congregations. Early on some congregations began specialized mission work to other minority ethnic groups, establishing small satellite congregations or Sunday school programs. During the 1940s and 1950s, some congregations used their choirs and music groups to advantage by establishing radio ministries while those in urban areas often participated in city evangelism crusades. A variety of evangelism programs were undertaken. Vacation Bible Schools became popular summer ministries aimed at children, while more elaborate Christmas productions and winter sweetheart banquets were aimed at adults. In more recent years, many congregations have found the Alpha program to be a helpful format for introducing friends and neighbors to the gospel and for incorporating them into the local church.

The tightly-knit community life of the congregation has often proven to be both the strength and weakness of Mennonite Brethren congregations. Its strength has been found in the strong sense of identity and belonging, the support and pastoral care for those within its circle, and the joy of shared vision and mission. At the same time, that strong sense of identity has sometimes

---

The Feet-washing Ceremony

When feet-washing was observed in the Mennonite Brethren Church in Henderson [Nebraska], it was always a part of the regular communion service. It occurred about twice a year.

This was the order of its observance: Because our communion services always ended with the exchange of the kiss of fellowship, the men and women were segregated for the service. It was appropriate, then, that they remained so for the washing of feet. After the observance of the Lord's Supper, the deacons who were serving brought in a number of towels and large basins of water, placing them on the floor by the front pew. In the meantime, the participants prepared for the washing. Neighbor asked neighbor for the privilege of washing his feet, each bared both feet, and in his turn walked down to the front of the church, where each washed the other's feet, dried them with the towel, and kissed him on his cheek. If there had been any hard feelings or differences between the two before, they were privately confessed at this time, and fellowship and love were restored. After each participant had taken his turn, the minister closed the service with a brief word bearing on the occasion, and the congregation sang the hymn, "Blest be the Tie that Binds," with joined hands.

—Ferne Hiebert

served as a barrier to those trying to break into the circle, or has seemed too confining to those most assimilated into North American society. Questions of church discipline during the early years of the conference often focused on issues of separation from the surrounding culture, even when that separation was from others who called themselves Christians. Both world wars forced congregations to struggle with questions of national loyalty, language and ethnic culture, as well as what it means to continue as a witness to peace. In mid-century, Canadian churches were faced with the challenge of assimilating another wave of Mennonite Brethren immigrants from South America and Russia just when the language transition from German to English was almost accomplished. Throughout Canada and the United States, congregations have struggled to make the transition from ethnic enclaves to more inclusive and diverse congregations and the question of what it means to be Mennonite Brethren has taken on new importance with the incorporation of other language groups such as the French, Chinese, Spanish, Koreans and Slavs, into the larger Conference. Congregations have struggled to separate theological identity from ethnic identity even as they tried to welcome and incorporate newcomers. Many congregations are engaged in a new transition as traditional worship formats give way to more contemporary styles of music and practice. Yet the mission emphasis that lies at the center of Mennonite Brethren congregations has given strong motivation to succeed at these challenges. In addition, the commitment to live together as a community of faith and to follow after our Lord in a life of obedient discipleship, continues to provide vision for Mennonite Brethren congregations.

12

Mennonite Brethren in a Changing Society

John H. Redekop

The twenty-two delegates who met in 1879 for the first North American Mennonite Brethren General Conference could not have imagined how this newly created organization would evolve. Since the first Mennonite Brethren had come to North America only five years earlier, they still looked back to their Russian experiences for guidelines, but they also looked forward. The ways this immigrant group defined its social, economic and political beliefs, how it evolved in these areas, and how society influenced its decisions constitutes fascinating history.

Urbanization

A crucial social change for North American Mennonite Brethren has been urbanization, a process that has greatly influenced individual, family, and denominational life. The first Mennonite Brethren immigrants all settled in rural areas, and remained there for several generations. A motto they carried from Russia and appropriately characterized them was "*Bibel und Pflug*" (Bible and Plow). Until World War II many retained a strong antipathy toward urban lifestyles; as late as 1920 there were virtually no urban congregations in the United States or Canada. The social and economic impact of the Great Depression and then of World War II began to change this situation. By the early 1970s, 56 percent of Mennonite Brethren in North America lived in towns of 2,500 residents or more, the highest percentage of any Mennonite group. By 2001 that percentage has apparently risen to well over 80 in Canada and to almost 80 in the United States.

The consequences of Mennonite Brethren urbanization during mid-century were substantial. Family life was often weakened because of differing community involvements, work schedules, diverse social activities, and the virtual disappearance of enclave settlement patterns. In rural settings the reality of families depending on one another in co-creating the crops had a deeper meaning than did working in a city factory. Also, in the country there were fewer challenges to traditional values.

Urbanization tends to weaken the sense of neighborhood and community. It also produces more marriages with people from outside the traditional faith or ethnic community. In an urban area there is also generally less knowledge of neighbors, less commonality of interests and values, and less communal activity. Further, the younger generation tends to be drawn to new values, especially after the memory of rural living has weakened. Where the number of urbanized group members is large and interactive, as for example in Winnipeg, these tendencies, although still strong, can be reduced.

The San Jose (Calif.) Mennonite Brethren Church was one of the earlier Mennonite Brethren congregations in a major urban area. Here, members pose in front of the American Legion Hall, where they met from 1940 to 1942.
(CMBS Fresno)

Adapting to the City: The Kerckhoff Community

Kerckhoff Avenue block party, Fresno, California, 1992. (CMBS Fresno)

As more Mennonite Brethren families moved to urban areas in the decades following World War II, some sought ways to preserve the face-to-face qualities of the small towns and rural areas from which they had come. One of the best examples of this effort can be seen in the "Kerckhoff Community" of Fresno, California.

Mennonite Brethren families first moved into homes on Kerckhoff Avenue, in an older part of Fresno, in the early 1970s. Some of these families had previously explored more intensive forms of community living, but had decided not to pursue those alternatives. Instead they chose to buy houses in close proximity to each other and to create a cooperative community in that way. In the summer of 1973 five families who had moved onto Kerckhoff Avenue, all part of the College Community Mennonite Brethren Church in Clovis, began meeting for weekly potlucks. Soon after, they also installed a community swimming pool in one of the yards.

Other families, mostly Mennonite Brethren but also from other church traditions, were drawn to the community on and around Kerckhoff Avenue. In addition to the weekly potlucks and swimming pool, the group gathered for annual Easter and Christmas events, sponsored traditional Russian Mennonite food festivals, created tool and food cooperatives, worked together to renovate and repair homes in the neighborhood, and hosted refugee families. While many of these activities no longer continue, the group still meets regularly for potlucks and holiday events.

In 1992 the Kerckhoff community organized a twentieth anniversary celebration, in which it invited back everyone who had ever participated in its activities. Over 230 people came from all over the United States to attend the three-day event, striking evidence of how important this effort to create an urban community has been for so many.

Examples of early Mennonite Brethren urban congregations: (top) Fresno, California [Bethany]; (upper left) Winnipeg, Man.[North End]; (upper right) Oklahoma City, Okla.; (bottom) Vancouver, B.C. (CMBS Fresno)

"The Shirtsleeve Millionaire"

The September 3, 1951, issue of *Life* magazine ran an article entitled the "Shirtsleeve Millionaires" that showcased newly-rich farmers of California's San Joaquin Valley. Among the ten profiled was Edward J. Peters. Born in Saskatchewan in 1905, Peters moved in 1920 with his father Simon Peters to Kern County in the south valley. In 1931 he married Elizabeth Willems, also of Saskatchewan. Soon after marriage he started Maple Leaf Enterprises by washing and grading potatoes for other area farmers. With time the company became a large diversified agri-business firm. The farming operations eventually grew to more than three thousand acres. Major crops included cotton, potatoes and alfalfa. His potato production made him one of the "potato kings" of the country. Other aspects of the business included a petroleum bulk plant, a cotton gin, a grain elevator, a radio-communications and farm equipment sales division, a radio broadcasting station.

One of the distinguishing features of KWSO, the radio station, was its commitment to classical music. Peters had inherited from his father what a local newspaper called "one of the state's finest private libraries of classical recordings." In an area more noted for its country western musical artists, KWSO ran programs entitled "Symphonic Treasures," "Portraits in Music," "Opera Library and Classics" and "Concert Hour and Music of the Masters." A typical program would include the music of the likes of Strauss, Dvorak, Schubert, Beethoven, Bach or Ravel.

The success of the various businesses, particularly potatoes, brought Peters local, state and national attention. In the early 1950s he was elected to successive terms as President of the National Potato Council and became a familiar figure in Washington, D.C. He received virtually every award that the local community and county could offer. Few in Kern County were as respected and as decorated as Peters.

He appeared on the Mennonite Brethren Conference scene in 1954 when he attended the General Conference sessions in Hillsboro, Kansas. His notoriety meant that people looked with curiosity and respect at this dignified and somewhat reserved gentleman. No issue at the 1954 conference was thornier than the question of Mennonite Brethren higher education. It is not surprising that he was elected chair of the newly organized US Board of Education. For the next eighteen years he chaired the board in what is surely one of the most creative periods in Mennonite Brethren higher education in North America. During this time Tabor College achieved regional accreditation, the Mennonite Brethren Biblical Seminary was established and also achieved accreditation and Pacific Bible Institute grew into a junior college and a senior college, also with accreditation.

(CMBS Fresno)

Other Mennonite agencies also benefited from his leadership and counsel. As a member of the Kern County Mental Health Board he was instrumental in the establishing of Kernview, the Mennonite Mental Health Hospital in Bakersfield. He was also one of the founding members of Mennonite Economic Development Associates (MEDA) and visited South America more than once to assess and nurture the organization's work in Paraguay.

Peter's most prosperous years were before he became involved in these various church-related organizations. He remarked on more than one occasion that precisely as he gave his attention to the work of the church his businesses declined. While the irony was striking, it in no way diminished his commitment to the work of the church or conference. Life, he said, "is too sacred a gift to be spent on selfish pursuits."

The Dilemma of Faith and Culture

"Many issues we faced during the 1940s and 1950s were cultural in nature, although we did not see them that way then. By making them cultural issues, some of them became occasions for acute conflict. Most Mennonite Brethren among whom I moved were immigrants who had come to Canada in the 1920s. Threatened by the new culture, they tried very hard to maintain the values of their European past.

"Crucial among these was the German language. In some houses English was strictly forbidden, though this was the language the children spoke in school. This caused deep rifts in some families. I spent Saturdays in German school for several years, and loathed it deeply. We young people were eager to shake off our European past and to identify with our Canadian friends at school. . . .

"The language conflict in church was often more acute than in the home, because the faith of our parents was somehow bound up with their mother tongue. For us as teenagers it sounded a bit comical to hear leading churchmen explain, that with the loss of German we also would lose our faith. . . .

"There were other tensions caused by clashes in cultural mores. There were certain European patterns of behavior that parents expected their children to perpetuate. Women were to dress conservatively, and sometimes a preacher who—as it was then said—was not afraid to speak the truth, aimed his wrath at the sisters who wore short-sleeved dresses. Also, it was thought bad form for women to wear their hair short, because of, what I consider a misinterpretation of 1 Corinthians. Once at the Canadian Conference, when I was moderator, I was taken aback when a woman got up and asked what we were going to do about the fact that she had been excommunicated years ago for cutting her hair. . . .

"The wearing of jewelry was generally taboo, particularly since, according to the book of Judges, the Midianites had worn earrings. (That Eleazar gave Rebekah a nose ring, weighing half a shekel, was overlooked.)"

—Adapted from David Ewert's "Theological Autobiography" in Bridging Troubled Waters: The Mennonite Brethren at Mid-Twentieth Century *(Kindred Productions, 1995).*

Although urbanization was having a major impact on most Mennonite Brethren in North America by mid-century, the General Conference did not seriously address the issue until 1978. Noting that 75 percent of society lived in urban centers, the Board of Reference and Counsel acknowledged that "the revolution which most challenges the North American Mennonite Brethren church today is the move from rural to urban to metropolitan." But in spelling out a response, the Board focused almost entirely on new ways of ministering in urban settings. It said virtually nothing about the impact on the Mennonite Brethren church itself.

Vocational diversification

Alongside urbanization, Mennonite Brethren also experienced wide-ranging vocational diversification. Until about 1920, approximately 80 percent of Mennonite Brethren lived on farms. Another 10 percent or so worked in farm-related vocations as mechanics, carpenters, cobblers, tailors, small-town retailers, grain elevator operators or domestics. Only about 10 percent worked in all other occupations.

Following World War II the situation changed drastically. By 1960 only about half of the Mennonite Brethren in Canada and the US were involved in agricultural pursuits. By 1990 the number declined to a third, and by 2001 Mennonite Brethren on farms were a small minority. Instead they can be found working in a broad diversity of vocations.

Changing Educational Patterns

The shift to urban lifestyles and vocations were accompanied by changes in education patterns. In the early decades, many Mennonite Brethren young people dropped out of school after grade eight and few pursued higher education. It is estimated that in Canada, until World War II, only two or three percent pursued education beyond high school or Bible school, which, until the 1950s, operated largely at the high school level. In the US the figure was higher but still probably below five percent. Because of urbanization, acculturation and prosperity, that pattern changed drastically after World War II.

By 1972, 36 percent of North American Mennonite Brethren had acquired education beyond the high school level and 11 percent had completed a graduate degree. By 1982 the percentage of Mennonite Brethren with post-high school education had reached 48 percent.

While higher education has led to some shifting in ethical values, basic Christian beliefs and practices have remained strong among more highly educated Mennonite Brethren. The suspicion among some in the denomination that higher education undermines Christian faith is statistical-

Generosity in times of need

C. A. DeFehr (CMBS Winnipeg)

Few businessmen have as successfully combined business acumen and churchly leadership as Cornelius A. DeFehr (1881-1979). He was born in South Russia just as Mennonite commercial and industrial enterprises began to flourish. After marrying Elizabeth Dyck (1885-1972) he moved in 1903 to Millerovo, and fast became a leader in the developing Mennonite Brethren church and Mennonite businesses of the area. He built a thriving machine factory that produced seeding machines, threshing machines, hydraulic oil presses, and many of the parts for cylindric mills. Before the onset of World War I more than one hundred employees worked in the factory and the annual business totaled more than one million rubles.

The animosity toward Germans during World War I, the ensuing civil war between the supporters and opponents of the Bolshevik Revolution, the nationalizing of industrial plants and personal threats forced the DeFehrs to leave Millerovo. After nightfall on December 7, 1919, together with other families, they left for what would be six years of uncertainty before arriving in Canada in 1925.

The trip to Canada involved a stopover in Hamburg, Germany. There DeFehr visited Herman Schuett, a Mennonite businessman in the city, whose company had supplied the motors for the mills that the factory had produced in Millerovo. Schuett knew that DeFehr was a man on the run, moving to a new country and facing the difficulties of any new immigrant. Yet confident of DeFehr, he gave him the following assurance:

"Our mutual business association began, Mr. DeFehr, when you started in a very small way in Millerovo. At that time I gave you my confidence, and I have never been disappointed. We will now make a new beginning. See what you can do in Canada. Order what you can use, and I will give you open credit on all your orders."

DeFehr had hardly settled his family in Manitoba when he began importing hardware through the Hamburg Export and Import Company of Heinrich Schuett. By the spring of 1926 DeFehr opened a business headquarters in downtown Winnipeg. Credit financing by Schuett quickly permitted him to develop a brisk business. The product lines soon increased to a variety of general hardware tools, household appliances and agricultural machinery. A growing dimension of the business was imported cream separators from the Westphalia Separator Company of Werner and Hugo Habig. The business quickly expanded from a small area in southern Manitoba across the Canadian prairies. By 1929 sales were approaching $75,000. The products were almost entirely European-made and mostly from Germany.

While the depression years took their toll, the business survived and then flourished in the post-World War II boom. By 1947 net profits were over $80,000. By then C.A. DeFehr's interests were largely focused on church and Mennonite agency work. His insights and financial support were important to the development of many Mennonite agencies and institutions in both North and South America.

In these prosperous years following the war DeFehr did not forget that his business partners in Germany were facing difficulty. Now DeFehr could reciprocate and assist them as the Shuett family had helped them in the 1920s. When the war started the Canadian government seized a large shipment of cream separators because they were deemed to be enemy goods. Eventually they were sold to DeFehr for pennies on the dollar. DeFehr, however, kept the original invoice and invested the amount in his company. The investment grew during the war and, when it was over, he extended the full credit to the Habig family. They came to Winnipeg and took back to Germany goods of an equal amount. In addition the Defehrs sent many aid packages to both the Habigs and Shuett families.

The relationship between members of the C.A. DeFehr clan and the Shuett and Habig families continues to this day. The continuing friendship is based not only on past business relationships but also on this rich history of businessmen, on both sides of the ocean, practicing mutual aid and extending financial credit to those in need.

—*Adapted from* Memories of My Life, *by C. A. DeFehr, (privately published, 1967) and conversation with Cornelius DeFehr.*

ly unwarranted. Studies in the 1970s and 1980s indicated that church members with more education actually rated higher in several key indicators of faith and religious devotion than did their less-educated counterparts. Higher education has not produced secularization.

Prosperity

The Mennonite Brethren immigrants who arrived in the 1870s and shortly thereafter generally were people of very modest means. Most of the thousands who fled Russia after the First World War or World War II were destitute.

While there was considerable prosperity in the 1920s, virtually all Mennonite Brethren in North America suffered serious financial setbacks during the Great Depression of the 1930s. Many Mennonite farmers lost their farms during those drought-plagued years.

With the end of the drought and the beginning of the war in 1939, prosperity returned. One of the great ironies in Mennonite history is the fact that these pacifists experienced unprecedented financial progress because of the war. It generated jobs at good wages, markets for crops with good prices, and business opportunities of unprecedented proportions.

When the war ended in 1945, many Mennonite Brethren in North America had become prosperous. The economic boom, furthermore, continued after the war. By 1960 most Mennonite Brethren in North America had moved into the middle class.

Due in part to this prosperity, one senses today a loss of suspicion toward "the world" by many Mennonite Brethren. In fact, some church members seem to be struggling with the cult of acquisitiveness. Upward mobility and affluence have also reinforced individualism and a sense of self-sufficiency. The extent to which Mennonite Brethren are preoccupied with how to spend their money suggests that new forms of hedonism have become serious temptations.

This new prosperity, however, also enabled Mennonite Brethren to support missions, schools, camps and many other denominational programs. It is not coincidental that the post-war period brought an institutional and programmatic expansion that to this day remains unparalleled. In many cases prosperity gave Mennonite Brethren the ability to put into practice many of their Anabaptist principles.

Have prosperity and wealth corrupted Mennonite Brethren? Evidence suggests that has not generally happened. Studies from the 1970s and 1980s suggest that in the areas of devotionalism—prayer, Bible study and "seeking God's will"—wealthy Mennonite Brethren rank only marginally lower than low-income respondents. In "closeness to God," however, they rank sixteen points lower. In church attendance and serving in church leadership posts, they rank significantly higher. In orthodoxy of belief the two groups are virtually identical. High income Mennonite Brethren evidence a greater regard for certain social ethics but also have greater toleration for some general practices such as moderate drinking and social dancing. In sum, the most affluent are not necessarily the least religious; in the maintenance of many areas they rank higher than other Mennonite Brethren.

It is noteworthy that until at least 1975 there is no recorded General Conference recommendation dealing with prosperity. Even after 1975 little was said or decided. The attentiveness of the US and Canadian conference has not been much better, although the Canadian conference in 1975 did hear a major paper on stewardship and the mobilizing of resources and passed two resolutions prescribing ethical guidelines. The General Conference Confession of Faith has also been notably silent in this area, until an article on this topic appeared for the first time in the 1999 edition.

Language Transition

The original Mennonite Brethren settlers in the US and Canada generally spoke both High German and Mennonite Low German. Church services were conducted only in High German. In rural areas these languages remained dominant, even though the children learned English in school.

The situation changed first in the US, largely because Mennonite Brethren had settled there earlier and because there had been little subsequent infusion of German-speaking Mennonite Brethren from Europe. By the 1930s English was rapidly replacing German in the homes and in some churches. When World War II broke out, with Germany an enemy country, English made increasing inroads in US Mennonite Brethren churches, especially in urban congregations. By the late 1940s, the transition was virtually complete.

In Canada, because Mennonite Brethren pioneers came later, the use of German persisted longer, and German remained the dominant language until well past World War II. The influx of thousands of German-speaking Mennonite Brethren from Europe and Latin America sustained the need for German. Not until the late 1950s did English make major inroads in the churches, and only in the late 1960s did it become dominant in most churches. German is still used in some six to eight Canadian Mennonite Brethren churches.

The language debate nearly split some congregations. Some advocates for the retention of German argued that German language and culture were of higher quality than English and should therefore be retained. Some tried to create a link between German and Christian values. The Canadian Conference *Kommittee für die Deutsche Sprache* ["Committee for the German Language"] vigorously advanced such arguments until its demise in 1963. Those who pressed for a speedy transition to English argued that it was necessary to retain young people, to be faithful to the Great Commission, and to enable new converts to join the church.

One reason why the language debate in both countries was not more divisive than it turned out to be was the exceptional goodwill and gracious spirit exhibited by many older Mennonite Brethren for whom German had remained their language of worship and prayer. Some elderly saints, almost in tears at the loss of what was very dear to them, stated at church business meetings, in halting English, that for the sake of the younger generation and the advancement of the Kingdom, English should be adopted.

Ethnic Identity

Many Mennonite groups, including the Mennonite Brethren, have historically been an ethno-religious community. Driven into seclusion in order to survive religious persecution, they also became a distinct ethnic group and brought this identity with them to North America. As long as most of these Mennonite Brethren lived in rural enclaves, the issue of ethnic identity was not controversial. Their particular fusion of faith and culture was a comfortable and mainly successful arrangement. As Mennonite Brethren began to more freely mix with the larger national cultures, in both the United States and Canada, the question of the ethnic and religious components of their identity became important. The fact that people of various ethnic groups began joining the Mennonite Brethren, either as individuals or entire congregations, also increasingly focused the question.

In Canada the matter of Mennonite Brethren and general Mennonite identity became important with the outbreak of World War II. The issue of exemption from military service fueled the public discussion. Were Mennonites German? A few Mennonites said that they were. Others

Nonresistance and Church Membership: The Dilemma of World War I

Mennonites who came to the United States in the 1870s did so with the vague promise that they would never be asked to serve in the nation's military. The United States' entry into World War I proved that promise to be false. The full-scale mobilization of troops during 1917 presented a serious challenge to nonresistant churches such as the Mennonite Brethren, and forced them to address issues that they had otherwise taken for granted. One of these issues for Mennonite Brethren had to do with its definition of church membership.

According to historian James C. Juhnke, "Many youths of draft age identified personally and culturally with the MB community but could not claim the conversion experience required for baptism and membership. [At this time it was not uncommon for Mennonite Brethren to wait for baptism and membership until in their twenties.] The Selective Service law required that to qualify as conscientious objectors, pacifists had to be certified as members of a well-established pacifist church or sect. How could MB sons who were not yet church members be certified? The MB Conference resolved the problem with a kind of halfway covenant. They arranged that a drafted youth might receive one of two official certificates. A bona fide member would receive a 'Certificate of Church Membership.' A nonmember might receive a 'Certificate of Church Relationship'—if he had at least one parent who was a church member, was a regular attender at worship services, and was registered in the church book as a 'child of our brothers and sisters.' . . . This arrangement satisfied draft authorities."

—Adapted from James C. Juhnke, Vision, Doctrine, War: Mennonite Identity and Organization in America, 1890-1930 *(Herald Press, 1989).*

described themselves as Dutch. Some said they were German-speaking but not German. Others said that they were simply Canadians with European background.

Beginning in the 1960s, Canadian governmental support for multiculturalism and the retention of ethnic identity sharpened the question. Mennonites in Canada were forced to rethink who they were. At the same time it became clear that, even after widespread transition to English, a strong sense of Mennonite ethnic identity persisted. Meanwhile, in the United States, the acculturation, but not social absorption, of Mennonite Brethren was continuing.

In both countries, however, the issue of ethnic identity became important as an increasing number of Mennonite Brethren churches dropped the term "Mennonite" from their name, choosing instead names such as "Bible Church" or "Community Church." Motivation for such action, in both new and long-standing congregations, seemed to be a desire to minimize pacifism and other distinctive beliefs and to be inclusive rather than ethnically specific.

By the 1970s, several additional realities focused this question, particularly but not only in Canada. First, the media began referring to certain artists, writers, politicians and others as Mennonites although those people were not church members or, in some cases, even Christians. The reality of "secular Mennonites," at least in public perception, could not be denied. Second, governments, at all levels, generally included Mennonites in their listings of ethnic groups. Third, encyclopedias and other scholarly works treated Mennonites as an ethnic, or at least an ethno- religious, group. Fourth, television programs and movies that focused on Old Order Mennonites or Amish conditioned the public to view Mennonites as ethnic. Also, certain Mennonite regions in the US and Canada successfully promoted themselves as tourist attractions. In Winnipeg and elsewhere, Mennonites set up ethnic booths in folk festivals. The perception of Mennonites as ethnic was reinforced when many Mennonite agencies, including inter-Mennonite and Canadian Mennonite Brethren entities, successfully applied to the Canadian and provincial governments for ethnic and multicultural grants.

A purely religious definition had become very problematic. More than a few people, not ethnically Mennonite, who were attending and joining Mennonite Brethren churches were perplexed. Many Mennonite Brethren churches responded by suppressing their Mennonite identity as well as their Anabaptist/Mennonite theology and changed their name.

In more recent years the paradox of minimizing the historic Mennonite identity rooted in Russia and elsewhere, while celebrating the rich cultural diversity of new congregations and new immigrant groups that have joined the conference, has become evident. We all are increasingly recognizing that faith is always embedded in culture and a Germanic Mennonite Brethren form is just as legitimate as other forms. Unfortunately, for some the complications continue because in

"From Cowering Fear to Spiritual Confidence": A Conscientious Objector in World War II

An eighteen-year-old naive farm boy. A committed church member. Head of the class academically, but socially considerably lower. President Franklin D. Roosevelt invited me to join the military for World War II. My congregation, the South Fairview (Okla.) Mennonite Brethren Church, suggested that I opt for alternative service work in Civilian Public Service.

Hints of trouble ahead came at my physical exam, where I was condemned to the nether parts by an examining Marine. My parents' home would be rotten-egged. The church's windows were shot through. Two of us departed for the CPS camp at Downey, Idaho, on a September night in 1943. We soon learned to avoid other passengers because they wondered why healthy young men were not in uniform. We sat on our luggage between the cars. We blinked several times upon entering camp, where a dozen Amish men were weaving rugs.

On my first furlough I was cursed at the wheat elevator. A group of younger peers planned to ambush me on my walk home one Saturday night. Thirty-two months later, after a thousand letters from my soon-to-be wife, and after holding rather responsible positions while so young, I returned home a convinced Anabaptist. I did not know that in the next year my congregation would thrust me into the ministry. Like a flower "forced" to blossom prematurely, I moved from cowering fear to spiritual confidence in an unfriendly world.

—*Marvin Hein*

Felling trees at Civilian Public Service Unit #31, Camino, California. (CMBS Fresno)

Alternative Service in Canada during World War II

"The first time I declared that I would not take up arms and go to war was at a supper table at Prairie Bible Institute in 1940. The men around the table (there was strict segregation of the sexes in the dining hall) thought it strange that a young man would be so unpatriotic, disloyal and cowardly as not to defend his country in time of war.

"I do not recall receiving any teaching or instruction about nonresistance either in the Coaldale MB Church or in the Bible school I attended for three years. Only during the 1950s did churches have peace conferences, seminars and lectures. However, when conscription and the prospect of a draft loomed in 1941, our church leader, Rev. B. B. Janz, asked all the eligible young men to remain in church after the morning service for an announcement.

"He then told us: 'Now you young brethren know that we are conscientious objectors and that we do not take up arms and go to war.' Measures would be taken so that we could do alternative service, but we would have to appear before a Selective Service Board for an interrogation or examination. To prepare us for the interview we had several meetings or briefings at which the historical position and a few Bible passages were given to us as the basis for this stance. . . .

"We had been briefed on biblical nonresistance but not on the philosophical base. The word pacifism was rarely used except when university trained men who had studied the philosophies of Tolstoy, Gandhi and Schweitzer espoused the evils of war. Some Mennonites began to use the term pacifism in place of biblical nonresistance, though I prefer the biblical base to the philosophical. . . .

"It seems to me that the whole matter of ASW [Alternative Service Work] was handled in an unproductive way. Both we and the government officials regarded it as a way to avoid discrimination. It removed us from the public eye.' . . . We thought we would be home after four months of basic training time as required of army recruits. However, men were soon called to serve for the duration of the war. . . .

"Most of us benefitted from the inter-church association and fellowship. We cultivated our own spiritual lives and learned from each other how to develop good devotional habits. By being responsible for much of our nurture, we learned leadership responsibilities. . . .

"Alternative Service during World War II played a greater role in our lives than we realized at the time. It added significantly to development in Mennonite history by impacting a whole generation of men who became pastors of our churches, teachers in our colleges and leaders in our conferences."

—Adapted from Henry R. Baerg in A. J. Klassen, ed., Alternative Service for Peace in Canada During World War II, 1941-1946, edited by A.J. Klassen *(Mennonite Central Committee-B.C. and Seniors for Peace, 1998).*

Canada, the United States and some other countries "Mennonite" refers to both a faith tradition and an ethnic group.

Political Stances

The early years of Mennonite Brethren life in North America produced a series of negative statements on political participation. In the first unofficial conference session, in 1878, the delegates decided "that members are not permitted to hold government offices or take any part in the polls. However, we appreciate the protection we enjoy under our Government." An 1888 resolution stated "that in regard to national political conventions, it is strongly advised that, while we desire to have a good government, members should be careful so as not to defile their conscience. However, the Conference does not want to form a definite resolution in this matter." In 1890, the conference recommended "that members of the church refrain from participation and involvement in the contentions of political parties, but are permitted to vote quietly at elections, and may also vote for 'prohibition.'" It was further agreed, in 1893, "that our brethren shall not hold the offices of justice of the peace or constable. A member may be a 'notary public.'" In 1900 the assembled Mennonite Brethren delegates agreed not to use courts of law to settle their disputes.

Despite the above decisions, one can identify a continuous strand of political activism. A major concern, given the Conference's peace position, dealt with exemption from military conscription. The Mennonite Brethren Conference frequently reviewed, debated and refined its stance concerning its pacifist relationship to the state. Numerous requests were relayed to the Canadian and US governments to establish alternatives to military service, and these generally were successful.

In 1924, in a marked departure from previous pronouncements, the Conference endorsed political activism, affirming that "we consider it our duty to maintain the position to our Government, stated in Jer. 29:7, and in I Tim. 2:1. This includes that we endeavor to influence our government, especially the legislative body, to maintain peace and to abstain from war."

After World War II, activism took on additional dimensions when the traditional Anabaptist definition of the peace position as avoidance of war was greatly expanded to include prescriptions of policy for national governments in Canada and especially in the US. In a watershed 1969 resolution The

Jake Epp: Politician Extraordinaire

As a thirty-two-year-old high school history teacher and municipal councillor, this son of a Mennonite Brethren minister, and member of the Steinbach (Man.) Mennonite Brethren Church, was first elected in 1972 to the Canadian House of Commons. After having been elected six times as the Progressive Conservative Member of Parliament for his home constituency of Provencher, Jake Epp decided not to be a candidate in the 1993 national election.

When the Progressive Conservatives briefly formed the national government in 1979-1980, Prime Minister Joe Clark appointed Epp as Minister of Indian Affairs and Northern Development, the first Mennonite member in a national Cabinet. Apparently he was also the first national Cabinet member who did not take the oath of office but instead spoke a simple statement of affirmation.

When the Progressive Conservatives regained power in 1984, Prime Minister Brian Mulroney appointed Epp as Minister of Health and Welfare, a position he held until 1989. From 1989 to 1993 he served as Minister of Mines and Energy.

It is generally agreed that Epp made his greatest contribution as Minister of Health and Welfare. One of his key achievements was the gradual elimination of smoking from air travel. In 1992 retired US Surgeon General C. Everett Koop lauded Epp as mainly responsible for the North America-wide smoking ban on airline flights.

While occasionally, although rarely, ridiculed for his faith convictions, Epp was respected and widely praised for his integrity throughout his twenty-one year tenure in national politics. It was said of him that "He has no enemies in Parliament." Nationally syndicated columnist Jeffrey Simpson described him as "a good and decent man." Another reporter in a national daily wrote that "if the Conservative Government were to be a person, it would probably want to be Jake Epp."

During Epp's twenty-one years in Ottawa he was the strongest and clearest evangelical voice in Canadian politics. Brian Stiller, long-time Executive Director of the Evangelical Fellowship of Canada, observed that Epp "has consistently and biblically provided leadership and given witness to the gospel more than any [other] person I know."

In an arena in which many individuals marginalize their moral principles, Jake Epp has consistently held to his convictions and his calling to Christian servanthood. For good reason he is widely respected as a Christian statesman.

(CMBS Winnipeg)

—*John Redekop*

Mennonite Brethren General Conference affirmed its "historic position on peace and non-resistance" but it also stressed the church's "ministry of reconciliation and restoration" as well as the need "to promote peace" and affirmed "that the church has a prophetic role in relation to the state. Whenever the government fails in its divinely ordained function of administering justice and promoting peace, it is the Christian's responsibility to express his concern, and to witness against the abuses of power and the miscarriage of justice." This endorsement of political activism has been incorporated into the 1999 Confession of Faith.

Even before the 1969 approval of political activism, the Conference had occasionally expressed political sentiments. In 1921 it wrote to President Harding "in recognition of the President's interest in the question of demobilization and abolition of war." In 1939 it agreed "that the delegates from Canada and the United States express their gratitude to the governments of our cherished lands for pursuing a program of liberty and justice toward all men." In 1943, amidst war fever, the Conference stated "that we affirm our undivided loyalty to our country and to our government, which has graciously provided [alternative service to] our young men." In 1951 the delegates stated "that we prove ourselves sincerely grateful to our God and to the rulers of our countries for the considerate provisions made for conscientious objectors to war."

In 1975 the Conference passed two significant resolutions. One expressed "a word of caution against the violation of our peace-position by an endorsement of either Israel or Arab militarism or terrorism." The other approved letters "thanking the USA and Canadian Governments for the freedom we enjoy and the assistance we received by way of material aid for our world-wide relief program."

Clearly, Mennonite Brethren attitudes toward governments have undergone a major shift. By the early 1970s, only 2 percent of Mennonite Brethren agreed that "The state (national, provincial, and state government) is basically an evil force in the world, an opponent or enemy of the church and its program." Only 26 percent agreed that "It is not the business of the church to try to influence the actions of government in regard to such issues as war and peace, race relations, poverty, etc."

Partisan Political Involvement

Already in the late nineteenth century Mennonite Brethren in the US began running for political office, mostly at the local level. It appears that in Canada such initiatives began in the 1920s. Participation increased slowly. Then, in the twenty years between 1940 and 1960, Mennonite Brethren entered the electoral arenas in large numbers, especially in Canada. This high rate of politica candidacies has continued, again especially in Canada.

Scores of Canadian Mennonite Brethren have run for partisan office and many have been elected. Two, the Hon. Jake Epp and the Hon. Raymond Chan, have served as federal cabinet members. Many have served in provincial cabinets and, of course, in provincial and national legislatures. In one case, two Mennonite Brethren, members of the same church in Swift Current, Saskatchewan, sat in the provincial legislature, one as a cabinet member and the other as a leading member of the official opposition.

While the situation in the United States has not been researched as thoroughly, many Mennonite Brethren have been candidates at local, state and even national levels, though not to the same extent as in Canada. Many have served with distinction in elective offices. Harvey Wollman served as Lieutenant Governor and as Acting Governor of South Dakota. His brother, Roger, who served as a Supreme Court Justice in that state, administered the oath of office.

The Wollman Brothers: Mennonite Brethren Politicians in South Dakota

Harvey Wollman
(The Christian Leader)

Roger and Harvey Wollman, long-time members of the Ebenezer Mennonite Brethren Church of Doland, South Dakota, each have served in several of the highest elective offices in South Dakota state government. Roger Wollman, the older of the two brothers, and a lawyer by profession, was elected Brown County State's Attorney in 1966, and served in that capacity until his election to the South Dakota Supreme Court in 1970. He served on the state's highest court from 1971 to 1985, including four years as Chief Justice. In 1985, he was appointed by President Ronald Reagan to the Eighth Circuit of the United States Court of Appeals, based in St. Louis, Missouri. Justice Wollman is still serving on the Appellate Court bench there, and was elected Presiding Judge in 1999.

Harvey Wollman, a farmer, rancher and businessman from Frankfort, South Dakota, was elected State Senator in 1968 and served in that capacity until 1974. In 1970 he was selected by his peers to be the Minority Leader, and in 1972 he became Senate Majority Leader. In 1975, he was elected Lieutenant Governor of South Dakota, and became Governor of South Dakota when the Governor then serving was appointed Ambassador to Singapore. Governor Wollman served in that office until January 1979. His swearing in at the Capitol in Pierre was a historic event, in that it was the first time in state history that one brother, as Chief Justice, administered the oath of office to another brother becoming Governor, in the presence of their father, Edwin Wollman, deacon at the Ebenzer Mennonite Brethren Church. The inauguration was also marked by the offering of the invocation by Reverend Edwin Goossen, pastor of the Ebenezer Mennonite Brethren Church. Another church and family connection at the inaugural was the singing of the national anthem by Anne Wollman, Harvey's wife and the choir director at the Ebenezer Church.

The Ebenezer Church is one of the former Krimmer Mennonite Brethren congregations that joined the Mennonite Brethren Conference in 1960. Harvey later served on both the General Conference Board of Missions and Services and the Mennonite Brethren Biblical Seminary Board of Directors.

—*Alan Peters*

Mennonite Brethren voting habits indicate a tendency to support conservative orientations. Mennonite Brethren in the United States have typically voted overwhelmingly for Republican candidates. In the early 1970s, 39 percent of Canadian Mennonite Brethren reported that they voted Conservative with another 32 percent supporting the Social Credit Party, another conservative group. Twenty-three percent voted Liberal while only 5 percent supported the democratic-socialist New Democratic Party. A 1992 investigation of earlier voting patterns in both the US and Canada revealed similar percentages.

In recent decades Mennonite Brethren have become politically informed and generally supportive of government. In a 1972 study some 98 percent agreed that Mennonite Brethren should vote in public elections, 84 percent said that Mennonite Brethren could hold local, state, provincial or national elective office, and 60 percent felt that Mennonite Brethren should witness directly to elected officials by writing letters and by other means.

Conclusion

Mennonite Brethren in the US and Canada have experienced major transitions since the General Conference was founded in 1879. Urbanization, rising education levels, prosperity, acculturation, upward social mobility, political opportunity, and various social pressures have all played a part. It is encouraging to see that amidst this kaleidoscope of transitions, the Mennonite Brethren Conference has struggled, with considerable success, to hold fast to what is true and praiseworthy in God's sight and to apply Christian truths to its times and surroundings.

13

Broadening Our Horizons

Wally Unger

The Mennonite Brethren Church of today is vastly different than the one that began in South Russia in 1860. In its early years the Mennonite Brethren were a people of Dutch and Germanic background. While they sojourned in different lands—Poland, Russia, North America and South America—they remained a bonded community. Today the Mennonite Brethren Church has become a mosaic of many cultures, languages and ethnic groups. Eight French-speaking churches in Quebec are a provincial conference of the Canadian Mennonite Brethren. The US Conference has six African-American congregations in its North Carolina District. Hispanic churches make up 23 percent of the US Conference with thirty-one congregations in California, Oregon and Washington. An additional eight churches comprise the Latin American Mennonite Brethren District in South Texas. Forty Slavic congregations, totaling about eight thousand individuals, have affiliated or are in the process of affiliating with the US Conference. Mennonite Brethren in North America now worship in more than twenty different languages.

In Canada, most church growth has occurred in British Columbia, mainly through the efforts of the Board of Church Extension. The BC Conference of Mennonite Brethren Churches doubled the number of congregations to 106 between 1991 and 2001. Most of this growth came through establishing or adopting churches of various ethnic identities—Chinese, Laotian, Arabic, Persian, Indonesian, Korean, Vietnamese and Punjabi. There are twenty Asian churches in the BC Conference.

A childrens' parade by the South Side Mission in Minnesota, date unknown.
(CMBS Fresno)

The goal is to become a church that embraces all cultures and ethnic groups, a reflection of the all-inclusiveness of the kingdom of God. Mennonite Brethren are beginning to broaden their horizons. How did this broadening of the vision evolve? The answer lies in the Anabaptist origins of the Mennonite Brethren, and the renewing of that vision in Russia and beyond.

The Great Commission—still binding

The early Anabaptists saw the Great Commission as binding upon all believers. Their zeal for evangelism was unique among sixteenth-century Christians. Many early Anabaptists left their families and jobs to become wandering missionaries, supported only by what fellow brothers and sisters gave them. These Anabaptists took the Great Commission seriously and shared their faith often at the cost of persecution and martyrdom.

By the end of the sixteenth century the Mennonite zeal for spreading the Gospel had waned. Not until the early part of the nineteenth century was the missionary spirit once again revived in Prussia through the influence of the Moravian Brethren. The Prussian Mennonite congregation that established the village of Gnadenfeld, Russia, in 1835 brought that interest in evangelism with it. In 1860 a group from the Gnadenfeld Church seceded to form the nucleus of the

Early Mennonite Brethren evangelistic work often focused on preaching to unconverted members within the church community. Here, itinerant evangelist John Harms (center) is standing with several people converted during evangelistic meetings in Anaheim, California, ca. 1905. (CMBS Fresno)

Mennonite Brethren Church, carrying the mission spirit to the new church.

Sharing their faith was very important to the members of the newly-established Mennonite Brethren Church. Only twelve years after the founding of the church, the Brethren met for their first conference. At this convention the delegates established an itinerant ministry for evangelism and church extension. One of these evangelists was Johann Wieler, who had a burden to evangelize Russians even though it was against the law to do so. To proselytize among members of the Orthodox Church bore the penalty of imprisonment or exile to Siberia. Nevertheless, Wieler witnessed to the Russians, as did other Mennonite Brethren. In 1883, after the conference rejected Wieler's proposal for further evangelistic efforts, he carried on an effective independent ministry among the Russians in the Odessa area. After baptizing a Russian woman, Wieler was sentenced to exile in Siberia. He escaped to Germany, however, where he ministered to Russian Baptists until his death in 1889.

Members of the Mennonite Brethren Church shared their faith primarily with their Mennonite neighbors and also with nearby German Lutherans. When numerous Russians were converted and baptized, the Brethren helped in establishing Baptist churches and converts were advised to join them. No Mennonite Brethren churches were established among the Russians. To do so would have been an infringement of the law and endangered the status of the Mennonite Brethren Church in Russia.

Relating to "the World"

"Another question that troubled us greatly was how to relate to our non-Mennonite neighbors—designated as the 'world.' In school we were with other ethnic groups, but after school we had next to no contact with them. We were constantly warned against friendship with the world and it would not have occurred to us to invite non-Mennonite neighbors (or even General Conference Mennonites) to our home.

"This became a serious theological problem for us when our teachers in Bible school encouraged us to witness to our faith in our community. Our efforts at missions had to be kept at a safe distance from the local church. One outlet for us was to teach Daily Vacation Bible School in country schools away from our community. Even if we had wanted to invite a neighbor-friend to church it would have been pointless, for our services in the 1940s were still in German."

—*Adapted from David Ewert's "Theological Autobiography" in* Bridging Troubled Waters: The Mennonite Brethren at Mid-Twentieth Century *(Kindred Productions, 1995).*

Mennonite Brethren ministers, deacons and missionaries in North Carolina, 1947.
(CMBS Fresno)

Early years in North America

Although there was a fresh missionary impulse in the Mennonite Brethren Church in Russia, there were also elements of conservatism and isolationism that restricted the zeal for outreach. Evangelistic work among the Russians was very limited and was done largely through individual efforts. Mennonite Brethren in Russia reflected an essentially rural piety that was reluctant to enlarge its horizons.

This isolationist spirit was carried to North America in the migrations of the 1870s. These immigrants moved to rural farming communities in the Midwest of the United States and the prairie provinces of Canada. The inclination toward rural settlement was reflected in Conference policy. At the 1883 Mennonite Brethren General Conference in Henderson, Nebraska, delegates passed a resolution on living in cities. The consensus was that while members could not be forbidden to move to the city, they should be warned of the dangers of such a move. Over the next half century, most Mennonite Brethren heeded this warning.

The first attempts in North America to go beyond Mennonite Brethren ethnic borders were mission endeavors among the Comanche Indians in Oklahoma Territory in 1896 and Russians in Saskatchewan in the early 1900s. City mission work was begun in Minneapolis in 1909 and in Winnipeg in 1913.

The Post Oak Mission in Oklahoma, initiated by the Board of Foreign Missions, was the first tangible step committing Mennonite Brethren in North America to becoming an all-nations church. The first missionary at Post Oak was Henry Kohfeld, followed after twelve years by Abraham J. and Magdalena Becker. The Beckers' thirty-seven year ministry had a significant impact on thousands of Comanches in Oklahoma. In 1959, the Post Oak Mission became an independent Mennonite Brethren Church.

Children arriving at Vacation Bible School in Dalmeny, Saskatchewan, 1959.
(CMBS Winnipeg)

Missionaries at Post Oak broadened their vision to reach people of Mexican background living on the fringes of Lawton, Oklahoma. A Mexican mission church was established there in 1937. In 1964 the Lawton Church became a member of the Southern District Conference. Also in 1937, Harry and Sarah

"Here Build Jesus House"

"Missionary Henry Kohfeld's initial efforts to gain Comanche support for a mission proved discouraging. From his base at the Deyo Comanche Mission, fifteen miles southwest of Fort Sill, he traveled extensively on horseback across the western section of the reservation seeking to win over the people. Apparently the Indians did not find the black-bearded foreigner, who spoke English with a German accent, very convincing. . . . After two-and-a-half months of fruitless endeavors, and with his expense account of $150 diminished, the missionary-designate was so frustrated he contemplated giving up. In that 'dark hour of temptation,' he later related, he fell on his knees on the hot, dry prairie and prayed for guidance. A voice told him not to 'flee like a Jonah,' but to 'put your trust in God who will give you victory.'

"Reinvigorated, Kohfeld decided to take his plea directly to Chief Quanah Parker, who apparently had been away from home much of this time. The Fort Sill Indian agent, who had given Kohfeld little assistance previously, cooperated by providing an interpreter [a Christian convert of the Dutch Reformed Mission] and a team and wagon. As they made their way toward Quanah's home, Kohfeld promised the interpreter his prized watch for help in persuading the chief to grant land for a mission. . . . Quanah was not at home when Kohfeld and the interpreter arrived, so they explained the purpose of their visit to family members and friends who were present. . . .

"The interpreter must have been persuasive, for according to Kohfeld's account, when the chief arrived, one of his wives spoke to him about the matter. 'My dear husband,' she said, 'we have lived together twenty years and have been happy. Here is Jesus man, sent from God to build a Jesus House and teach us the way to heaven. If you hinder him, I shall never be happy again.' A woman named Tessika, whose husband had considerable influence with Quanah, also interceded on behalf of the missionary quest.

Henry Kohfeld

"Chief Parker discussed the issue with some ten to twelve of his tribesmen and reached a decision. He ordered Kohfeld to mount a horse behind an Indian. The chief led the party in a southwesterly direction, racing full speed for several miles over rough terrain and through a creek—a frightening experience Kohfeld would never forget. The horsemen stopped at a prominent post oak tree. Quanah cut several branches on the tree and said, 'Here build Jesus House.' Kohfeld produced a document authorizing 160 acres of land to be granted the Mennonite Brethren Church for missionary purposes and secured the signature or marks of Quanah and several other headmen of the Comanches. Post Oak Mission was born."

—*From* Comanches and Mennonites on the Oklahoma Plains: A. J. and Magdalena Becker and the Post Oak Mission, *by Marvin E. Kroeker (Kindred Productions, 1997).*

Sunday school class in South Texas, date unknown. Maria Peña is the teacher. (CMBS Fresno)

Neufeld began ministry among Latinos in South Texas. Over the next several years several congregations were established in South Texas and across the border in Mexico. In 1960 these congregations were organized into the Latin American Mennonite Brethren Conference.

Meanwhile in California, other Mennonite Brethren individuals were beginning outreach to Latinos. In 1926 Mennonite Brethren in Los Angeles established the City Terrace Mission in East Los Angeles. Though intended originally as a mission to Jewish people, it evolved into a primarily Latino congregation as the demographics of that area changed. Work among Latinos in California accelerated after World War II. In 1951 an outreach effort by Pacific Bible Institute students and faculty members resulted in the Sunset Gardens Church southwest of Fresno, a multicultural congregation with strong Latino focus. The first entirely Latino congregation was founded in 1955, in the small Fresno County farm community of Parlier, largely through the work of Dr. Arnold W. and Ann Schlichting. The Parlier congregation was followed by Spanish-speaking churches in Reedley (1962), Orosi (1963), Dinuba (1963), and Orange Cove (1965).

These endeavors marked the beginning of a broadening horizon for the Mennonite Brethren Church. It is clear, however, that the Mennonite Brethren still were focused inwardly. Well into the twentieth century, they remained a conservative, rural people concerned with establishing themselves in a new land. Outreach to others was not a high priority and was restricted by the cultural boundaries they so carefully maintained. However, urbanization would change this.

By the 1940s rapid urbanization overtook Mennonite Brethren. In 1941 only about 10 percent of North American Mennonite Brethren lived or worshiped in or near cities of fifty thousand or more residents. By 1960, almost 24 percent of them did so. By 1960, California was home to more urban-dwelling Mennonite Brethren Church members than any other state or province in North America. Manitoba was a close second. Ontario and British Columbia were third and fourth among Mennonite Brethren urban dwellers.

Enoch and Grace Wong: Chinese Church Planters

On September 24, 2000, more than three hundred people of the Pacific Grace churches hosted a celebration to commemorate the twenty years of leadership of Enoch and Grace Wong and the six Pacific Grace churches that they have established in British Columbia. That's right—six churches all bearing the same name, but in different locations: Burnaby, Port Moody (2), Vancouver, North Vancouver and South Vancouver. The occasion coincided with the thirty-fifth wedding anniversary of Enoch and Grace and the seventy-fifth birthday of Rev. Wong.

After graduation from the Hong Kong Alliance Bible Seminary in 1962, Enoch Wong began his ministry at the Cheung Chau Peak Alliance Church and the Scripture Union of Hong Kong. In 1980 Enoch came to pastor the Vancouver Pacific Grace Mennonite Brethren church, which then was a small congregation of thirty members. Pastor Wong reorganized the ministries of the church, developed new fellowships, Sunday school, gospel camps and challenged the congregation with the vision of mission and church planting. After seven years the congregation had grown to a membership of 155.

However that was just the beginning. Wong formally retired in 1987 and was succeeded by Rev. David Chan. In reality Enoch and Grace only nominally retired. They continued to assist in the establishing of the daughter churches. The prospect of Hong Kong being transferred from British control back to the People's Republic of China and the Tiananmen massacres of 1989 resulted in a large influx of Chinese immigrants into the Vancouver area. The opportunities were great and the Wongs were only too ready to assist in the establishing of the other five congregations.

One of the major strengths of Enoch and Grace has been their emphasis on Bible studies. In their twenty-plus years of ministry with Pacific Grace, they have led numerous Bible study groups. The Wongs also worked hard at mentoring seminary students and new pastors. A goodly number of the members of the six Pacific Grace churches were taught and cared for by the Wongs. Among them, are at least five pastoral couples now working in various churches and Christian organizations.

The celebration of Enoch and Grace Wong's twenty years in ministries ended with testimonies from both of them. Grace was a nurse in Hong Kong before coming to Canada and also taught in a nursing school for several years. She remarked: "I am proud of my contributions in the nursing career. However, the twenty years of pastoral ministries are much more memorable than the thirty-eight years of nursing work. Nursing for the soul is definitely a much more vital job than nursing for the physical body alone."

—*Adapted from an article written and translated by Joseph Kwan*

Church camps often served as a method of outreach among Mennonite Brethren churches. Pictured here are scenes from Hartland Camp in California (1979) and Lake Winnipeg Camp (today Camp Arnes) in Manitoba.
(CMBS Fresno and Winnipeg)

At first most Mennonite Brethren saw the city as the place where they settled, earned their livelihood and worshiped with fellow Mennonite Brethren. Others saw the city as a place to evangelize and they established programs to accomplish this. The outreach efforts were aimed primarily to people of lower socio-economic backgrounds with no church affiliation. Programs were often directed to children, who were generally more receptive to the Gospel than adults, and who the workers hoped would influence their parents to accept Christ. Most urban church planting projects in the 1950s, however, were primarily intended to retain existing members in the Mennonite Brethren fold and only secondarily for reaching others.

The period from 1945 to 1960 might be characterized as the era of "arms-length evangelism," a transitional time on the path to direct involvement in evangelism and church planting. This approach involved spreading the Gospel but not bringing newcomers into local Mennonite Brethren congregations. Examples of such evangelism in this period are tract distribution, evangelistic radio broadcasts, work among children (camping, Daily Vacation Bible School), evangelistic crusades (both in Mennonite Brethren churches and union crusades) and "colonization evangelism."

There was a proliferation of radio programs, particularly in Canada, with twenty-one separate programs produced across the country between 1941 and 1962. *The Gospel Light Hour* (now named the "Family Life Network") is the sole survivor, while in the United States the *Words of the Gospel* had a longstanding and significant impact.

"Colonization evangelism" involved groups of Mennonite Brethren voluntarily transplanting themselves for the purpose of evangelizing in a new area. Teachers, doctors and other professionals in "mobile professions" were encouraged to move into areas lacking a strong Gospel witness. In many instances, mission churches were established by such efforts. The group in Prince George, British Columbia, with a nucleus of fifteen teachers, joined the BC

Turning sod for a new Mennonite Brethren Church in St. Jerome, Quebec, ca. 1963-1964.
(CMBS Winnipeg)

Conference only a few years after is first informal meetings in 1959. Today Westwood has over four hundred members and an outreach ministry among the Chinese in the city. Other efforts at "colonization evangelism" ended when the professionals moved away.

There was a growing sense among Mennonite Brethren leaders of the time that something needed to be done regarding adult evangelism and more effective follow-up of the many child conversions. Concern for the post-conversion status of special ethnic peoples—Russians, Japanese, Native Indians and Latinos—raised the question of what should be done with such converts. The category "mission churches" was developed, and steps laid out whereby such groups could progress toward independence and eventual full membership in the Mennonite Brethren Church. The challenge of integration was just beginning.

Church Growth Evangelism

Fresh impetus to reach out, win and integrate other people came in the 1960s and 1970s through several church growth programs widely adopted on both sides of the border. The articulation of these new ideas came from the Board of Church Schools (later the Board of Evangelism) of the US Conference and its Executive Secretary Elmo Warkentin. The program was adapted to the Canadian constituency by George Konrad. The program slogan was "Double in a Decade," and 1965 to 1975 was to be a "Decade of Enlargement." The challenge was to place an immediate emphasis on evangelism.

The goal to "double in a decade," if achieved, would have resulted in a 7 percent annual attendance growth rate. Instead there was only a 2 percent annual growth rate, and actually a downturn in new church plants in the middle portion of the decade. Many pastors had been encouraged through the Decade of Enlargement to remain active in witnessing for Christ and many lay people had sensed the need to reach beyond themselves. Yet as Marvin Hein has noted, different ways and means of urging men and women to do the work of enlargement were necessary. According to Hein, "no technique, apart from the presence and working of the Holy Spirit (who is never limited by techniques or methods) will ever enable us to do the work of enlargement. We need the power of God's Spirit in every facet of the work of the kingdom."

In Canada, there was an outstanding example of broadening the horizons to win those of a different ethnic background when evacuated Belgian Congo missionaries initiated church planting work in Quebec. The "Quiet Revolution" in the 1960s saw the transfer of power from the Roman Catholic Church to the province. With this came the resurgence of Quebec nationalism and the goal of building a new society. There was a spirit of openness to new ideas and social change, along with disillusionment with the Roman Catholic Church. All of these factors combined to make people open to the Gospel. From 1964 to 1989 twelve Mennonite Brethren churches were planted, all but one French-speaking. At its peak, the Quebec churches grew to over seven hundred members and about one thousand people in attendance. In 1984, the Quebec churches united as an association and joined the Canadian Mennonite Brethren Conference. The Quebec Association has its own theological school, camp, and periodical to serve the Quebec churches.

Also in 1984 the Canadian Mennonite Brethren Board of Evangelism began publishing *Evangelism Canada*, edited by James Nikkel. This publication made church growth a top priority. Various programs of evangelism and church growth influenced Mennonite Brethren efforts in the late 1970s and 1980s, perhaps none so much as the Church Growth Movement. Promoted by Donald McGavran, C. Peter Wagner and Win Arn of Fuller Theological Seminary, it used a scientific approach to understand and describe the factors that caused failure or success in evangelism and church growth. One of McGavran's basic principles was that people like to become Christians without crossing racial, linguistic or class barriers. Thus church membership would be composed of basically one kind of people. This "homogeneous unit principle," much debated in evangelical circles, has been a guiding principle in most Mennonite Brethren church planting efforts in the past two decades.

Church Planting and Church Adoption

North American Mennonite Brethren have devoted considerable energy to church planting and church adoption during the 1980s and 1990s. In the United States, district home mission boards held seminars in church growth and church planting. The Pacific District Board of Home Missions became strongly committed to funding new Latino church planting projects, both in rural and urban communities. By 2000 there were more than thirty Latino congregations in the district.

In 1988, the US Conference created the Integrated Ministries program, headed by Loyal Funk. This program focused on new immigrant people groups coming to the United States. The goal was that by 2000, thirty viable church starts among these people groups be achieved and that there be at least a 20 percent population growth in these ethnic churches.

At the 2000 US Conference convention, Integrated Ministries reported that the new church starts and adoptions included twenty Slavic/Russian churches, seven Korean churches, ten Hispanic churches, two Japanese churches, five Ethiopian churches, and one Chinese church, with a total of over 18,000 attendees.

Canadian Mennonite Brethren were no less visionary regarding reaching out with the Gospel to Anglos as well as immigrant groups. In 1997 the Canadian Board of Evangelism introduced the Key Cities Initiative and named Calgary as the first key city for a multiple church plant focus. The goal, set together with the Alberta Board of Church Extension, was to establish ten new churches in five years. At mid-point in this program (early 2001) five churches had been planted.

The Key Cities Initiative has chosen Toronto as its next target in what has been labeled "Love Toronto." Toronto is the fifth-largest city in North America with 2.5 million people. It is one of the most ethnically diverse cities in the world, receiving 70,000 new immigrants every year. In partnership with the Ontario Board of Church Extension, the goal is to establish five new churches in Greater Toronto in five years.

The British Columbia Board of Church Extension (BOCE) has achieved exceptional outreach to a wide variety of ethnic groups. By 2001, about half of the new initiatives of the BOCE were cross-cultural, non-English speaking church plants. Unique ministries included work among Kosovar refugees, and another among Chinese boat people who arrived illegally on the shores of Vancouver Island. Greater Vancouver has the largest number of Chinese Mennonite Brethren churches anywhere in North America. A key factor here is that Chinese churches have been planting daughter churches. "Churches Planting Churches" was BOCE's millennium priority, known as "Project 2000." Having doubled the number of BC congregations in the previous decade, BOCE's goal is to again double in the next decade, bringing the total number of churches over the two hundred mark by 2011.

The US Conference devoted the early 1990s to assessing how it could become more successful in evangelism and church planting. A formal proposal to launch a new program, "Mission USA," was adopted by the 1994 convention. Under the leadership of Ed Boschman, appointed Executive Director of Mission USA in 1996, new church plants have sprung up in several cities, including Phoenix, Salt Lake City and Wichita. In 1998, Mission USA unveiled an aggressive program, MetroNet 2005, in which twenty new churches are to be planted in five years. The strategy calls for planting a network or cluster of churches in major metropolitan areas. Multiplication would be the key to the plan, with the majority of the first new church plants needing to birth new churches within the five-year period.

Phoenix, where Mission USA had previously planted Copper Hills Community Church, was chosen as the first major thrust of MetroNet 2005. "Mission Phoenix" began planting two new congregations in close proximity to Copper Hills, which donated $8,000 to help support the project. Mission USA has also begun working with church planters in Tulsa, Oklahoma, and Asheville, North Carolina, and is meeting with local churches regarding a plant in the San Francisco Bay area of California.

North American Mennonite Brethren Church Planting and Church Growth Models

Integration
All language groups meet together for worship
Leadership includes minority representatives
English is the "power language"
Simultaneous translation provided
Small groups and some Sunday school classes meet in language-specific groups

Adoption
A conference adopts already-formed congregations
These congregations meet on a semi-independent basis
They relate to conference through the director of Integrated Ministries

Parenting
Mother church nurtures a "start-up" group until they are ready to launch a new church
Mother church provides moral and initial financial support

Partnership
Two churches cooperate in a new church planting project
Each provides resources and personnel

Shared Use of Facility
Existing church rents facilities
Space use is staggered according to mutual agreement
Occasional joint services may occur

Independent, Self-supporting Group
New group has acquired its own building
Controls its internal affairs

Separate District
A group of ethnic minority churches form a separate district
Internal worship and administrative patterns are unique
May send representatives to MB conference conventions

Mennonite Brethren Worship Languages In North America

Albanian
Amheric
Arabic
Cantonese
English
Ukrainian
French
German
Hindi
Hispanic
Indonesian
Japanese
Lao
Khmu
Korean
Mandarin
Persian
Punjabi
Russian
Vietnamese

The Mennonite Brethren Mosaic

Many challenges face the Mennonite Brethren mosaic of twenty different nationalities and cultures. The first challenge is moving beyond historic Mennonite Brethren ethnic hegemony, which suggests that people should look like us and worship like us if they are going to be a part of our larger fellowship. Such a shift in thinking is gradually occurring. A new spirit of inclusion is taking hold, seeking ways of truly integrating transcultural congregations into the denomination. The dominant Germanic ethnic group that holds the reins of leadership and power is beginning to invite others to take on leadership roles and find their place as equals in denominational structures and ministries.

Second, we must remain flexible about how new church plants should function, particularly those of diverse ethnic groups. One model will not suit every situation. We must avoid the assumption that Hispanics, Slavs and Chinese will quickly assimilate into Canadian or American culture and therefore also soon integrate into traditional Anglo Mennonite Brethren congregations. Most will acculturate and learn English, but very few will completely assimilate in the near future.

Third, we need to respect ethnic identities and the various ways they are expressed. Unity as Mennonite Brethren does not mean uniformity. Thus we bless the fellowship and worship of each individual segment of the Mennonite Brethren mosaic as it celebrates God's presence and then bless the coming together of all the parts in times of corporate fellowship and worship. At the same time, we must not allow ethnicity to become the distinctive identifier of who we are in Christ—neither Hispanic, Chinese, Slavic, German/ Russian or Anglo is the essence, but faith in Christ. If we retain this scriptural priority, ethnicity, including that of the dominant culture, need never be a hindrance to evangelism and church growth.

A final challenge is to maintain a holistic perspective on church growth, avoiding an undue emphasis on numeric growth. When we build up the quality of congregational life, evangelism will be the result. We must be cautious of slogans and bandwagons, especially if confidence seems to reside more in techniques than prayer and reliance on the Holy Spirit. The 1965-1975 "Double in a Decade" slogan was only that. The 1980 Southern District Conference goal of starting twenty-five churches during the decade began well, with ten church plants having taken root by mid-decade. By 1996, however, all ten churches had shut down.

At the 1989 national convention, Church Extension and Evangelism Commission chairman Lynn Jost asked, "Why have we been so spectacularly unsuccessful at church planting, especially in larger cities?" Mission USA, with its emphasis on church planting and church renewal, is rising up to the challenge of reversing the trend Jost lamented. The Canadian Conference, with its emphasis on evangelism and developing healthy churches, is answering the call with successful church plants in several large Canadian cities. In both countries, growth is coming from various ethnic groups who are drawn to the Mennonite Brethren Confession of Faith and its church polity.

The Mennonite Brethren Church of North America is gradually becoming a beautiful mosaic of all nations. In celebrating its diversity of ethnic groups and cultures and in its unity centered on Christ, it is adorning the doctrine of God and showing forth the attractiveness of the teaching of God our Savior (Titus 2:10).

Afterword:
A Future with Promise

Herb Kopp

A time to be born, a time to die.

The words of Qoheleth, the Preacher, are true for every generation, "For everything there is a season, and a time for every matter under heaven: a time to be born, and a time to die" (Ecclesiastes 3:1-2a). Movements and institutions, like human beings, are born, they mature, become old and die.

The recommendation of the General Conference at Wichita in 1999 was easy enough to understand: "That the General Conference of Mennonite Brethren Churches be dissolved." By this action of the convention, a small conference born in 1879 has come full circle after more than 120 years of ministry. It was born out of necessity, it staggered uneasily through its early years, then matured into a useful, meaningful institution and now is about to die.

Years ago, I stood at the bedside of a godly woman who was soon to die. She said, in a weak, frail voice, "It is easier to die when you live on through your children's children who contribute to the well-being of the world." The United States and Canadian churches met together, at the General Conference level, sixty-two times. We remember with fondness its robust work, its successes. We also remember and grieve its failures. We met together to plot world evangelism strategies, to discern educational needs and bring institutions into reality. We processed the meaning of our Anabaptist faith in the context of growing economic security and wealth. We debated the wording of the revised and new Confessions of Faith; we published materials to represent our particular theological worldview.

More than anything, we reached across an international boundary to work at the issues we held in common. For the most part, we were able to see beyond local interests to deal with world issues. We were compelled, both by our history and our theological understandings, to have a vision for something greater than merely our present, common good. We collaborated and worked with unity as we built a superstructure on the "foundation already laid," Jesus Christ. When ministries came to an end, we had the courage to close institutions, to eliminate or restructure boards, and even approve the movement of missions personnel to more promising locations.

In the end, the "children" have grown up and are taking their place in the world. The national churches, which we helped create, are growing up. Today there are eighteen national conferences where once there were only two. So, while we grieve the passing of the General Conference, we also celebrate its effectiveness.

Dislocation and Reconfiguring

The second recommendation passed by the delegation at Wichita '99 was also clear: "That the General Conference Executive develop an orderly process of transferring the ministries to national control by 2002." When an institution dies a natural death we tend to celebrate its passing. It lived well and it died well. We thank God for effective ministry. However, when we intentionally end the life of an institution, particularly an institution that is still capable of life and productivity, we have mixed feelings. The General Conference, as the convention minute records show, was still a viable institution. That we lament its passing, and wonder if its ministries can function as effectively under national governance as they did under General Conference governance, is understandable.

It is clear from the 1999 resolution that ending the functional life of the General Conference was not a mandate to dismantle its ministries. Change, radical change, has a way of unsettling even the most secure ministries. Therefore, it is to be expected that the four ministries of the General Conference—Mennonite Brethren Missions/Services International, the Board of Faith and Life, the Board of Resource Ministries, and the Mennonite Brethren Biblical Seminary—which at dissolution were healthy, necessary ministries, will experience considerable dislocation as they find a new life within the two national conferences.

During the next decade the process of reconfiguring these ministries will accelerate. National churches, without the benefit of cross-boundary dialogue, will make independent choices about mission, education, theology and Anabaptist beliefs. The pragmatic urge to have something close to home, to make something work better, and to cost less will inform much of the agenda.

While the two national conferences are assuming responsibility for these various ministries we do recognize that there exist other competing geographical realities. The critical mass of the national membership for both Mennonite Brethren conferences lies on the West Coast. This western growth seems to be accelerating. The United States Midwest and the Canadian Prairies increasingly and proportionately have less influence than earlier. A trend that seems to be gaining momentum is that churches have a local and international consciousness. What appears to be weakening is a national ministry consciousness. Denominationally, we can probably expect regionalization to strengthen and national cooperation to weaken. Churches want their "conference dollars" to work locally where their affect can be monitored, or internationally where they are seen as "missions." The missions component of this giving, however, must be answerable back to the local congregation. So while we are embracing a national mission in this reorganization we do recognize other realities on the horizon.

Dare to Dream a Dream

When an institution dies it leaves an open space where it once held prominence. For many decades the General Conference cut a wide swath through our denomination. It anchored us in ministries larger than ourselves. It kept reminding us that the world is comprised of life experiences larger than merely our viewpoint and interests. It insisted that life is best when it takes into account the life experience of national churches different from us. The divestiture process has forced every region of both Canada and the United States to rethink its mission, publishing and educational goals. When one vision dies, another needs to be created to fill the void.

The Mennonite Brethren Church needs a new vision, a vision that does not only have a distinctly national flavor, but rather, a vision that embraces the global reality. For the Mennonite Brethren Church to flourish and grow we need a vision greater than what the old General Conference represented, and what we presently possess. We need a rekindled passion fueled by the needs of the world, a faith that insists on disciplined discipleship, an identity that gives us a secure place to stand, and an ideology that transcends local needs. This new vision must be global, mission-focused and attainable. It requires four new leaps of faith.

First, a new International General Conference needs to emerge. The International Committee of Mennonite Brethren (ICOMB) represents the beginning of something new and potentially powerful. The time has come for the eighteen Mennonite Brethren national conferences to come together for fellowship and in ministry and mission. ICOMB, the international committee representing the world-wide Mennonite Brethren church is fragile and not strongly organized. It is very much in infancy, but it has taken its first steps. The days of colonialism are gone. The days when the old General Conference (that is, Canada and the United States) controlled the agenda have vanished. A new partnership of equals is becoming a reality. This will take a new way of thinking. True, the majority of funding will still originate in North America, but the agenda will be global.

Second, this new International General Conference must model New Testament Christianity. The genius of the first-century church is that it broke down many of the barriers that the Greek and Roman cultures had erected. The revolutionary message of the first-century church was that in Jesus Christ there is equality, in the church there is no distinction between slave or free, male or female, educated or uneducated, Jew or Greek, rich or poor. To sit as equals means more than adjusting our personal biases and viewpoints, it also means equality at the decision-making table, a place where rich and poor nations, large and small national churches, have equal power. To sit as equals means we work by consensus, not democracy; we work together, respectful of each other as human beings and respectful of our viewpoints.

Third, a new international confession of faith will need to be developed. What does it mean to be an evangelical Anabaptist in the world where we live? What does it mean to be Mennonite Brethren where we live? One way to answer that question is to ask: "Where, in the world, do we live?" If we live in North America, then one way to respond to that question is to refer to our new *Confession of Faith*. For North American Mennonite Brethren it meant adding two articles to the Confession: "The Sanctity of Life" and "Christianity and Other Faiths." For us it means strengthening the article on "Stewardship" to address the disproportionate percentage of wealth we hold, and to adjust the "Lord's Supper" article to accommodate changing patterns of worship in our congregations. But to hear our Congolese brothers and sisters speak, might mean that an article on "The Meaning of Suffering," or "Contentment" be included in a new Confession. Somehow, we will need to discover what it is that we hold in common, and what the issues are that help us understand the life experience of brothers and sisters in another part of the Mennonite Brethren world.

ICOMB has taken a large step in this direction by appointing a task force to begin work on a new international confession of faith. This will quickly test our willingness to be instructed theologically and biblically by brothers and sisters who do not share our life experience.

Finally, we need a new partnership in mission. The time has come for a new partnership in mission, where every national conference becomes a "sending" church. The strength of the new charter granted to MBMSI, through the divestiture process, has set the stage for this to emerge. While in the short run, some reconfiguring and restructuring will need to occur, in the long run the decision to consolidate operation to one locality might be wise.

Final Things

Human beings are born, they grow up, they grow old and they die. Likewise, institutions are born, grow up, grow old and die. Young children and new institutions replace the old. Ministries are reconfigured and renewed. One dream ends and a new dream emerges. Old realities are left behind, new realities are faced and addressed. And life goes on in the Mennonite Brethren Church, as it should. Thanks be to God!

Permissions

"Margaretha Froese Wiens Klassen: Mother of the Mennonite Brethren Church?" Adapted from Alan Peters, "Margaretha Froese: 'Mother' of the MB Church?," in *Mennonite Brethren Historical Society of the West Coast Bulletin* (no. 18, November 1987). Reprinted by permission.

"Mennonites or Baptists?" Adapted from Abe Dueck, *Moving Beyond Secession: Defining Russian Mennonite Brethren Mission and Identity, 1872-1922* (Winnipeg: Kindred Productions, 1997). Reprinted by permission.

"The Birth of the Krimmer Mennonite Brethren." Adapted from Paul Toews, "The Long Road to Union" in *The Christian Leader* (November 12, 1985). Reprinted by permission.

"Heinrich Voth and the first Mennonite Brethren Church in North America." Adapted from J.A. Froese, *Witness Extraordinary: A Biography of Elder Heinrich Voth, 1851-1919* (Winnipeg: Board of Christian Literature, 1975). Reprinted by permission.

"Sister Anna." Adapted from Frieda Esau, "Providing a Home Away From Home," in *Looking Back in Faith: A commemorative collection of photos and writing to mark the centennial of Mennonite Brethren in Manitoba, 1888-1988*, edited by Helmut Huebert, Harold Jantz, John Longhurst (Winnipeg: Manitoba Mennonite Brethren Centennial Committee, 1988). Reprinted by permission.

"Benjamin B. Janz." Adapted from John B. Toews, "Benjamin B. Janz (1877-1964)." *Profiles of Mennonite Faith* no. 5, (Fresno: Historical Commission of the Mennonite Brethren Church, 1998). Reprinted by permission.

"Finding one's way in a new world," in Rudy Wiebe, *Peace Shall Destroy Many* (Grand Rapids, Mich.: William B. Eerdmans, 1962). Reprinted by permission.

"C.F. Klassen: helping his people." Adapted from Herb and Maureen Klassen, "C.F. Klassen: Gott Kann." *Profiles of Mennonite Faith* no. 8, (Fresno: Historical Commission of the Mennonite Brethren Church, 1999). Reprinted by permission.

"Map of approximate migration route of Mennonites leaving the Soviet Union, 1943-45" from William Schroeder and Helmut T. Huebert, *Mennonite Historical Atlas,* 2nd ed. (Winnipeg: Springfield Publishers, 1996). Reprinted by permission.

"Biblical or Systematic Theology?" Adapted from J.B. Toews, *JB: A Twentieth-Century Mennonite Pilgrim* (Fresno: Center for Mennonite Brethren Studies, 1995). Reprinted by permission.

"A theological autobiography." Adapted from David Ewert, "Theological Autobiography" in *Bridging Troubled Waters: the Mennonite Brethren at Mid-Twentieth Century*, edited by Paul Toews (Winnipeg: Kindred Productions, 1995). Reprinted by permission.

"Sin with a small 's'," in Katie Funk Wiebe, *The Storekeeper's Daughter: A Memoir* (Scottdale, Pa.: Herald Press, 1997). Reprinted by permission.

"Abraham H. Unruh." Adapted in part from David Ewert, *Stalwart for the Truth: The Life and Legacy of A.H. Unruh* (Winnipeg: Board of Christian Literature, 1975). Reprinted by permission.

"From Brotherhood to Congregational Autonomy," Adapted from J.B. Toews, *JB: A Twentieth-Century Mennonite Pilgrim* (Fresno: Center for Mennonite Brethren Studies, 1995). Reprinted by permission.

"Mennonite Hospitality: 300 Families Put Up 3000 Guests." Adapted from *The Daily Oklahoman*, (October 23-24, 1939). Reprinted by permission.

"P.C. Hiebert and the Grand Cross of the Order of Merit." Adapted from Wesley J. Prieb, "Peter (P.C.) Hiebert," in *Something Meaningful for God*, edited by Cornelius J. Dyck (Scottdale, Pa: Herald Press, 1981). Reprinted by permission.

"Adjusting to a new culture." Adapted from A.K. and Gertrude Wiens, *Shadowed by the Great Wall* (Winnipeg: Board of Christian Literature,1979). Reprinted by permission.

"A New Direction in Missions." Adapted from J.B. Toews, *JB: A Twentieth-Century Mennonite Pilgrim* (Fresno: Center for Mennonite Brethren Studies, 1995). Reprinted by permission.

"The wandering editor: John F. Harms." Adapted from Orlando Harms, *Pioneer Publisher: The Life and Times of J. F. Harms* (Hillsboro, Kan.: Center for Mennonite Brethren Studies, 1984). Reprinted by permission.

"Reflections on education in Canada." Adapted from David Ewert, "Theological Autobiography," in *Bridging Troubled Waters: The Mennonite Brethren at Mid-Twentieth Century*, edited by Paul Toews (Winnipeg: Kindred Productions, 1995). Reprinted by permission.

"Why a Bible College?" in Catalog of Mennonite Brethren Bible College (1944). Reprinted by permission.

"Reshaping the Seminary." Adapted from J.B. Toews, *JB: A Twentieth-Century Mennonite Pilgrim* (Fresno: Center for Mennonite Brethren Studies, 1995). Reprinted by permission.

Cover of Rudy Wiebe, *Peace Shall Destroy Many* (Grand Rapids, Mich.: William B. Eerdmans, 1962). Reprinted by permission.

Photo of Peter M. Friesen, *The Mennonite Brotherhood in Russia, 1789 - 1910*, translated and edited by J.B. Toews, et al. (Fresno: Board of Christian Literature, 1980). Reprinted by permission.

"The End Times" by David Waltner-Toews, in *Liars and Rascals: Mennonite Short Stories*, edited by Hildi Froese Tiessen (Waterloo, Ont.: University of Waterloo Press, 1989). Reprinted by permission.

"Obituaries: the story of a life." Originally printed in *Zionsbote*, June 14, 1950. Reprinted by permission.

Cover of Anna Reimer Dyck, *Anna: From the Caucasus to Canada*, translated and edited by Peter Klassen (Hillsboro, Kan.: Mennonite Brethren Publishing House, 1979). Reprinted by permission.

"Mennonite Music" by Jean Janzen, in *Words for the Silence* (Fresno: Center for Mennonite Brethren Studies, 1984). Reprinted by permission.

Cover of Esther Loewen Vogt, *Turkey Red* (Winnipeg: Kindred Press, 1986). Reprinted by permission.

Review by Peter Klassen of Rudy Wiebe, *Peace Shall Destroy Many*, originally published in *Mennonite Brethren Herald* (October 12, 1962). Reprinted by permission.

"Generosity in Times of Need." Adapted from C.A. DeFehr, *Memories of My Life* (Winnipeg: privately published, 1967) and conversation with Cornelius DeFehr. Reprinted by permission.

"The Dilemma of Faith and Culture." Adapted from David Ewert, "Theological Autobiography," in *Bridging Troubled Waters: The Mennonite Brethren at Mid-Twentieth Century*, edited by Paul Toews (Winnipeg: Kindred Productions, 1995). Reprinted by permission.

"Alternative Service in Canada during World War II." Adapted from Henry R. Baerg, *Alternative Service for Peace in Canada During World War II, 1941-46*, edited by A.J. Klassen (Abbotsford, B.C.: Mennonite Central Committee and Seniors for Peace, 1998). Reprinted by permission.

"Relating to the 'world.'" Adapted from David Ewert, "Theological Autobiography," in *Bridging Troubled Waters: The Mennonite Brethren at Mid-Twentieth Century* (Winnipeg: Kindred Productions, 1995). Reprinted by permission.

"Here Build Jesus House." in Marvin Kroeker, *Comanches and Mennonites on the Oklahoma Plains: A.J. and Magdalena Becker and the Post Oak Mission* (Winnipeg: Kindred Productions, 1997). Reprinted by permission.

"Nonresistance and church membership: the dilemma of World War I." Adapted from James C. Juhnke, *Vision, Doctrine, War: Mennonite Identity and Organization in America, 1890-1930* (Scottdale, Pa: Herald Press, 1989). Reprinted by permission.

About the Authors

Abe Dueck is currently Director of the Centre for Mennonite Brethren Studies, Winnipeg, Manitoba. For many years he was a Professor of History and Academic Dean at Mennonite Brethren Bible College/Concord College in Winnipeg. He is the author and editor of numerous books and articles including *Moving Beyond Secession: Defining Russian Mennonite Brethren Mission and Identity, 1872-1922* (Kindred Productions, 1997).

Kevin Enns-Rempel is Archivist at the Center for Mennonite Brethren Studies, Fresno, California and teaches United States History at Fresno Pacific University. He is the author of many articles dealing with the migration and settlement of Mennonites in the western half of the United States.

Lynn Jost is Associate Professor of Biblical Studies at Tabor College, Hillsboro, Kansas. He was the last chair of the General Conference Board of Faith and Life, and in that capacity directed the development of the most recent *Mennonite Brethren Confession of Faith*.

Doreen Klassen is an Assistant Professor in the Social Science Division of Memorial University of Newfoundland. She is the author of *Singing Mennonites: Low German Songs among the Mennonites* (University of Manitoba Press, 1989), editor of *International Songbook, 1990* (Mennonite World Conference, 1990) that was utilized for the 10th Assembly of the Mennonite World Conference in Winnipeg, Manitoba.

Herb Kopp is the last Moderator of the General Conference of Mennonite Brethren Churches of North America. He has pastored several churches in Canada and edited the *Mennonite Brethren Herald* (1985-1988). He currently resides in Winnipeg, Manitoba, and is Conference Pastor for the Manitoba Conference of Mennonite Brethren Churches.

Wally Kroeker has been a newspaper reporter and magazine editor for thirty-five years. From 1975 to 1985 he was editor of *The Christian Leader*, a publication of the United States Mennonite Brethren Conference. He currently is director of publications for Mennonite Economic Development Associates, Winnipeg, Manitoba, and editor of its magazine, *The Marketplace*.

James Pankratz is currently the Dean of Mennonite Brethren Biblical Seminary, Fresno, California. He is a past President of Concord College (now part of the Canadian Mennonite University). He has also served in various overseas assignments. He has written on many topics relating to the life and witness of the church. His column "Christian Mind" ran in *Mennonite Brethren Herald*, 1980-1997.

John H. Redekop is currently Professor of Political Science at Trinity Western University, Langley British Columbia. He is also Professor Emeritus at Wilfrid Laurier University. He is a former moderator of Canadian Conference of Mennonite Brethren Churches and has served on many conference boards at various levels. He is an author of numerous books and articles, including

A People Apart: Ethnicity and the Mennonite Brethren (1987). His column "Personal Opinion" has run in *Mennonite Brethren Herald* for the past 37 years.

Valerie Rempel is an Assistant Professor at the Mennonite Brethren Biblical Seminary, Fresno, California. She has been active in various General Conference Boards and the Executive Committee. She is also the author of several articles dealing with the history of Mennonite Brethren women.

John B. Toews is the author of many books on Russian Mennonite history and especially the story of the early Mennonite Brethren. Recent contributions include *Perilous Journey: The Mennonite Brethren in Russia, 1860-1910* (1988); *Journeys: Mennonite Stories of Faith and Survival in Stalin's Russia* (1998) and *The Story of the Early Mennonite Brethren (1860-1869): Reflections of a Lutheran Churchman* (2002). He is currently Professor of Church History and Anabaptist Studies at Regent College, Vancouver, British Columbia.

Paul Toews is Professor of History at Fresno Pacific University, Fresno, California, and Executive Director of the Historical Commission of the Mennonite Brethren Churches of North America. He is the author of numerous books and articles on diverse aspects of Mennonite history, including, *Mennonites in American Society, 1930-1970: Modernity and the Persistence of Religious Community* (1996).

Walter Unger is President Emeritus of Columbia Bible College, Abbotsford, British Columbia. He is also the author of many articles dealing with various aspects of Mennonite Brethren history and theology. His column "Christian Mind" was featured in the *Mennonite Brethren Herald*, 1981-1996.

Katie Funk Wiebe is a lover of the beauty and power of words and of the church. In 2000 the Mennonite editorial staff chose her as one of the twenty people who had "the most forceful influence on the life and belief" of the General Conference Mennonite Church and the Mennonite Church in the twentieth century by raising the credibility of Mennonite writing. She is professor emerita of English at Tabor College, Hillsboro, Kansas.